CAMPAIGN
WARRIORS

CAMPAIGN WARRIORS

The Role of Political Consultants in Elections

JAMES A. THURBER
CANDICE J. NELSON
Editors

BROOKINGS INSTITUTION PRESS
Washington, D.C.

Copyright © 2000
THE BROOKINGS INSTITUTION
1775 Massachusetts Avenue, N.W.
Washington, D.C. 20036
www.brookings.edu

Library of Congress Cataloging-in-Publication data
Campaign warriors : the role of political consultants in elections /
James A. Thurber and Candice J. Nelson, editors.
    p.   cm.
Includes bibliographical references and index.
ISBN 0-8157-8454-6 (alk. paper)
ISBN 0-8157-8453-8 (pbk. : alk. paper)
    1. Campaign management—United States   2. Electioneering—United
States.   3. Political consultants—United States.   4. Campaign
management.   5. Electioneering.   6. Political consultants.   I. Thurber,
James A., 1943–   II. Nelson, Candice J., 1949–
    JK2281 .C323 2000   99-050915
    324.7'0973—dc21   CIP

9 8 7 6 5 4 3 2 1

The paper used in this publication meets minimum requirements of the American National Standard for Information Sciences—Permanence of Paper for Printed Library Materials: ANSI Z39.48-1984.

Typeset in Sabon

Composition by Harlowe Typography
Cottage City, Maryland

Printed by R. R. Donnelley and Sons
Harrisonburg, Virginia

Contents

Acknowledgments

The editors are indebted to the Pew Charitable Trusts for its support of the Improving Campaign Conduct project, which funded the research in this volume. Special thanks go to Paul C. Light, who was with Pew at the beginning of this project and now heads the Governmental Studies division at Brookings Institution, for his commitment to this book and to the enterprise of improving the way our election campaigns are waged. Sean Treglia and Michael Delli Carpini of the Pew Charitable Trusts provided important support for the research reported in this volume. We would also like to thank Rebecca Rimel, president of the Pew Charitable Trusts, for her confidence in this project and her outstanding leadership in improving public policy-making, campaign conduct, and our democratic processes.

At American University, we extend thanks to Cornelius M. Kerwin, provost, who played a special role in supporting this project. We would also like to acknowledge the assistance, comments, and encouragement received from Jennifer Dyjak, Marni Ezra, Leslie McNaugher, Stuart Rothenberg, Claudia H. Thurber, Carol Whitney, and Fred Yang.

At the Brookings Institution Press we express our gratitude to Nancy Davidson, Christopher Kelaher, and Robert Faherty, as well as Kerry V. Kern, who edited the manuscript, Deborah Patton, who provided the index, and Inge Lockwood who proofread the pages.

CHAPTER ONE

Introduction to the Study of Campaign Consultants

JAMES A. THURBER

Elections are arguably the single most important event in American democratic life, an opportunity for Americans to both give their consent to be governed and to hold their representatives accountable for past performance. Modern competitive elections for local, state, and national office are often dominated by professional campaign consultants structuring what candidates say and do. The strategies, tactics, and the management techniques of these professionals have had a fundamental impact on the quality of American elections and the nature of our democracy. The rapid rate of change in modern campaigns has been reflected in the development of specialized expertise, division of labor, and the diversification of professional needs to win an election. Although there has been a rapid growth in campaign consulting, it is often out of public view, which in turn prohibits in-depth knowledge of the extent of such activities.

The first political consultants were most likely volunteers in the elections of John Adams and Thomas Jefferson who gave their candidates advice about debates, circulating printed materials, making speeches, and getting out the vote. Campaigns have needed consultants, whether volunteers or paid professionals inside or outside a party organization, from the beginning of our democracy. However, paid professional political consultants outside political parties who make a living from campaigns are relatively new to American politics. Political parties, the center of campaign activity until three decades ago, have now taken a back seat to the campaign consultants. Major changes in financing campaigns and dramatic changes in campaign technology have helped the rapid growth of campaign consulting. Campaign consulting is a relatively new profession that continues to evolve and redefine itself in each election cycle. Political consultants have an impact on candidates, voters, the outcome of elections, and ultimately on governance and public policy. Who are the political consultants? What do they believe? What will they do to win? Are political consultants hurting or helping the conduct of election campaigns and democracy?

The primary theme of the essays in this book is that political consultants have an important impact on campaigns and elections. Consultants have helped to redefine the role of political parties and have transformed the way candidates communicate with voters and the way voters judge candidates. They are at the core of the electoral process in the United States and in many other nations. This is, of course, not news to political consultants or candidates running for office. Candidates and consultants know they need each other and the rapid growth and diversification of the profession reveals that sense of interdependence. Although professional political consulting outside of political party organizations has been around since the 1930s, it has only recently sparked interest among political scientists, journalists, and the public. Relatively little is known about the world of political consultants.

Studies have treated campaigns as symbolic events, as propaganda activities with the power to change voter preferences, and as a determinant variable in elections, but there is little known about the role consultants play in campaigns. Studies about campaigns and elections have focused on voting behavior and the determinants of vote choices, recruitment (or why people run for office), the role of the media, campaign finance (why contributors give, how much they give, to what effect, and the need for reform), party activists and the role of party organization in elections, special interest groups in elections, the impact of negative advertising on the electorate, and the incumbent advantage in elections.

When voters moved away from partisan cues as the basis of voting, campaigns and electioneering began to matter. When campaigns and electioneering started to make a difference, so did the profession of political consulting, but empirical political science research on consulting did not keep up with the growth and influence of the industry. Campaign activities and political consulting deserve close analysis. Dan Nimmo noted that "campaigns may no longer be battles between candidates but between titans of the campaign industry, working on behalf of those personalities."[1] With the rise of candidate-centered elections, political parties have become less important; at the same time, the amount of money spent by candidates has skyrocketed. Consultants have taken the place of parties in most areas of campaigning, and they are spending vast amounts of money to make sure that candidates are competitive and win. It is essential to understand the individuals, and their beliefs, who are playing such a major role in modern elections. Only by doing so can we understand their importance on modern American democracy.

We need to know more about consultants, but much of the writing about the political consulting industry is atheoretical, produced by journalists or by practitioners whose writing consists of insider accounts of campaigning and "how to" books. Some scholars have attempted to combine the insider knowledge of practitioners with that of political scientists in their study of campaign management.[2] Although the scholarly literature about consulting is much more theoretical than that of the practitioners, it is also primarily descriptive in nature, based exclusively on case studies, interviews, or surveys of members of the industry.[3] Since the state of knowledge and theory about political consultants is limited, it is difficult to examine their influence in campaigns. The intent of this book is to analyze consultant influence from a variety of perspectives.

The essays in this volume collectively present original data and analysis describing the world of campaign consultants and their impact on elections. Each chapter analyzes campaign consulting from a different perspective. Chapter 2, by James Thurber, Candice Nelson, and David Dulio, presents results from two hundred in-depth interviews with consultants and describes who consultants are and their attitudes on the consulting business, voters, the media, ethics, and the need for campaign reforms. Dennis Johnson, in chapter 3, presents a comprehensive description of the diversification and complexity of consulting as a business. In chapter 4, Martin Hamburger, a veteran campaign media consultant, provides a rare insider's perspective of the consulting industry and describes lessons he has learned from many years in the campaign business. Paul Herrnson, in chapter 5, tests the impact of consultants on fund-raising, strategy, communications, and electoral success in congressional elections. In chapter 6 Stephen Medvic builds on Herrnson's study by analyzing the importance of consultants and candidates in the outcome of congressional elections. Robin Kolodny reports on her analysis of consultants as electoral partners with state political parties in chapter 7. In chapter 8 David Magleby and Kelly Patterson analyze the role of consultants in initiatives and referenda. Shaun Bowler and David Farrell in chapter 9 report on the internationalization of election campaign consultancy and the spread of political consultancy worldwide.

Classic Works on Consultants

The earliest works on modern political consulting explore the origins of the consulting industry and the background of campaign consultants. Historic accounts of elections as early as the 1828 contest between John Quincy Adams and General Andrew Jackson reveal the evidence of involvement of a variety of political consultants. The historic accounts are based on secondary sources and observations that tell us little about the role and impact of the consultants. Many studies of the role of political parties and their activists are in effect analyses of the role of consultants within parties. Reports of discussions with consultants and case studies about their role in campaigns within the past fifty years have provided a rich picture of their importance but have not provided systematic data on the profession.

Past studies explored whether consultants came from public relations backgrounds, as opposed to public service or careers in the political parties.[4] These analyses found that consultants with public relations backgrounds dominated the political world in the middle of this century and that political consultants were effective because they provided information and communication expertise to campaigns.[5] Nimmo also found that consultants became much more specialized in the 1960s and were not only experts in technology and communication but resource allocation as well: "Their major contribution to a campaign is rationality in allocating scarce resources—time, money and talent."[6]

Aside from historic works about specific elections and the accounts of journalists and practitioners, the world of political consulting remained virtually unexplored by academics prior to the 1970s.[7] As a result of Larry Sabato's work and the heightened media attention given to the increased importance of consultants in the late 1980s and early 1990s, political consulting began to attract the interest of more academics who initiated studies into the impact of consultants upon elections.[8] Chapter 2, "Portrait of Campaign Consultants," stems from two hundred in-depth interviews from a national sample of general campaign specialists, pollsters, media experts, and campaign fund-raisers and presents the first detailed description of the backgrounds, attitudes, and reported behavior of consultants.

Consultant Influence on Electoral Outcomes

What impact do campaign professionals have on electoral politics? Up to now there have been primarily two lines of research concerning the impact political consultants can have on elections. The first explores whether the use of consultants leads to increased funds for campaigns.[9] The second examines whether retaining political consultants leads to a higher percentage of the vote for a candidate.[10] These lines of research are extended in this volume with Herrnson's work, as reported in chapter 5, and Medvic's study of professionalization in congressional campaigns in chapter 6.

Herrnson in chapter 5 explores the financial implications of campaign professionalization. Candidates' viability is based on judgments concerning campaign organizations. He finds that campaign professionalization has an important impact on candidates' fund-raising success. The more consultants a campaign hires, the more money the campaign is able to raise.[11] Political parties, political action committees (PACs), and individuals who make large contributions want to invest their money in campaigns that have the highest chance of success, and they look to campaign professionalization as one potential indicator.

Herrnson finds that professionalism has a significant impact for both incumbents and nonincumbents on the ability of campaigns to raise funds from PACs and political parties. However, professionalism only significantly affects incumbents' ability to raise funds from individual contributors. It does not significantly improve nonincumbents' chances for raising money. Evidence is mixed regarding whether use of consultants can increase a candidate's share of the vote in elections to the U.S. House of Representatives.

Medvic in chapter 6 finds the strongest evidence that, for both challengers and open seat candidates, a more professionally run campaign equals a greater percentage of the vote. He also finds that the simple presence of professionals leads to a significant increase in the total vote, even after controls for the impact of money and quality of candidate are applied. Further, he finds that using consultants benefits Republican nonincumbents but not Democratic nonincumbents. When nonincumbents are further separated into challenger and open seat categories, Medvic finds that both Republican challengers and open seat candidates benefit from consultant use, but Democratic candidates do not.

Although Dabelko and Herrnson did not find support for the professionalization hypothesis in their study of the 1984 House election, Herrnson used more recent data and reports in chapter 5 that candidates who waged amateur campaigns had an abysmal record and those who mounted highly professional campaigns had a much higher probability of winning, especially in open seats.[12]

Relationship between Consultants and Political Parties

There is general agreement that the decline of political parties has led to a rise in the use of political consultants (see chapters 4 and 5 in this volume). Political consulting firms have taken over many of the traditional party functions. However, there is disagreement over whether the increased use of political consultants is good or bad for political parties. Some scholars suggest that consultants weaken political parties by encouraging candidate-centered campaigning.[13] Others disagree and argue that consultants help parties achieve collective party goals by providing services to candidates that the parties cannot do themselves (see chapter 6). Still others find that consultants depend on political parties for future business.[14]

Kolodny, in chapter 7, explores the two basic views of the relationship—the adversarial versus allies—between consultants and parties. Are consultants little more than "advertising agencies" for candidates, only interested in their own win/loss record, or are consultants interested in promoting a particular ideology and party goals?

Kolodny finds that Republican consultants were more likely than Democrats to have worked for the party organization. She also finds that consultants who worked for the party prior to becoming consultants were more likely to have the party as a client and were more likely to coordinate their efforts with the party. Finally, those who worked for the party organization had a more positive opinion of the party than those who did not. Overall, Kolodny's research lends support to the allies view of the relationship between parties and consultants.

Consultant Use in Initiative Campaigns

The growth of the initiative industry is fueled by the difficulty of qualifying a measure for the ballot. Firms that specialize in initiatives are concentrated in California and Washington, D.C.; however, D.C. firms tend to do a mixture of candidate and initiative work. Signature gathering firms are necessary to get enough names to qualify. "To meet these signature requirements, initiative proponents in large and small states routinely hire signature-gathering firms"; if sufficient funds are available, any issue can qualify for the ballot.[15]

Magleby and Patterson describe in chapter 8 the role that consultants play in initiatives and referendums. First, they inquire whether citizens or consultants are the force behind initiative campaigns. Most consultants report that their role is to respond to the needs of citizens, not to create needs. However, it is possible that ideas for initiative campaigns have come from consultants. Second, Magleby and Patterson examine who hires consultants for initiatives and find that they are frequently hired by organized interests.

In addition, they query consultants about their feelings toward the initiative process. The consultants interviewed support the initiative process but note that initiatives have the potential to undermine representative government when they become too frequent. In California elected officials will not act on important matters because they can place the tough decisions in the hands of voters. Others complain that the initiative process is purely emotional and that voters make ill-informed decisions.

Further, the authors find that consultants who work on initiative campaigns do not work solely with members of their own party. In this, they differ from consultants who work on candidate elections. The latter group of consultants typically work only with other consultants of the same party.

Comparative Works: The Future of Consulting?

Sabato was the first to comment on the growing tendency for consultants to work overseas.[16] The International Association of Political Consultants (IAPC), founded in 1968, has grown from fifty to almost two hundred members over the past thirty years. The association meets regularly to exchange ideas and tactics. There is some baseline scholarship from political scientists in other nations who explore the role of political consultants in their nations;[17] however, little research from American scholars explores the way in which U.S. consultants have exported their talents overseas and to what effect.

Bowler and Farrell in chapter 9 examine some of the reasons for the internationalization or "Americanization" of consulting. In addition, they describe some of the limitations facing consultants who try to "go international." They survey the members of the IAPC to probe the role that overseas consultants play, which services are in demand, and the level of cooperation between U.S. consultants in overseas campaigns.

Conclusion

Although election campaigns are a major event in American democratic life and much is written about those battles, we know little about the campaign consultants who help to structure the strategy, theme, and message of those important events. Campaign consultants are major players in modern elections, but we know little about who they are, their role, and their influence. Collectively, each chapter in this book helps to fill the gap of knowledge about campaign consultants. Each author brings original, new data and systematic observation about political consultants that helps to expand the empirical and theoretical work about campaign consultants and their impact on elections.

Notes

1. Dan Nimmo, *The Political Persuaders: The Techniques of Modern Election Campaigns* (Prentice Hall, 1970), p. 50.

2. See James A. Thurber and Candice J. Nelson, *Campaigns and Elections American Style* (Westview Press, 1995); Daniel M. Shea, *Campaign Craft: The Strategies, Tactics, and Art of Campaign Management* (Praeger, 1996); and Karen S. Johnson-Cartee and Gary A. Copeland, *Inside Political Campaigns: Theory and Practice* (Praeger, 1997).

3. See Stanley Kelley Jr., *Professional Public Relations and Political Power* (Johns Hopkins University Press, 1956); Nimmo, *The Political Persuaders*; Larry J. Sabato, *The Rise of Political Consultants: New Ways of Winning Elections* (Basic Books, 1981); Frank I. Luntz, *Candidates, Consultants, and Campaigns: The Style and Substance of American Electioneering* (Basil Blackwell, 1988); Mark P. Petracca and Courtney Wierioch, "Consultant Democracy: The Activities and Attitudes of American Political Consultants," paper presented at the annual meeting of the Midwest Political Science Association, Chicago, Ill., 1988.

4. Kelley, *Professional Public Relations*; Nimmo, *The Political Persuaders*.

5. Kelley, *Professional Public Relations*.

6. Nimmo, *The Political Persuaders*, p. 41.

7. For accounts of journalists, see Sidney Blumenthal, *The Permanent Campaign: Inside the World of Elite Political Operatives* (Beacon Press, 1982). For practitioners, see H. M. Baus and W. B. Ross, *Politics Battle Plan* (Macmillan, 1968); J. M. Perry, *The New Politics: The Expanding Technology of Political Manipulation* (New York: Clarkson N. Potter, 1968); G. Wyckoff, *The Image Candidate* (Macmillan, 1968); Joe McGinnis, *The Selling of the President 1968* (New York: Trident Press, 1969); Robert Agranoff, *The New Style in Election Campaigns* (Boston: Holbrook Press, 1972); Joseph Napolitan, *The Election*

Game and How to Win It (Doubleday, 1972); S. J. Guzzetta, *The Campaign Manual: A Definitive Study of the Modern Political Campaign Process* (Anaheim, Calif.: Political Publishing Company, 1987); Gary Selnow, *High Tech Campaigns* (Praeger, 1994); and Mary Matalin and James Carville, *All's Fair: Love, War, and Running for President* (Random House, 1994).

8. Sabato, *The Rise of Political Consultants;* Mark P. Petracca, "Political Consultants and Democratic Governance," *PS: Political Science and Politics,* 22 (1989), p. 11–14; Petracca and Wierioch, "Consultant Democracy."

9. Paul S. Herrnson, "Campaign Professionalism and Fund-Raising in Congressional Elections," *Journal of Politics,* 54 (1992), pp. 859–70.

10. Stephen K. Medvic and Silvo Lenart, "The Influence of Political Consultants in the 1992 Congressional Elections," *Legislative Studies Quarterly,* 22 (1997), pp. 61–77; Stephen K. Medvic, "Is there a Spin Doctor in the House? The Impact of Political Consultants in Congressional Campaigns," Ph.D. dissertation, Purdue University, 1997; Stephen K. Medvic, "Party Support and Consultant Use in Congressional Elections," paper presented at the annual meeting of the American Political Science Association, Washington, D.C., 1997; Kirsten la Cour Dabelko and Paul S. Herrnson, "Women's and Men's Campaigns for the U.S. House of Representatives," *Political Research Quarterly,* 50 (1997), pp. 121–35;

11. Herrnson uses two-stage least squares (TSLS) to capture the reciprocal causality that certainly exists between professionalism, money, and competitiveness.

12. Dabelko and Herrnson, "Women's and Men's Campaigns for the U.S. House of Representatives."

13. Sabato, *The Rise of Political Consultants;* Luntz, *Candidates, Consultants and Campaigns;* Robin Kolodny and Angela Logan, "Political Consultants and the Extension of Party Goals," paper presented at the annual meeting of the American Political Science Association, Washington, D.C., 1997.

14. Sabato, *The Rise of Political Consultants;* Luntz, *Candidates, Consultants and Campaigns;* Kolodny and Logan, "Political Consultants and the Extension of Party Goals."

15. David Magleby and Kelly Patterson, "Consultants and Direct Democracy," paper presented at the annual meeting of the American Political Science Association, Washington, D.C., 1997.

16. Sabato, *The Rise of Political Consultants.*

17. See Shaun Bowler and David Farrell, chapter 9 in this volume; Shaun Bowler and David Farrell, eds., *Electoral Strategies and Political Marketing* (Houndmills, Basingstoke: Macmillan, 1992); David Farrell, "Political Consultancy Overseas: The Internationalization of Campaign Consultancy," paper presented at the annual meeting of the American Political Science Association, Washington, D.C., 1997. Also see David Butler and Austin Ranney, eds., *Electioneering: A Comparative Study of Continuity and Change* (Oxford University Press, 1992); Fritz Plasser, "Tracing the Worldwide Proliferation of American Campaign Techniques," paper presented at the annual meeting of the International Association of Political Consultants, Milan, Italy, 1999.

CHAPTER TWO

Portrait of Campaign Consultants

JAMES A. THURBER

CANDICE J. NELSON

DAVID A. DULIO

Political consultants are an essential part of election campaigns, but political scientists have all but ignored them
as a focus of research until recently.[1] For almost fifty years political scientists have been studying both American elections and American electoral behavior. From the earliest analyses in *Voting* and *The American
Voter* to the more recent studies of *The Changing American Voter, Why
Americans Don't Vote,* and *The New American Voter,* scholars have
examined the factors that influence voters' decisions at the polls and how
these factors have changed over time.[2] There are also many studies of
elections generally—presidential, congressional, state and local, primary,
and general.[3] However, there have been few studies over the years that
examine the individuals who are responsible for delivering, and often creating, the messages that voters receive—namely, political consultants.[4]

In the earliest days of the United States, candidates were able to, and
did, talk directly to voters. In past generations, political party officials
played a major role in electoral campaigns. They chose candidates; raised
money; provided expertise, labor, and voter lists; and helped get out the
vote. Today the parties play a diminished role and political consultants
often operate in their place. As the country grew, it became more difficult for candidates and potential voters to communicate directly with

An earlier version of this chapter was presented at the annual meeting of the American
Political Science Association, Boston, September 1998.

each other. With the advent of radio and then television, the broadcast media became an increasingly important tool of campaign communication.[5] As the use of television and radio ads increased, the need for specialists with expertise to develop such ads grew. Similarly, as campaigns became larger and more sophisticated, other expertise also developed— survey and opposition researchers, direct-mail providers (both for fundraising and persuasion mail), fund-raisers and financial consultants who contact donors, get-out-the-vote specialists, and speech writers, to name just some of the political consultant specialties that have developed over the last thirty years.[6] These professionals have become major repositories of political experience and employers of skilled labor. Although they have become important elements in election campaigns, we know little about these political consultants.

In order to fully understand American elections at the start of the new century, we need to understand this group of people who help to develop and deliver a candidate's strategy, theme, and message to the electorate. Just as we study the media to understand how people receive and process political information, we need to study the role consultants play in delivering these campaign messages to voters.[7]

This analysis defines who the consultants are and what they believe; it is a portrait of the profession. This study reports on the first wave of a survey that examines four types of political consultants—media consultants, pollsters, fund-raising consultants, and general consultants. We examine how these consultants view the candidates for whom they work, the voters with whom they try to communicate, the media who report on campaigns, previously proposed campaign reforms, and campaign ethics. However, we begin with a description of the political consulting industry.[8]

The analyses conducted in this chapter are meant to be mainly descriptive, as we are still exploring consultants as individuals. In our data analysis we control for a number of variables in order to provide a fuller picture of the consultants in our sample. These variables include consultants' self-reported party identification, consultant type, and consultants' age and experience in the profession. These controls are well founded in theory and previous scholarly work.[9] For example, the political consulting business is a partisan business. While some consultants might work for candidates of both parties (Dick Morris, for example), most are loyal to one party. In addition, because of the division of labor, all consultants do not share the same expertise and characteristics, and thus experiences. Because of the duties each performs, poll-sters, media consultants, fund-raisers, and general consultants can be differentiated. Each has his or her own specialty in a campaign, and this may lead to distinct attitudes and behavior when compared to another type of consultant. We entered the analysis of consultant attitudes with a number of expectations, many having to do with these explanatory variables. These expectations are highlighted in our discussion of the survey findings.

Who Are Political Consultants?

Before discussing any relationships discovered in the survey data, it is important to give a demographic description of the political consulting industry, something that has been lacking until this point. The sampl-ing procedures described in appendix A yielded a sample that accu-rately reflects the partisan make-up and type of consultant. This procedure allows us to assemble a picture of an industry that is very much a part of election campaigns in the United States, yet one that is understudied.

This survey showed that principals in the major campaign consulting firms are primarily white and male. Dennis Johnson also reaches this con-clusion in chapter 3 of this book. Of the principals responding to the survey, 98 percent were white and 82 percent were male. The consulting industry therefore is similar in demographic characteristics to the indi-viduals for whom they work—the candidates and officeholders.[10] Politi-cal consultants earn hefty salaries, with more than one-half (52 percent) reporting an average annual family income in 1996 and 1997 of more than $150,000 and two-thirds reporting more than $200,000.

Principals in the major political consulting firms are relatively young and highly educated, like their clients the candidates. Only 6 percent reported *not* having a college degree, while 42 percent reported having a college degree, 26 percent said they had a master's degree, and 14 percent reported having either a law degree or a doctorate. Seventy-eight percent of the respondents were under the age of 50, and 40 percent were under 40, with an average age of just under 43.

Political consultants are not very religious, relative to the general pop-ulation. A full 22 percent describe themselves as either atheist or agnos-tic, compared to only 8 percent of the general population; 10 percent described themselves as "born-again" Christians, while 33 percent of all Americans classify themselves this way.

Party organizations are a major training ground for political consultants. In fact, the most common past experience or training cited by professional consultants was working for a national, state, or local party or party committee. These data confirm the work done by Robin Kolodny, presented in chapter 7 of this volume, and others, which asserts that the party organizations are the breeding ground for the next generation of political consultants.[11] This may be changing, however, with the rise of training organizations, such as American University's Campaign Management Institute, George Washington University's Graduate School of Political Management, the Women's Campaign School at Yale, and others. More than one-half (54 percent) of the consultants responding to the survey report having worked for an elected official at the federal, state, or local level, and the same amount reported working in government themselves. Only 30 percent of the principals in major consulting firms reported working for some kind of media organization.

Although consulting is a partisan business, and consultants usually work for candidates on only one side of the aisle, most consultants describe their political beliefs as toward the middle of the ideological spectrum. Nearly one-third (28 percent) of all respondents describe themselves as moderates. Nearly 80 percent of Republicans describe themselves as either conservative or moderate; only 18 percent said they were very conservative. Seventy-four percent of Democrats characterized themselves as either liberal or moderate; only 22 percent categorized themselves as very liberal.

The portrait of American political consultants painted by this research is one of well-educated, ideologically moderate, young, and politically experienced professionals. Understanding the attitudes of these campaign elites will help to explain their role in election campaigns. In the following sections, we analyze consultants' attitudes toward three key players in elections: candidates, voters, and the media. We also examine consultant opinions about campaign reform and ethics, two important factors influencing the future of campaigns in America. The section on reforms focuses on campaign finance and what consultants would do to change the system. Finally, the section on ethics examines the conventional wisdom that consultants are devious and unethical creatures who are out to "win at all costs."

Consultant Attitudes toward Candidates:
Everyone Deserves Representation

A central focus of any election campaign is the candidate. The relationship between candidates and consultants is a critical link to understand when studying modern campaigns in the United States. When we analyze the views of consultants, we find that they do not think very highly of their clients, the candidates. Nearly 48 percent of them rate their congressional candidates as "fair" or "poor" (see table 2-1). While only 17 percent of consultants feel candidates for office have gotten better since they first entered politics, 42 percent said the candidates have gotten worse in that time (see table 2-2). Republican consultants reveal a more positive view of their clients than the Democratic consultants, with 71 percent of the Republicans saying their candidates are "excellent" or "good," versus 40 percent of the Democrats saying the same. Fifty-three percent of the Democrats say their candidates have gotten worse over time, compared to only 27 percent of the Republicans expressing that view.

A possible explanation for these partisan differences may be both parties' electoral fortunes prior to the 1998 elections. Prior to 1998 the Democrats took some hits in congressional elections—losing their majority in 1994 and failing to regain it in 1996. The fact that Democratic consultants have not been successful in getting their clients elected lately may be the root of their negative feelings about candidates. Democratic consultants may be attributing the blame for their party's recent misfortune to the candidates. In the same vein, these findings may show that Republican consultants are attributing their recent success in congressional elections to their candidates.

The Democratic party's gains in the 1998 congressional elections may have provided a venue to test this hypothesis. While they did not win back control of Congress, their performance was better than expected. If elec-

Table 2-1. *Political Consultants' Views of Today's Candidates*[a]

Percent

Rating	Republicans	Democrats	Total
Excellent/good	71	39.5	52.3
	(56)	(45)	(101)
Fair/poor	29	60.5	47.7
	(23)	(69)	(92)

a. Sample sizes are in parentheses. Pearson's Chi-square = 18.45, degrees of freedom = 1, $p = .000$. Fisher's exact test $p = .000$ (two-tail).

Table 2-2. *Political Consultants' Views of the Changes in Candidates for Office*[a]

Percent

Rating	Republicans	Democrats	Total
Gotten better	33	6	17.2
	(26)	(7)	(33)
Gotten worse	26.5	53	42
	(21)	(60)	(81)
Stayed the same	40.5	41	40.9
	(79)	(114)	(79)

a. Sample sizes are in parentheses. Pearson's Chi-square = 27.109, degrees of freedom = 2, $p < .000$.

toral fortunes drive these beliefs about candidates, we would expect to see consultants' views change somewhat. In the next wave of the survey, we might expect to see Democratic consultants' opinions of candidates be more positive and those of Republican consultants be more negative.

Consultants of both parties say it is difficult to sell a mediocre candidate's stands on issues. A majority of consultants of both parties (69 percent of Republicans and 58 percent of Democrats) report it is either "somewhat difficult" or "very difficult" to elect a mediocre candidate. While equal frequencies were found across party, those consultants who said it was somewhat or very difficult to elect a mediocre candidate were older (mean age 44.3) than those who said it was either "very easy" or "somewhat easy" to elect less-than-stellar candidates (mean age 40.6).

While professional campaign consultants share few characteristics with other professionals, they are similar to lawyers, for example, in that their business allows them to accept some clients and reject others.[12] We asked professional political consultants how important certain considerations were in their decisions to take on a client. Consultants were asked about the candidate's chances of winning, ability to govern once in office, political beliefs, and ability to raise money to pay for the campaign. The probability of a candidate winning is important to consultants of both parties, with 78 percent of all consultants (83 percent of Republicans and 75 percent of Democrats) saying that it is very or somewhat important in their calculus for selecting their clients. More media consultants (85 percent) and general consultants (86.5 percent) said this was an important consideration in their taking on a client than did pollsters (64 percent) or fund-raisers (77 percent).

Table 2-3. *Importance of Candidate's Ability to Raise Money in Political Consultants' Calculus of Whether to Take on a Race*[a]

Consultant's party	N	Mean ranking[b]	Standard deviation
Republicans	79	7.9	1.4
Democrats	115	8.5	1.3

a. t - test for equality of means = –2.99, degrees of freedom = 192, p = .003 (two-tail).
b. Scale is 1 (not at all important) to 10 (very important).

The importance of a candidate's ability to govern is also a factor in a consultant's calculus to accept a client or not, with 82 percent saying that it is very or somewhat important. More surprising, however, was the finding that 44 percent of consultants said they have helped a candidate get elected that they were later sorry to see serve in office, with the Democrats (47 percent) showing more regret than Republicans (40.5 percent).

The greatest consensus among consultants was found in their responses to the question of a candidate's political beliefs and ability to raise money. A full 97 percent of all consultants (no difference between Republicans and Democrats were found) said a candidate's political beliefs were either "very important" or "somewhat important." And 98 percent (again no partisan differences were found) said a candidate's ability to raise money and pay the bills was either very or somewhat important. In addition, Republican consultants gave a candidate's ability to raise money a mean ranking of 7.9 (on a scale of 1–10); Democrats gave it a ranking of 8.5 (see table 2-3).

The message is clear—consultants like to work with potential winners who can pay. They want candidates who can govern (the ultimate reason for an election), but they have second thoughts about some of their clients after they are elected. Many consultants say they get involved in campaigns for the thrill of the competition rather than political ideals, money, political power, or influence, but they are still concerned about getting paid. Almost one-third of the respondents indicate that the thrill of the game is the main reason their fellow consultants entered the profession. Political beliefs and money tie, at 26 percent each, as the next reason for getting involved in the campaign consulting business, and the power and influence that is associated with the position was the least cited reason, with only 8.5 percent citing it.

Table 2-4. *Political Consultants' Views of*
How Well Informed the Electorate Is[a]

Percent

Rating	Republicans	Democrats	Total
Very well informed/	44	25	32.5
somewhat well informed	(34)	(28)	(62)
Somewhat poorly informed/	56	75	67.5
very poorly informed	(43)	(86)	(129)

a. Sample sizes are in parentheses. Pearson's Chi-square = 8.048, degrees of freedom = 1, p = .004. Fisher's exact test p = .007 (two-tail).

Consultant Attitudes toward Voters

Because one of the most important roles of consultants is to persuade potential voters to vote for their clients, we were interested in the consultants' perceptions of the American electorate (see table 2-4). We found that while consultants do not think the American people are very well informed about major policy issues facing the country, they do trust the judgment of the American people on both domestic policy issues and their electoral choices on election day.

We found that only 32.5 percent of our consultants thought voters were "very well informed" or "somewhat well informed," whereas 67.5 percent thought voters were "somewhat poorly informed" or "very poorly informed." There were significant differences between Republican and Democratic consultants. Forty-four percent of Republican consultants thought voters were very or somewhat well informed about major policy issues, whereas only 25 percent of Democratic consultants thought voters were very or somewhat well informed. While more than half (56 percent) of Republican consultants thought voters were somewhat or very poorly informed on major policy issues, three-quarters of Democratic consultants so viewed voters. Perhaps the perception that Republican voters are better educated, and thus better informed on issues than Democratic voters, is reflected by the consultants in this study.

In addition to the political party affiliation of consultants, we also controlled for age, experience as consultants, and the type of consultants. While we found no differences among consultants of different ages or among consultants with different years of consulting experience, we did find some differences among types of consultants. Fifty percent of fund-raising consultants responded that voters were "very well informed" or "somewhat well informed," compared to only slightly more than 30 percent of pollsters and general consultants and 25 percent of media consultants. Because pollsters measure voters' information about policy issues, their perceptions may be the most accurate of those interviewed. Because media consultants are charged with developing advertising campaigns focused on informing the electorate, it is not surprising that 75 percent of these consultants perceive voters as somewhat or very poorly informed. However, because the number of respondents in each tabular cell was small, we draw no conclusions, and these findings should at best be considered speculative.

While the political consultants in our survey do not consider American voters well informed about policy issues, they do trust the judgment of the voters on major domestic policy issues.[13] When asked how much confidence they have in the judgment of the American people on major domestic policy issues, 79 percent of the consultants said they had "a great deal" or "a fair amount" of confidence, while just 20 percent said they had "not very much" or no confidence in the American people. Moreover, there is little difference between Republican and Democratic consultants on this question. Eighty-two percent of Republican consultants trust the judgment of the American people "a great deal" or "a fair amount," while 77 percent of Democratic consultants have the same view.

When controlling for both age and experience as a consultant, we find some difference among the respondents. Older consultants and those with more experience as consultants are more likely to trust the judgment of the American people on domestic policy issues than are their younger or less experienced colleagues. Those consultants who said they had either "a great deal" or "a fair amount" of trust had almost 18 years of experience and an average age of 43; those who said they had "not very much" or no trust had only 15.5 years experience and an average age of nearly 41. Type of consultant also revealed differences in the confidence of the judgment of the American people, with media and general consultants having somewhat more confidence in voters than pollsters and fund-raising consultants.

Finally, we asked our sample how much trust and confidence they had in the wisdom of the American people when it came to making choices on election day. We found that 85 percent of the consultants had "a great deal" or "a fair amount" of confidence in the choices of the American people. Here we saw some differences between Republican and Democratic consultants, with 89 percent of Republican consultants reporting "a great deal" or "a fair amount" of confidence, compared to 82 percent of Democratic consultants. Perhaps these findings reinforce our earlier result, which illustrated that Republican consultants see voters as better informed on major issues than do their Democratic colleagues. If Republican consultants see voters as better informed on policy issues, it is not surprising that they would have more trust and confidence in voters' decisions on election day.

No differences were found between younger and older consultants, but consultants who said they had either "a great deal" or "a fair amount" of trust in the electorate on election day were more experienced (18 years experience on average) than those who said they did not have very much or no trust in the American people (15.5 years experience on average). Again, this may reflect an earlier result. Recall that the more experienced consultants were more likely to trust the judgment of the American people on domestic policy issues. Finally, we found fund-raising consultants were somewhat *less* trusting than other types of consultants, but still three-quarters of fund-raising consultants trusted the judgment of the American people on election day.

One maxim that guides many political consultants is to never underestimate the judgment of the American people, but to never overestimate their interest in politics. Our findings seem to support this point of view. While a majority of consultants believe the American people are not very well informed about politics, a majority nevertheless trust the judgment of voters on domestic policy issues and have trust and confidence that the American people will make the right choices on election day. This begs the question, if voters are not well informed about politics yet are viewed as capable of making the correct choice on election day, what mechanism is functioning to allow them to do so? Our findings lend support to the theories that argue voters use shortcuts when they make their choice at the polls. These shortcuts, or heuristics, are efficient ways to get around the lack of knowledge voters have during a campaign.[14]

Political Consultants and the Media: Oil and Water Do Not Mix

Compared to the trust and confidence political consultants have in the electorate and the mixed ratings they give to today's candidates, consultants' views of the media are full of negativity. Political consultants give today's political journalists poor ratings and think that they have gotten worse over time. We felt it important to investigate consultants' attitudes about political journalists, and the media in general, for a number of reasons. During an election cycle, both media outlets and political consultants (some more than others) provide voters with information about candidates and the upcoming election. Out of this, an adversarial relationship often develops, where many political journalists (either in the recent phenomenon of "ad watches"—journalistic accounts of candidate advertisements designed to educate the public as to the accuracy of the ads—or in conventional columns) may question the work and tactics of consultants. Therefore, while they have two different motivations, they are forced to come together as important actors during an election cycle.

We asked our sample a number of questions relating to the media, but when asked about the quality of political journalists today, political consultants gave a resoundingly negative response. A full 68 percent of consultants rated political journalists either "fair" or "poor." The response was almost identical across parties, with 68 percent of Republicans and 67 percent of Democrats offering one of those two responses. Just 32 percent of both Republicans and Democrats rated political journalists as "good," and only 1.5 percent of *all* political consultants rated them as "excellent" (there were zero Republican responses in this category). We believe that these negative ratings may stem from the adversarial relationship that has developed between the media and political consultants and campaigns in general. At a conference for political consultants and political journalists at American University in June 1998, campaign consultants consistently blamed print and broadcast journalists for the negative views the American public has of campaigns and elections, and the journalists blamed the consultants.

A key hypothesis about the relationship between consultants and the media is that, like voters who develop stronger partisan attitudes as they grow older, political consultants who have been around longer develop more concrete attitudes toward the media.[15] The experiences or run-ins they have had over the years may have reinforced their beliefs about journalists. It may be that more experienced consultants have had one or two specific instances that caused them to feel the way they do. On the other hand, those consultants who do not have as much experience may not have experienced a defining encounter with a journalist.

When we controlled for the age and the experience of consultants, interesting patterns and differences appeared. When looking at the "excellent" and "good" ratings taken together, and the "fair" and "poor" ratings together, no differences in age or experience were found. However, when all four response categories were examined, a pattern presented itself, with older and more experienced consultants congregating at both extremes—the ratings of "poor" or "excellent." The mean age of consultants who rated journalists as "excellent" was 48; those rating them as "poor" had a mean age of 44; and those rating political journalists as "good" or "fair" had an average age of 42. Here, a similar pattern is found, with more experienced (and likely older) consultants having extreme views of the media, rating them as either "excellent" (mean experience of 23 years) or "poor" (mean experience of 21 years). The middle ratings groups ("good" and "fair") show average years of experience around 17.[16] Taken together, consultants who rated political journalists as either "excellent" or "poor" (the extreme categories) have an average experience of 22 years. This would place them entering the consulting industry in the 1976 election cycle, just after the Watergate crisis.

As in the analyses of candidates and voters, we also controlled for type of consultant. While there were few differences found, one interesting contrast presented itself. Compared to all other consultant types, pollsters are shown to be more likely to give today's political journalists favorable ratings. Forty percent of pollsters rated political journalists as "excellent" or "good," compared to only 29 percent of media consultants, 24 percent of general consultants, and 28 percent of fund-raisers.

Why might we see this type of relationship? We believe pollsters rate political journalists more favorably because their work, at times, resembles that of journalists. In a way, both occupations are based on research—journalists for their stories and pollsters for their campaign's message and tactics. In addition, news stories about campaigns often rely on polling data. In other words, the relationship between pollsters and political journalists may not be as adversarial as other types of consultants. Both rely on interpreting facts and systematic observation. In addition, pollsters, compared to all other types of consultants, often have the least amount of contact with the campaign. Polling firms are often based in cities like Washington, D.C., where they contract out sampling and telephone interviews to be done in a state or district, bringing the data back to analyze it in house. Ultimately, this may result in pollsters

Table 2-5. *Political Consultants' Rating of Political Journalists*[a]

Percent

Rating	Worked in media	Did not work in media	Total
Excellent/good	25	35	31.8
	(15)	(48)	(63)
Fair/poor	75	65	68.2
	(45)	(90)	(135)

a. Sample sizes are in parentheses.

not having much of a presence in the district or state. Thus they are often removed from the campaign and therefore from all the actors involved, including the media. This lack of contact may also lead to the more generous ratings.

We also asked our sample what they did before becoming a political consultant—had they worked for a national, state, or local party or party committee; for a government official; or for the news media? We hypothesized that those who had worked for a news organization would rate today's journalists more favorably, given that they had some experience with the job. The first important finding is that few political consultants had ever worked for any news organization. As noted above, only 30 percent of the respondents reported ever having worked in the media. Not only were the consultants who had worked in the media not more likely to rate political journalists more favorably, they actually gave more *negative* ratings. Seventy-five percent of those consultants who had worked for the news media, compared to 65 percent of all other consultants, rated today's political journalists as "fair" or "poor" (see table 2-5).

The results obtained when we asked the consultants in our sample whether the quality of political journalists had gotten better, worse, or stayed the same since they entered politics nearly mirror those just described. There were virtually no differences when controlling for party: older and more experienced consultants were slightly more inclined to say journalists had gotten worse, and pollsters were slightly more likely to say journalists had gotten better over the years.

Consultants reinforced their negative rating of the media, with 50 percent (46 percent of Republicans and 53 percent of Democrats) saying that political journalists had gotten worse over time. Only 10 percent of Democrats and 11 percent of Republicans said that political journalists had gotten better. The balance said the quality had stayed the same.

Finally, we again controlled for type of consultant and found few differences. In a similar finding to the one outlined above, pollsters were more likely to give political journalists a favorable rating and say they have gotten better over time. More than 17 percent of pollsters gave this response compared to only 2.5 percent of general consultants, 8.75 percent of media consultants, and 10 percent of fund-raisers. Again, we believe the less generous ratings from general consultants, media consultants, and fund-raisers stem from the more adversarial relationship that they have with the media, relative to the pollsters' relationship.

Our final analysis relating to political consultants' attitudes toward the media centered on the effects political journalists can have on political consultants. We asked political consultants how much "ad watches" have made campaigns more careful about what they put into their campaign ads. Ad watches are one of the best connections between journalists and political consultants and clearly show the relationship between the two. Here political journalists offer a critique of sorts of the accuracy and ethics of political consultants' work.

Considering the evidence put forth above, the results are striking. Political consultants disliked the media and gave them low ratings for quality. However, 56 percent of them said that ad watches have affected campaigns "a great deal" or "a fair amount." The percentages were also consistent across party, although slightly more Democrats (60 percent) than Republicans (51 percent) said ad watches had the effect of making campaigns more careful in deciding what goes into the content of their television ads. While political consultants do not like political journalists, they do give ad watches credit for making their peers more careful and for affecting their behavior somewhat.

When we controlled for the age and the experience of political consultants, we found no differences between those who said ad watches had an effect on a campaign's decisions and those who said they had little or no effect. This may be due to the fact that ad watches are still a relatively new phenomenon, and unlike other results reported above, more experienced consultants probably do not have any more experience or exposure to ad watches than do younger or less experienced consultants.

Finally, we again controlled for the type of consultant. Here we hypothesized that media consultants, and possibly pollsters, would be more likely than fund-raisers and general consultants to say that ad watches have had an effect on campaigns and what they decide to put into their television spots. Because pollsters, and especially media consultants, are closely tied to what goes into a campaign commercial—pollsters describe issues that are salient with the voters and media consultants script and produce the advertisements—they are the ones most likely to feel the pressure of ad watches that act as watchdogs of sorts over their work. General consultants, and especially fund-raisers, have less contact with campaign spots and are less likely to see or feel the effect of ad watches.

As expected, pollsters (62.5 percent) and media consultants (61 percent) were more likely to say that ad watches have made campaigns more careful in their decision about the content of their ads than are fund-raisers (45.5 percent) and general consultants (40.5 percent). These differences also reach marginal statistical significance. The relationship between ad watches and consultants is easily seen here, with those consultants who are more closely tied to and affected by ad watches being more likely to see their effect on campaigns and campaign ads.

Campaign Reform: The Status Quo Is the Way to Go

Campaign reform has been a major concern to journalists, academics, elected public officials, and the voters during the last decade. Whether reforms are successful or not depends to a large extent on candidates and consultants and their willingness to fulfill them. Thus, we were especially interested in the opinions of political consultants on the need for reform and their suggestions for improving campaigns, since they play a central role in elections.

For the most part, political consultants favor the status quo when it comes to how elections are waged in the United States. We asked consultants their opinions on five different campaign finance reforms: creating public funding for candidates who accept spending limits, providing free television time to candidates, eliminating soft money, increasing individual contribution limits, and limiting spending by issue advocacy groups (see table 2-6). Few of the proposed reforms investigated in the survey received support from consultants generally. Increasing individual contribution limits received the greatest support (67 percent of all consultants said this was either an "excellent" or "good" idea), while the other proposed reforms all saw 51 percent or fewer of the consultants reporting these were either "excellent" or "good" ideas (see appendix A for complete results).

Table 2-6. *Partisan Differences on Proposed Campaign Reforms*[a]

Percent

Reform and rating	Republican	Democrat	Total
Creating public finding for candidates who accept spending limits[b]			
Excellent/good	7	65	41
	(5)	(75)	(80)
Fair/poor	94	35	59
	(74)	(40)	(114)
Providing free televison time to candidates[c]			
Excellent/good	26	68	51
	(20)	(78)	(98)
Fair/poor	74	32	49
	(58)	(37)	(95)
Eliminating soft money[d]			
Excellent/good	12	46	32
	(9)	(53)	(62)
Fair/poor	88	54	68
	(74)	(62)	(131)
Increasing individual contribution limits[e]			
Excellent/good	79	59	67
	(62)	(67)	(129)
Fair/poor	21	41	33
	(17)	(40)	(63)
Limiting spending by issue advocacy groups[f]			
Excellent/good	14	37	27
	(11)	(41)	(52)
Fair/poor	86	63	73
	(68)	(70)	(138)

a. Sample sizes are in parentheses.
b. Pearson Chi-square = 67.018, degrees of freedom = 1, p = 0.000 (two-tail). Fisher's exact test p = 0.000 (two-tail).
c. Pearson Chi-square = 33.092, degrees of freedom = 1, p = 0.000 (two-tail). Fisher's exact test p = 0.000 (two-tail).
d. Pearson Chi-square = 25.442, degrees of freedom = 1, p = 0.000 (two-tail). Fisher's exact test p = 0.000 (two-tail).
e. Pearson Chi-square = 7.776, degrees of freedom = 1, p = 0.005 (two-tail). Fisher's exact test p = 0.008 (two-tail)
f. Pearson Chi-square = 12.296, degrees of freedom = 1, p = 0.000 (two-tail). Fisher's exact test p = 0.000 (two-tail).

As in other areas, the consultants we talked to exhibited great partisan differences in their attitudes toward campaign reform. Democratic consultants were more in favor of ending soft money and establishing public funding and free television than were Republicans, while Republicans were more in favor of increasing individual contribution limits than were Democrats.

These partisan differences among consultants generally mirror the partisan differences expressed by Republican and Democratic officeholders on the same topics. For the most part, most Democrats in Congress have favored eliminating soft money, providing free television time, and providing public funding, and most Republicans have favored increasing individual contribution limits more so than Democrats.[17]

The partisan differences found between Democratic and Republican consultants on the question of limiting issue advocacy spending are again large, but what is more interesting and important is that 49 percent of consultants said this was a "poor" idea. The fact that consultants help to elect our representatives in this democracy may mask the other fact: that political consulting is a business. Consultants depend on this industry for their livelihood. Therefore, it is not surprising to find that consultants would reject a proposed reform that would limit spending from issue advocacy groups. In today's electoral context, issue advocacy is a big business. Any limitation on this spending is a lost opportunity for consultants to further their business.

This may be more so the case for some consultants than for others. For example, media consultants play a large role in issue advocacy campaigns, as they are the ones issue advocacy groups turn to for their television advertising. This may also be true for the proposed reform that would establish free television time for candidates. Free television time for candidates would mean that the media consultants who write and produce the spots that go on television would not receive their percentage (usually about 15 percent) of the purchase of air-time, which is the most significant portion of their payment (relative to the retainer).

However, the results simply do not support this idea. The percentage of media consultants who said limiting issue advocacy spending was an "excellent" or "good" idea (40 percent) was the *highest* of all four consultant types investigated—pollsters (21 percent), fund-raisers (36 percent), and general consultants (11 percent). In addition, more than one-half of media consultants said that providing free television time was either an "excellent" or "good" idea. Only pollsters (59 percent) were more supportive of this reform. Therefore, the evidence does not permit us to conclude that potential monetary threats lead media consultants to reject reforms that may limit their ability to create business with any greater likelihood than other types of consultants. However, we must not lose sight of the fact that nearly half of all consultants rejected a reform that would limit issue advocacy spending. As noted earlier, this is the more important result. While one type of consultant is no more likely to be against this reform, it is surely a common concern.

The idea that economic concerns help drive consultants *is* supported by the finding that, even in the face of the clear partisan differences, the majority of all consultants agreed that increasing the individual contribution limits was a good idea. Across all types of consultant, more than 35 percent said this was an "excellent" idea, and when those who responded that this was a "good" idea are added in, this figure increases to more than 60 percent. Whether this result is a signal that consultants have a "greater good" in mind—that is, better run campaigns—or that they simply see an opportunity to bring in more money to elections and therefore fill their pockets is beyond the scope of this study.

Campaign Ethics: Consultants Are Not So Bad

In general, much of the conventional wisdom concerning professional consultants claims that they are unethical in their business practices and try to "win at all costs." It also paints campaigns as breeding grounds for unethical behavior. For example, recent journalistic accounts of campaigns and campaign consultants have raised the issue of push polling (the practice of calling potential voters, describing the opponent in unflattering terms, and then asking the potential voter if this information would make them less likely to vote for that candidate) and have claimed that it is a common occurrence.[18] Even scholars such as Larry Sabato have said this practice is very common.[19] However, our data are more encouraging; consultants appear to be aware of and concerned about unethical behavior in campaigns.

Only one-half of the consultants surveyed said that unethical practices occur either "very often" or "sometimes" in campaigns. The only difference identified here was across type of consultant. A greater percentage of fund-raisers (54 percent) said that unethical practices occurred "not very often," "rarely," or "never" compared to other types of consultants—pollsters (47 percent), media consultants (49 percent), and general consultants (43 percent). Fund-raisers can surely be confronted by ethically uncertain situations—taking an illegal contribution, for example. However, media (and possibly general) consultants are likely to have more of an opportunity to see unethical behavior due to their omnipresent role in campaigns.

Data on consultants' attitudes toward some specific questionable campaign practices do not support the negative view of their profession portrayed in the popular media. It can be argued that campaign tactics, such as making factually untrue statements about an opponent, taking an opponent's statements out of context, using scare tactics, suppressing voter turnout, and using push polls, are unethical. If campaign consultants truly want to "win at all costs," we would expect acceptance of these types of practices as valid campaign tactics. This is not the case. Push polls (71.5 percent) and making untrue statements (97.5 percent) are undeniably considered unethical by the vast majority of consultants. Other tactics, such as focusing on criticisms of one's opponent (which may be termed a "contrast") and focusing on the opponent's personality, are found to be acceptable campaign practices. An opponent's record and personality are considered fair game in modern elections.

While these results show that professional consultants do not accept some of the most egregious campaign tactics, we do not know whether the consultants who report these tactics as unethical use them or not. This could be a situation in which consultants think certain practices are unethical, yet, at the same time, they feel free to use them to gain an advantage in an election. This is the most important question to ask. To say that using these practices is unethical is one thing; actually avoiding and refusing to use them in a tight race is another. If consultants are actually employing these unethical tactics when they identify them as unethical, there is a serious problem for the industry and democratic elections.

One side of this may be the proclivity for campaigns to "go negative." A debate in the literature exists over what "going negative" means and what its effects are.[20] However, it is clear that consultants do "go negative" and that they find it a useful and acceptable campaign tactic, as 98.5 percent say it is not unethical. We know consultants use this tactic, no matter how it is defined, likely because they feel it works. It is less clear, however, whether the questionable tactics such as those discussed above are employed even though they are considered to be ethically questionable.

In general, there is agreement across party and consultant type as to the acceptability of going negative in a campaign. Consultants' judgements about the acceptability of other tactics are mixed. One of these instances is in the use of scare tactics during campaigns (see table 2-7). Democrats and Republicans show some interesting differences. More Democrats than Republicans said that using scare tactics is acceptable.

Table 2-7. *Partisan Differences in Consultants' Attitudes toward the Use of Scare Tactics in an Election*[a]

Percent

Rating	Republican	Democrat	Total
Acceptable	31	43	38
	(23)	(48)	(71)
Questionable	51	46	48
	(38)	(52)	(90)
Clearly unethical	18	11	13
	(13)	(12)	(25)

a. Sample sizes are in parentheses. Pearson Chi-square = 3.339, degrees of freedom = 2, p = 0.183 (two-tail).

In the case of push polls, more Republicans than Democrats said that using them was acceptable. The most interesting results, however, are found in the responses to the tactic of suppressing turnout. Just prior to the 1998 election, Republicans were accused of planning to try to suppress black turnout in some solid Democratic and black districts. However, Democrats were more likely to say suppressing turnout was an acceptable practice (see table 2-8). While 48 percent of consultants from both parties said this was "clearly unethical," Republicans were more likely to say this was "questionable," while Democrats were quicker to view the practice as "acceptable" (27 percent to 15 percent).

Some evidence shows that younger consultants are more accepting of questionable ethical behavior than their older colleagues. A slight difference based on age was found in consultants' attitudes toward focusing on criticisms of one's opponent. The mean age for those saying this is an acceptable practice (N = 162) was 41.8 and the mean age for those who said this was a questionable practice (N = 35) was 46.5.[21] However, this is contradicted by the finding that older consultants were *more likely* to accept push polls than were younger professionals. The mean age of those who said using push polls was "acceptable" (N = 13) was 46.0, the mean age of those who said it was "questionable" (N = 41) was 41.3, and the average age of those who said it was "clearly unethical" (N = 140) was 42.5.[22]

The final portion of this analysis focuses on political consultants' membership in their professional organization, the American Association of Political Consultants (AAPC). A great number of the campaign consul-

Table 2-8. *Partisan Differences in Consultants' Attitudes toward the Suppression of Voter Turnout*[a]

Percent

Rating	Republican	Democrat	Total
Acceptable	15	27	22
	(11)	(31)	(42)
Questionable	36	25	30
	(27)	(29)	(56)
Clearly unethical	49	47	48
	(36)	(54)	(90)

a. Sample sizes are in parentheses. Pearson Chi-square = 4.907, degrees of freedom = 2, p = 0.086 (two-tail).

tants surveyed *do not* belong to the AAPC—only 52 percent of the total reported being members. More Democrats than Republicans report being members, but this difference does not reach statistical significance. Fundraising consultants are less likely to be members, compared to all other types of consultants. No other differences were detected in terms of membership in the association.

This is not a surprising finding. Membership in the organization is voluntary and has little effect on consultants' ability to attract business—either positively or negatively. Moreover, the AAPC offers no monetary or purposive selective benefits to its members.

The literature on group membership offers a variety of theories of how and why groups form, attract, and maintain members that apply to belonging to the AAPC.[23] Membership in the AAPC seems to be a clear victim of the problems Mancur Olson identified when he began writing about group formation and membership.[24] One could argue, however, that members can receive solidary benefits through the fraternal nature of the organization. But the lack of selective benefits offered by the AAPC would lead us to expect few consultants would report being members.

In addition, the AAPC requires that all its members sign a code of ethics each year when they renew their membership. The code is designed to encourage consultants to abide by ethical standards while conducting their business.[25] However, this code is for all intents and purposes unenforceable and is only general guidance for consultant behavior.

Surprisingly, however, an overwhelming majority, 81 percent, of the consultants in this sample agreed that there *should* be a code of ethics. There were no differences detected across party or consultant type. However, consultants who favored a code of ethics were less experienced

Table 2-9. *Partisan Differences in Consultants' Attitudes toward a Strong Code of Ethics That Allows for a Sanction of Censure[a]*

Percent

Response	Republican	Democrat	Total
Yes	62	79	72
	(39)	(70)	(109)
No	38	21	28
	(24)	(19)	(43)

a. "Should a professional organization be allowed to censure those who violate the code of ethics?" Sample sizes are in parentheses. Pearson Chi-square = 5.1, degrees of freedom = 1, p = 0.024 (two-tail). Fisher's exact test p = 0.029 (two-tail).

(mean years of experience = 17.0) than were those who opposed a strong code (mean years of experience = 20.3).

An even more surprising finding is that these same consultants say that the code should be enforceable by allowing the professional organization to censure violators (see table 2-9). More than 70 percent of all consultants favored a censure sanction. Partisan differences surface again, with Democrats more likely than Republicans to be in favor of a strong code that allows for some kind of sanction or punishment.

When asked whether or not there should be a code of ethics for consultants, 7 percent of all consultants volunteered that one already exists. This indicates that many consultants may already be familiar with the AAPC code of ethics. Indeed, 61 percent of consultants surveyed *were* familiar with this code. While Democrats and Republicans know about the AAPC code with relatively the same frequency (about 60 percent), fund-raisers and those who reported power and influence as the main motivation of consultants were less likely to be familiar with the AAPC code of ethics.

So, most consultants know about the code of ethics, but does the code matter? Does the code affect the behavior of consultants? As noted above, the code, as it stands now, is for the most part unenforceable. But this does not necessarily preclude consultants from letting their behavior be affected by it. Consultants report that the AAPC code affects their personal behavior (46 percent said it affects their behavior "a great deal" or "a fair amount") but not that of their peers (87 percent said the code affects their peers' behavior "not very much" or not at all). This is a classic example of a respondent saying I would not do that, but everyone else would.

Conclusions

The growth in the number of consultants has been dramatic in the past three decades, and this has had a fundamental impact on American elections. The development of expertise in polling, fund-raising, grass-roots organizing, media production, advertising strategy, direct mail, website design, and general campaign management, just to name a few growth areas, has professionalized campaigns and increased the cost of elections at all levels in the United States.[26] The rising costs of campaigns is directly related to the increase in the number of consultants and the expensive technology they bring to election battles. Since consultants have increasingly replaced amateurs and political party professionals at all levels of politics, it is essential to understand who these professionals are and what they think about their critical role in election campaigns. The comprehensive survey of American campaign consultants in this chapter begins to answer these questions and leads us to several important conclusions about these elite political professionals.

First, consultants think money is important in a campaign, but it is not enough to get a candidate elected. The quality of a candidate's strategy, theme, and message are equally, if not more, important. Issues and the way they are handled by candidates matter; they are central to democratic elections. Despite popular conceptions that political consultants can sell any candidate to the voters, our survey finds that more than half of these professionals think it is difficult for a mediocre candidate or a candidate with unpopular stands on issues to win an election. When asked which was a more serious problem in a campaign—a candidate with a weak message or a candidate who is a poor campaigner—an overwhelming majority of the consultants said that a candidate with a weak message was more serious than one with poor campaign skills. However, a candidate's ability to raise money and pay bills, as well as the political beliefs of the candidate, are important considerations in the consultants' decision to get involved in a campaign. The candidate's chances of winning and his or her ability to govern effectively were considerably less important.

Second, Democratic and Republican campaign consultants exhibit serious differences in their views on candidate quality. Many more Republicans than Democrats gave a positive review of today's candidates. Similar differences were found when consultants were asked about the change in candidate quality over time—more Republicans reported that they felt candidates had gotten better over time, while most Democrats said that candidates had gotten worse. One area of consensus among consultants in their attitudes about candidates was that many said they had worked for a candidate they were later sorry to see serve in office; this is a disturbing conclusion by those helping to get these public officials elected.

Third, just as consultants respect the difficulty in getting candidates elected, consultants also respect the judgments voters make on election day. While consultants do not think voters are very well informed on major policy issues, they nevertheless reported a great deal of confidence in the judgment of the American people in their choices at the ballot box. This is encouraging, coming from a group of political professionals who are typically described as believing they can fool voters into electing any candidate at any time.

Fourth, when it comes to the media, consultants are much less positive. The consultants in the survey showed little respect for the quality of political journalists. They do not respect the coverage of campaigns and think that the quality of journalists has gotten worse during the years they have been involved in politics. However, they do give journalists credit for using ad watches to help make campaigns more careful about the content of their campaign commercials. It seems as though the symbiotic relationship described by Sabato has turned more toward an adversarial one that leads consultants and journalists to be on opposing sides, at least from the point of view of the consultants.[27]

Fifth, most professional campaign consultants want little change in the way in which campaigns are waged in the United States. Partisan differences surfaced on the topic of campaign reform, although they seemed to mirror the partisan differences expressed by elected officials on the same topic. Greater proportions of Republicans favored increasing individual contribution limits than Democrats, and more Democrats were in favor of eliminating soft money and providing public funding for candidates than Republicans. Political consulting is a profession and a business, and those senior-level consultants who participated in this survey have been successful under current campaign regulations and thus are more likely to support the status quo. Consultants' attitudes about campaign reform   reflect those of the officeholders they have helped to elect. Just as incumbent officeholders have been elected under the current rules, campaign consultants know how to win with the current laws and to bring any change would not be in their self-interest.

Sixth, consultants' views on campaign ethics were found to be much more encouraging than conventional wisdom might project. Not only do consultants favor a code of ethics for their profession, but they favor a strong code that could sanction a consultant for an ethics violation. In addition, consultants view many deplorable campaign tactics—such as push polling, making false statements, and suppressing voter turnout—as clearly unethical. This evidence is a strike against the conventional wisdom that political consultants only care about winning and will try to "win at all costs."

Conventional wisdom also often indicts professional political consultants as causing low voter turnout and public cynicism, as well as reducing complex debates to negative sound bites. We find this to be inaccurate. Indeed, consultants do have other interests than just winning—they favor a strong code of ethics, dislike unethical campaign tactics, trust the judgment of the electorate, and care about the in-office performance of those they help to elect. In today's electoral context, political consultants contribute a significant amount to the quality of the discourse in campaigns. They help elect candidates, but they also help voters and democracy by communicating those same candidates' messages. Consultants do not have control over candidates and incumbent elected officials in elections. Without a doubt, some unethical consultants help to foster cynicism and apathy in the electorate through their tactics, but the attitudes and opinions expressed by the senior professionals in this survey reveal they are not taking part in the destruction of our electoral system. Those few consultants who will do anything to win are not the norm in the profession. Winning is fundamental to any campaign consultant's capacity to survive in the profession, but, surprisingly, the consultants in this survey are still concerned about the impact of their advice on our democracy. Political consultants believe they are an essential and valuable part of the electoral process and our representative democracy and they say that they want to improve the way election campaigns are fought. They want to win without damaging our democratic life.

Notes

1. James A. Thurber, "The Study of Campaign Consultants: A Subfield in Search of Theory," *PS: Political Science and Politics*, 31, 2 (1998), pp. 145–49.

2. Bernard R. Berelson, William N. McPhee, and Paul F. Lazarsfeld, *Voting: A Study of Opinion Formation in a Presidential Campaign* (University of Chicago Press, 1954); Angus Campbell, Philip E. Converse, Warren E. Miller, and Donald E. Stokes, *The American Voter* (University of Chicago Press, 1960); Norman H. Nie, John R. Petrocik, and Sidney Verba, *The Changing American Voter* (Harvard University Press, 1976); Frances F. Piven and Richard Cloward, *Why Americans Don't Vote* (Pantheon Books, 1988); Warren E. Miller and J. Merrill Shanks, *The New American Voter* (Harvard University Press, 1976).

3. For presidential elections, see Steven J. Rosenstone, *Forecasting Presidential Elections* (Yale University Press, 1983) and Samuel Popkin, *The Reasoning Voter: Communication and Persuasion in Presidential Campaigns* (University of Chicago Press, 1991). For congressional elections, see Gary C. Jacobson and Samuel J. Kernell, *Strategy and Choice in Congressional Elections* (Yale University Press, 1981); Gary C. Jacobson, *The Politics of Congressional Elections* (Harper Collins, 1997); and Paul S. Herrnson, *Congressional Elections: Campaigning at Home and in Washington*, 2d ed. (Washington, D.C.: CQ Press, 1998). For state and local elections, see Mildred A. Schwartz, "Electoral Success versus Party Maintenance: National, State and Local Party Contributions to Illinois Legislative Races," *Publius*, 24 (1994), pp. 79–92. For primary elections, see Marni Ezra, "*The Benefits and Burdens of Congressional Primary Elections,*" Ph.D. dissertation, American University, 1996; and Paul S. Herrnson and James G. Gimpel, "District Conditions and Primary Divisiveness in Congressional Elections," *Political Research Quarterly*, 48, 1 (1995), pp. 117–34.

4. Notable exceptions include Larry Sabato, *The Rise of Political Consultants: New Ways of Winning Elections* (Basic Books, 1981); Frank Luntz, *Candidates, Consultants, and Campaigns: The Style and Substance of American Electioneering* (Basil Blackwell, 1988); James A. Thurber and Candice J. Nelson, eds., *Campaigns and Elections American Style* (Westview Press, 1995); Robin Kolodny and Angela Logan, "Political Consultants and the Extensions of Party Goals," paper presented at the annual meeting of the American Political Science Association, Washington, D.C., 1997; and Thurber, "The Study of Campaign Consultants."

5. See, for example, Shaun Bowler, Todd Donovan, and K. Fernandez, "The Growth of the Political Marketing Industry and the California Initiative Process," *European Journal of Marketing*, 30, 10/11 (1996), pp. 173–85; Robert Friedenberg, *Communication Consultants in Political Campaigns* (Praeger, 1997); or Shaun Bowler and David Farrell, "The Internationalization of Election Campaign Consultancy," chapter 9 in this volume.

6. See Dennis W. Johnson, "The Business of Political Consulting," chapter 3 in this volume, and Herrnson, *Congressional Elections*.

7. See, for example, Shanto Iyengar and Donald Kinder, *News that Matters* (University of Chicago Press, 1987); Kathleen Hall Jamieson, *Dirty Politics: Deception, Distraction and Democracy* (Oxford University Press, 1992); and Stephen Ansolabehere and Shanto Iyengar, *Going Negative: How Attack Ads Shrink and Polarize the Electorate* (Free Press, 1995).

8. A description of the sampling methodology and sample results can be found in appendix A.

9. Sabato, *The Rise of Political Consultants*; Mark P. Petracca and Courtney Wierioch, "Consultant Democracy: the Activities and Attitudes of American Political Consultants," paper presented at the annual meeting of the Midwest Political Science Association, Chicago, Ill., 1988.

10. See, for example, Norman J. Ornstein, Michael J. Malbin, and Thomas Mann, *Vital Statistics on Congress* (Washington, D.C.: Congressional Quarterly, 1997).

11. See also Robin Kolodny and Angela Logan, "Political Consultants and the Extension of Party Goals," *PS: Political Science and Politics*, 31, 2 (1998), pp. 155–59. For anecdotal evidence, see Martin Hamburger, "Lessons from the Field: A Journey into Political Consulting," chapter 4 in this volume, or Candice J. Nelson, "Inside the Beltway: Profiles of Two Political Consultants," *PS: Political Science and Politics*, 31, 2 (1998), pp. 162–70.

12. We realize that those consultants who have just entered the business may not be in the position to pick and choose their clients, but the subjects of this survey–principals in the top firms–do likely enjoy this option.

13. Robert E. Lane, *Political Ideology: Why the American Common Man Believes What He Does* (Free Press, 1962).

14. See, on schemas, Paul M. Sniderman, Richard A. Brody, and Phillip E. Tetlock, "The Role of Heuristics in Political Reasoning: A Theory Sketch," in Sniderman, Brody, and Tetlock, eds., *Reasoning and Choice: Exploration in Political Psychology* (Cambridge University Press, 1991); Pamela Johnston Conover and Stanley Feldman, "How People Organize the Political World: A Schematic Model," *American Journal of Political Science*, 28 (1984), pp. 1357–80.

15. For evidence supporting the "impressionable years" theory of political socialization, see Donald O. Sears, "Whither Political Socialization Research? The Question of Persistence," in Orit Ichilov, ed., *Political Socialization, Citizenship Education and Democracy* (Teachers College Press, 1990).

16. A one-way ANOVA test showed significant differences between the four groups at the $p < .01$ level ($F_{3, 193} = 3.859$).

17. See Anthony Corrado, Thomas Mann, Dan Ortiz, Trevor Potter, and Frank Sorauf, eds., *Campaign Finance Reform: A Sourcebook* (Brookings, 1997).

18. See Charles E. Cook, "Christensen's Low Blow Holds a Lesson for Other Campaigns," *Roll Call*, May 18, 1998; Bill Hall, "Those Liars Posing as Pollsters Pollute our Politics," *Lewiston Morning Tribune*, July 8, 1996, p. 8A.

19. Sabato quoted in Marie Cocco, "Suppression Phone Calls Corrode the Campaign," *Bergen Record* (N.J.), February 19, 1996, p. A19.

20. See Kathleen Hall Jamieson, Paul Waldman, and Susan Sherr, "Eliminate the Negative? Defining and Refining Categories of Analysis for Political Advertisements," in James A. Thurber, Candice J. Nelson, and David A. Dulio, eds., *Crowded Airwaves: Political Advertising in Elections* (Brookings, forthcoming); Ansolabehere and Iyengar, *Going Negative*.

21. A t-test ($t = -2.938$, d.f. $= 195$, $p = .004$ [2-tail]) is reported here rather than an f-test because only two categories were included in the analysis as a result of only one respondent appearing in the third category and saying that this practice was "clearly unethical."

22. Even though an f-test ($F = 1.407$, $p = .247$ [2-tail]) fails to reach statistical significance, a post hoc least-significant difference (LSD) pairwise multiple comparison test indicates a significant difference between the first two groups ($p = 0.09$ [2-tail]) and a nearly significant difference between the first and third groups ($p = 0.160$ [2-tail]).

23. See, for example, David B. Truman, *The Governmental Process* (Knopf, 1951); Mancur Olson, *The Logic of Collective Action* (Harvard University Press, 1965); Robert H. Salisbury, "An Exchange Theory of Interest Groups," *Midwest Journal of Political Science*, 13 (1969), pp. 1–32; Paul A. Sabatier, "Interest Group Membership and Organization: Multiple Theories," in Mark P. Petracca, ed., *The Politics of Interests* (Westview Press, 1992).

24. Olson, *The Logic of Collective Action*.

25. See American Association of Political Consultants, "Code of Ethics," AAPC manual, 1998, or at *www.theaapc.org*.

26. For data on the rising costs of campaigns see, for example, Ornstein, Malbin, and Mann, *Vital Statistics on Congress*.

27. Larry Sabato, "Political Influence, the News Media and Campaign Consultants," *PS: Political Science and Politics*, 22, 1 (1989), pp. 15–17; Sabato, *The Rise of Political Consultants*.

CHAPTER THREE

The Business of Political Consulting

DENNIS W. JOHNSON

A s we head into the 2000 campaigns, political consulting has developed into a maturing multibillion dollar business. More than ever, candidates for office rely on the services of campaign professionals. Increasingly, professional consultants handle ballot initiatives and issue advocacy campaigns; they assist corporate and nonprofit clients and work for international candidates and causes. In the early 1980s Larry Sabato described the strategies, techniques, and personalities that dominated this relatively new industry.[1] Since then, the business of political consulting has grown dramatically, expanding into a second and third generation of firms, many offering technologically sophisticated services unheard of two decades ago.

The business of political consulting traces back to the California team of Clem Whitaker and Leone Baxter, who in 1933 formed Campaigns, Inc. They were the first to work in statewide elections and initiative-referendum politics. Whitaker's first role as a consultant in a candidate campaign was in the 1934 "Campaign of the Century"—the governor's race in California that saw reform candidate Upton Sinclair shake the California political establishment. Whitaker and Baxter were hired, not to promote a candidate, but to ensure that Sinclair was not elected governor. The campaign was filled with attacks against immigrants and poor people; Sinclair was falsely linked to a fictitious California Communist party and slandered in other ways; the Hollywood film establishment created sensational news clips attacking Sinclair. With this inauspicious beginning, the age of media politics and campaign consulting had begun. Whitaker and Baxter's career blossomed with this win and their victory in the Central Valley water referendum in 1933. Throughout their twenty-year career, Whitaker and Baxter were enormously successful, winning seventy of seventy-five campaigns they managed.[2]

With the exception of the work of Whitaker and Baxter, most early political consulting was conducted as a sideline by public relations firms. In 1957 Alexander Heard found forty-one public relations firms offering campaign services; nearly half of them were located in California, Texas, and New York.[3] By the mid-1950s, however, a new specialty was emerging: the professional campaign manager. David L. Rosenbloom found that by 1957 about thirty or forty professionals were managing campaigns on a regular basis.[4]

In the 1960s professional campaign management became more routine, especially at the presidential, gubernatorial, and senate levels. Professional campaigning was also coming to congressional races, especially for incumbents. By 1960 a total of 188 congressional campaigns received some level of professional services; by 1968 that number had jumped to 650, and an estimated 900 campaigns used professional campaign services in 1970.[5] These figures, however, have to be read with some caution. In many cases in the 1960s professional services meant only a salaried staffer who had worked on campaigns before and now was providing some measure of experience and expertise. Many of these so-called professionals would not be considered consultants today; they would more likely be considered campaign staffers. Despite some of the difficulties with terminology and deciding just who constitutes a professional consultant, we find that in the next two decades campaign professionals were used much more often and campaign-oriented firms began to flourish.[6]

In the mid-1980s many political consulting businesses were created, often by younger members of established firms or operatives who had worked for the national political parties. The new firms were mostly in the fields of media advertising and polling. By the late 1980s political consultants were employed by candidates for public office at all electoral levels, including state legislators, mayors, city councillors, county commissioners, and even school boards.[7]

In looking at congressional races, Paul Herrnson found that 1992 campaigns, especially those of incumbents, had become highly professionalized.[8] Members of Congress seeking reelection had the biggest advantage, employing paid campaign staffs and political consultants, with specialists in polling and media advertising. Seventy-seven percent of the 120 incumbent campaigns surveyed used professional polling consultants, while 76 percent used media consultants.

By the mid-1990s many consulting firms began assisting candidates in races well below the statewide or congressional level. For example, the Republican polling firm of Wirthlin Worldwide, with branch offices in Hong Kong and London, worked for Ronald Reagan and Margaret Thatcher, but they also worked for sheriff candidates in Charlotte City and Palm Beach City, Florida. Whistlestop Communications, a Republican media firm based in Indianapolis, in 1996 worked for in-state mayoral candidates in Wabash and Carmel, for auditor and treasurer candidates in Howard County, and for a variety of Indiana state senate and house candidates. Candidates for the school board in St. Johns City, Clay City, and Duval City, Florida, all received professional polling assistance from Jacksonville-based Populus, Inc. City council candidates in San Marcos, California, mayoral candidates in Huntsville, Alabama, and Warren, Michigan, and a circuit court clerk candidate in Chesapeake, Virginia, were assisted by professional consultants. Hundreds of candidates for state legislative seats, municipal and state court positions, and those supporting local and statewide ballot initiatives used the services of professional consultants.

Political Consulting Today

Not all political consultants are alike, and not all contribute the same value of services to a campaign. In campaign studies, this elemental fact is sometimes lost and, as a consequence, consultants of all stripes tend to get lumped together in the same category and are then added together. When social scientists fail to make critical distinctions about the work of professional consultants, they often end up with simplistic and unrealistic conclusions about the role and impact of consultants. The business of political consulting has three fairly distinct tiers.

Strategists, Specialists, and Vendors

In the top tier are the *strategists*, the key consultants who develop the campaign message, communicate it to voters, and provide strategic advice and support throughout the campaign. In an elaborate, well-funded campaign the strategist might include the general consultant, campaign manager, the media consultant, the pollster, and the direct-mail specialist. If they communicate well with each other, these consultants will provide the candidate with coordinated message and strategy development. In a smaller campaign the strategist might be the professional campaign manager or the pollster. When scholars and the public focus on campaign consultants, they usually think of strategists, and much of the discussion throughout this chapter focuses on these consultants.

In the second tier of consultants are the *specialists,* who provide essential campaign services: fund-raising, candidate and opposition research, media buying, voter contact, initiative and referenda legal services, petition and signature gathering, and speech writing. These skills are extremely important to a campaign but do not, in themselves, form the strategic core of services. Campaigns cannot run without money, and professional fund-raisers can make the difference between a robust, well-funded campaign and one that is poorly funded and barely able to communicate with voters. However vital their services, fund-raising professionals are not at the strategic core. The same can be said for candidate and opposition research. Research professionals distill enormous amounts of information about voting, public service, and increasingly about candidates' private lives; they create order and direction out of mounds of factual information, which becomes the raw data used in political communications. However, researchers are not strategic decisionmakers for campaigns. Most ballot initiatives could never get certified without the work of professional signature gatherers; without the services of television time-buyers, campaign commercials would lose their impact, failing to hit the targeted audience and time. Vital as these and other campaign services are, they, too, fall into the category of specialists.

The third tier of consultants is comprised of *vendors* who supply campaign products and services: website developers, voter files and mailing list firms, campaign software and computer services, print and promotional materials, media tracking, and other services. Most specialists and strategists work for just one political party, while many vendors offer products and services for anyone who will pay for them.

In addition, there is a small industry of political newsletters and magazines. For the consulting industry, the most prominent is Congressional Quarterly's *Campaigns & Elections* magazine and its newsletter, "Campaign Insider," both edited by Ron Faucheux. Consultants, journalists, and campaign junkies can turn to *National Journal's* web-based hotline, various politically oriented websites and on-line services, plus political newsletters focusing on congressional elections or state politics.[9]

Campaigns range greatly in the professional political consulting services they employ. A top-flight, highly professionalized statewide race with a $6 million budget might easily employ this range of consultants, providing these services:

STRATEGISTS

General consultant	Overall campaign coordination
Campaign manager	Day-to-day management of campaign staff
Polling firm	Polls, focus groups, strategic advice
Media firm	Create media communications, develop theme and message
Direct mail firm	Create mail communications, develop theme and message

SPECIALISTS

Research team	Opposition and candidate research
Telemarketing firm	Phone banks
Fund-raising firm	Raise campaign funds
Media buying firm	Buy television time
Speech writer	Craft announcements and stump speeches

VENDORS

Website developer	Create website
Printing firm	Printing promotional materials
Voter file firm	Lists of voters, addresses
Campaign solftware	Software for Federal Election Committee filings, database management, other uses

At the other end of the electoral food-chain, a campaign for a local office—school board, for example—may have only $30,000 to spend but still can be considered professional:

STRATEGISTS

Campaign manager	Plan and execute all phases of strategy and message development, manage the all-volunteer campaign.

VENDORS

Printing firm	Provide handbills, posters, bumper stickers

Both of these are examples of professional campaigns, but they could not be further apart in the degree of skill and depth of specialization.

In chapter 6, Stephen K. Medvic argues that political consultants should be "treated in the aggregate as a campaign resource."[10] My experiences as both a consultant and a student of campaigning make me resist strongly such aggregate analysis.

Do consultants make a difference? As Herrnson notes in chapter 5, political consultants have an important but not overwhelming impact on congressional races. The same can be said for other races in which professionals are employed. Modern campaigns require sophisticated communications and technological expertise, especially in statewide and competitive congressional races. Without consultants in these races, candidates stand little chance of competing, let alone winning. Do consultants provide the margin of victory? Here we get into much murkier territory. In rare cases, consultants have engineered election miracles. And when an election miracle happens for one side, an election disaster occurs on the other. One example is the come-from-way-behind victory masterminded by general consultant James Carville and his associates of Democrat Harris Wofford in the 1991 special election for the Senate seat in Pennsylvania. (On the other hand, Wofford's opponent, Richard Thornburg, squandered a 44-point lead, and his consultants were incapable of preventing the meltdown). But electoral miracles rarely happen; more common are the close contests that were won because of the talents and skills of individual consultants.

Even the best consultants lose several contests each election cycle, and many have suffered bitter defeats. The 1996 presidential campaign of Robert Dole was a revolving door of consultants who were unable to put together a consistent message; the consultants for Michael Dukakis in the 1988 presidential campaign were incapable of responding to negative advertising; Al Checchi's high-powered consulting team spent $40 million dollars—a record amount—and Checchi still came in third in the 1998 California gubernatorial primary; and Jesse Ventura's mainstream opponents and consultants did not understand the power and attraction of this former wrestler's persona.

The business of political consulting is a dynamic niche market within the larger world of marketing and communications. It differs from the larger world in a number of ways.

1. *A fraction of the communications market place.* The businesses of commercial polling, media advertising, direct mail, and telemarketing are

vast multibillion dollar enterprises in the United States. Many of the techniques developed in the commercial world have been applied to the specialty world of campaigns and elections. However, the core election activities—polling, media advertising, direct mail, and telemarketing—constitute only a fraction of the total market for those industries. Private political polling, for example, represents only 2.5 percent ($100 million) of the entire $4 billion annual survey research industry.[11] Political advertising is similarly dwarfed by the advertising in the general consumer market. The most successful political media firms may have $15 million in billings during a two-year election cycle. By contrast, the London-based advertising firm of Saatchi and Saatchi earned $274 million in the United States in 1996 alone and was only the third-largest commercial firm in U.S. billings.

The amount of money spent on political television advertising, the most expensive item in a statewide or presidential campaign, pales in comparison to advertising generated by commercial interests. For example, during the seven-month period of April through October 1996, when the presidential elections and the other campaigns were in full swing, only 1.2 percent of all television commercials were for candidates and political causes.[12] Put in perspective, the total amount of funds spent on the 1996 presidential election was $883 million, with some estimates of indirect spending ballooning that to approximately $2.4 billion. Commercial product advertising on national media was $66.7 billion in 1996; General Motors Corporation spent the most, $1.71 billion in media advertising, while Procter and Gamble was second at $1.45 billion.[13]

Direct mail is a booming $31.2 billion market, dominated by such industry giants as Banta Corporation, Wallace Computer Services, and Webcraft Technologies. By contrast, political advertising through direct mail is approximately 2 percent of that market, approximately $750 million a year.[14] Commercial telemarketing is a huge $385 billion annual market; this does not include the large mail order catalogue and inbound telemarketing business.[15] Of this, political telemarketing is far less than 1 percent.

2. *Small business operations.* In the commercial world, a business that generates less than $50 million is considered a small enterprise. By that measure, every political consulting firm is a small business. Most of the estimated 3,000 firms that specialize in campaigns and elections have very small staffs—perhaps two or three partners, a total staff of ten—and generate several hundred thousand dollars in revenue annually. Only a few

firms, such as media consultant Squier, Knapp, and Dunn, generate millions of dollars in revenue, and most of this passes through the consultants' hands to pay television advertising costs. Leading polling firms, such as the Tarrance Group or Public Opinion Strategies, may have forty to eighty employees; most are support staff working the telephones and part of the back office operations.

Quite a few firms are cottage enterprises—one- or two-person boutiques, often in specialty markets, such as event planning, opposition research, fund-raising, or media buying. Many political consulting firms operate out of the basement of the principal's home, with no more than telephone lines, computers, fax machines, and on-line access. For example, even after he became famous as Clinton's principal political adviser, James Carville and his assistants worked out of the "bat cave," a basement studio apartment on Capitol Hill that served as Carville's home and nerve-center for his far-flung political operations.

3. *A highly cyclical market.* Firms that rely solely on campaign cycles are exposed to the roller coaster of cash-flow: many lean months, with little money coming in from clients, countered by a few fat months, with the bulk of the revenues pouring in. In addition to the on-off flow of cash is the pressure of juggling many candidates during the last crucial weeks of the campaign cycle and the enormous time pressures of a busy campaign season. Some consulting firms have around-the-clock operations during the last critical weeks of the campaign—political emergency rooms geared to handle any last-minute crisis. But the cyclical nature also works in the opposite direction: there are long stretches when there is no business, few campaign opportunities during the "off-year" cycles, and professionals and support staff who have to be paid or let go until the cycle picks up again.

One of the most difficult, but necessary, tasks is to smooth out the steep curves in the election cycle so that money and resources flow more predictably. Consultants have adapted several strategies. First, many campaigns now last months longer than before; consultants are entering the campaigns earlier and staying longer. Second, consultants are searching for off-year races especially down the electoral ladder—mayoral and general assembly races, and other local contests that in past years would not have had professional assistance. Third, consultants are getting more involved in the growing business of initiatives, referendums, and issues management. Many of these campaigns are tied to the same election cycle as candidates' campaigns, but others are tied to local, state, or congressional issue cycles. Fourth, political firms turn to trade association, corporate, issue advocacy, and international clients to smooth out the peaks and valleys of the election cycle.

4. *Shifting from candidate to issues management.* Many consulting firms limit the amount of business they do with candidate campaigns. A study conducted in 1972 found that 58 percent of the 360 campaign management firms surveyed depended on candidate campaigns for less than 50 percent of their business.[16] By the 1980s, firms were shifting away from heavy reliance on candidate campaigns. For example, Matt Reese, who had worked for more than 400 Democratic candidates, changed his firm's direction after the 1982 elections to concentrate on corporate and trade association clients. Republican consultant Eddie Mahe shifted his business from 100 percent candidate-based in the early 1980s to about 15 percent candidate-based in the early 1990s, picking up corporate and other clients in place of candidates. The Clinton Group, a pioneering political telemarketing firm, in the mid-1970s gained 90 percent of its work from candidates but since has moved dramatically away from candidates to issues and corporate work. Newer consulting firms such as Winner/Wagner and Francis, and established ones, such as the Todd Company, Garin-Hart-Yang Research, and many others have considerable business stakes in non-candidate campaigns.[17]

As corporations have discovered the value of grass-roots lobbying and issues management, consultants who specialize in direct mail and political telemarketing shifted focus to legislative and issues work. Corporate and trade association organizations took special notice of the successful political consultant-orchestrated grass-roots campaign run against the Clinton health care proposal. Such work is often far more lucrative, more reliable, and less stress-inducing than working for candidates in the competitive election cycle. Some of the most successful political consulting firms have less than one-half of their revenue coming from candidate campaigns.[18]

5. *The business of winning.* Politics, like sports, is a zero-sum game: someone wins and someone loses. In political consulting, success is not measured by increases in market share or profitability to shareholders, but in winning. However, winning is not enough. Perception and expectation play an important role as well. A consultant's reputation can be hurt when a client barely wins, when he or she was expected to win by a wide margin. Consultant's sometimes tout their winning streaks, but when the streak is ten easy wins, with little or no real competition, the

streak loses its luster. The consulting firm that takes on the tough fight, steers the dark horse to victory, or puts up a much better fight than expected will build its reputation. For the political professional consultant, losing is part of the game. Campaign consultants can be "hot" for two or three election cycles and then suffer crippling losses. Even the most successful firms have suffered major defeats.

There is not a great deal of stability for political consulting firms. The best are sometimes toppled by their own mistakes, by the tides of politics, or by lackluster performances of their clients. Consultants working for marginal candidates may not get paid on time, may not get paid the full amount for services rendered, or may not get paid at all. Some consultants simply lack the business skills or patience to keep their companies afloat. Busy firms have gone bankrupt and firms have folded because partners are impatient with internal business details. In the end, many political consultants are more interested in and adept at politics than running a small business.[19]

6. *Fluid business and increased competition.* It is relatively easy to break into the political consulting business and in every campaign cycle scores of new firms are created. Following each election cycle there is a substantial turnover of personnel at the national party political operations, and ambitious (and sometimes soon-to-be unemployed) campaign operatives join established consulting firms or decide to begin their own business in polling, research, fund-raising, and other special services. Often junior partners, chafing at their underling status in established consulting firms, set up their own operations. Some of the best known consulting firms have had acrimonious disputes among partners, with the firms splitting and dividing up their client base.

Looking at the Democratic polling firms alone, Stuart Rothenberg observed that "change is so endemic ... because most firms are merely collections of individuals who stay together for convenience. When disagreements about personality, money, or the direction of the firm crop up, there are few institutional loyalties to keep the firm together."[20]

Since the 1980s the increasing number of consulting firms has led to greater competition and, in many cases, a stagnation in prices charged for professional services. Polling firms, in particular, have been affected. With increased technological sophistication, inexpensive software and laptops are used instead of multimillion dollar mainframe computers, and pollsters increasingly subcontract their telephone interviewing to telemarketing specialists.

7. *Technology driven*. Sound political judgment, timing, determination, and raw courage are necessary ingredients in any campaign. But increasingly campaigns depend on specialists who also can provide a technological edge. This comes in many forms: use of on-line retrieval systems and websites, computer-assisted telephone technology, voter and demographic databases, statistical analysis of demographic information, and precinct mapping. It was an extraordinary revelation when the first set of computer-aided maps were prepared, matching 1980 census information with voting histories. In an instant party leaders, strategists, and candidates could tell what districts would look like and discern probable voting patterns. Those days of marvel are history, like the early days of the 286 processor or the 1200-baud modem. Now strategists are able to use predictive technologies, such as the Chi-Square Automatic Interaction Detection (CHAID); traditional statistical techniques, such as regression analysis; and new artificial intelligence technologies, such as neural nets and genetic algorithms to target potential voters.[21] Other technologies have led to vast improvements in candidate and opposition research, direct mail targeting, telephone banks, polling, media analysis, focus group and dial group research, and other tools of the modern campaign.

8. *Demographics of the business*. The political consulting business for its first twenty-five or thirty years has been dominated by white men playing serious games of politics. While Leone Baxter was quite literally the first lady of campaign consultants, she was also the only woman for a very long time. Few women and fewer minorities were involved at any significant level of political consulting during the first decades.

Those demographics are changing, especially with the emergence of women consultants. In 1993 *Campaigns & Elections* profiled seventy-four women who have made a significant impact on politics and public policy, and others have made their mark since then.[22] There have been few African American or other minority political consultants.[23] Political consulting is also a young person's business where individuals can establish themselves in a relatively short period of time.[24] In chapter 2 James A. Thurber, Candice J. Nelson, and David A. Dulio provide further information about the demographics of the consulting business as well as insight into the attitudes and priorities of campaign consultants.

Many political consulting firms are clustered in Washington or in the nearby suburbs close to the White House, Congress, the national political parties, and national issues. Most consulting firms are not located in Washington, but in Denver, Austin, Sacramento, Atlanta, or any number of other locations, usually the state capitol. For these firms, political consulting is sometimes confined to the state or region, while others may have clients throughout the nation and internationally. California is also home to many major firms, with emphasis on media, polling, initiative, and referendum specialists. New York also has been the home to a number of well-established political consultants. Major firms often have Washington (or New York) and West Coast offices to handle their clients.

An Emerging Profession?

While there has been great growth in political consulting, has a true profession emerged? Surveying the sociological literature on the definition of professions, Margaret Scammell has found these essential criteria: "collective control over entry into the profession, a self-policed ethical code and core skills, and definable, theoretically-based bodies of knowledge."[25] Using this definition, political consulting falls short of being a profession.

Law, medicine, accounting, and several other fields fulfill these requirements. Journalism, starting decades earlier than political consulting, has its own set of standards, graduate and undergraduate education, body of knowledge, and awards and honors. While these all lead to a fully credentialed profession, they do not fulfill all criteria. Yet, like journalism, political consulting does not meet the first requirement: control over entry into the profession. Anyone may become a political consultant, without need of formal training, licensing, or accreditation. During each election cycle, new consulting firms are created, while others break up, regroup, and fall by the wayside.

There now is academic and practical training in nearly all aspects of campaign specialties. There are a number of short training institutes, such as those given by both political parties at the national, state and local levels; courses in practical politics at several universities; and a full-fledged masters degree program in political management. The emphasis is on practice and technique, with relatively little integration of social science research.[26]

The sense of consulting as a profession has been fostered by the creation in 1967 of the American Association of Political Consultants (AAPC) and its international counterpart, the International Association of Political Consultants (IAPC), established in 1968. In 1980 there were about 50 AAPC members ; by 1990 there were some 700. Approximately 400 consultants belong to the IAPC. Two regional organizations recently have been formed, the Latin American Association of Political Consultants (LAAPC) and the European Association of Political Consultants (EAPC).[27] Each of these organizations has the requisite institutional trappings, such as by-laws, annual meetings, boards of directors, and awards and honors.

Every member joining the AAPC is required to adhere to a code of ethics. But it is a code without much teeth. For all the charges of dirty campaign tactics, there has never been a disciplinary action by the AAPC against any of its members, nor has there been much emphasis on enforcement of ethical behavior within the profession itself.[28] In 1996 the AAPC took a firm stand, however, denouncing "push polls"—the practice of having a telemarketing company make thousands of last-minute telephone calls, under the pretense of being pollsters, to spread sharply negative and at times false information about opponents.[29]

The Future of the Political Consulting Business

Since the 1950s the business of political consulting has made several transformations. The first campaign consultants were primarily generalists who worked almost exclusively on candidate campaigns. As the business began to mature, many of the earlier generalists repositioned themselves, taking on corporate clients, issues management work, or international candidates. A second generation of consultants began flooding the market in the 1980s, especially in the specialty markets of polling and media. They brought both a greater technological sophistication and a more activist commitment than the pioneers had a decade earlier. The 1990s have seen another wave of consultants, many of them in the specialty markets.

Consultants have seen business grow because of the superheated fundraising activities of the national Democratic and Republican parties and the explosion of soft money and issues advocacy. For years Congress has had campaign finance reform on its agenda, and in the aftermath of the 1996 presidential races there has been increased pressure for reform. Many federal reform packages were discussed, but none were enacted into law. Several states have not waited for federal campaign reform and have enacted their own campaign spending limits and restricted reporting requirements. While not highly probable, major finance reform could severely restrict the amount of funds available for campaign activities, and by extension restrict business opportunities for political consultants.

Several trends suggest, however, that there will be growth opportunities for the consulting business: increases in ballot initiatives, grass-roots issues management, and other forms of direct democracy; more competition in state legislatures, particularly in states where the margins between the two parties are small; and increased communication challenges through cable television, talk radio, and the Internet. Further fueling the growing marketplace for campaign consultants is the simmering distrust of politicians, the impact of term limits, and, ultimately, the survival instinct of incumbents to protect themselves against challengers by hiring as much professional advice as they can afford.

Notes

1. Larry Sabato, *The Rise of Political Consultants: New Ways of Winning Elections* (Basic Books, 1981). See also Karen S. Johnson-Cartee and Gary A. Copeland, *Inside Political Campaigns* (Greenwood Publishing Group, 1997), and Robert V. Friedenberg, *Communication Consultants in Political Campaigns: Ballot Box Warriors* (Praeger, 1997).

2. Dan Nimmo, *The Political Persuaders: The Techniques of Modern Election Campaigns* (Prentice Hall, 1970), p. 36. For a discussion of the first years of campaign management as a business, see also Stanley Kelley Jr., *Professional Public Relations and Political Power* (Johns Hopkins University Press, 1956); David L. Rosenbloom, *The Election Men: Professional Campaign Managers and American Democracy* (Quadrangle Books, 1973), chap. 4; and Sabato, *The Rise of Political Consultants*, pp. 10ff. On Whitaker and Baxter, see Carey McWilliams, "Government by Whitaker and Baxter," *Nation*, April 14, 21, and May 5, 1951.

3. Alexander Heard, *The Cost of Democracy* (University of North Carolina Press, 1960), p. 418.

4. Rosenbloom, *The Election Men*, p. 51.

5. Ibid., pp. 52–53. Robert J. Huckshorn and Robert C. Spencer noted that few challengers in congressional races—only 4 percent—employed salaried managers for their campaigns, while 22 percent of the candidates in marginal races used salaried campaign managers. *The Politics of Defeat* (University of Massachusetts Press, 1977).

6. Edie Goldberg and Michael Traugott, *Campaigning for Congress* (Washington, D.C.: CQ Press, 1984), pp. 17–24. In 1978 the authors found that paid media consultants were hired in 39 percent of the 146 congressional campaigns surveyed, while 52 percent of the campaign managers for incumbents were members of their congressional staffs assigned to the elections. While not focusing on the role of outside professional consultants, this study suggested that relatively few professionals, apart from media consultants, were used in congressional campaigns. See also Jerry Hagstrom and Robert Guskind, "Changing the Guard," *National Journal*, October 22, 1986, p. 2660.

7. Mark P. Petracca, "Political Consultants and Democratic Governance," *PS: Political Science and Politics* (March 1989), pp. 11–14, and Walter De Vries, "American Campaign Consulting: Trends and Concerns," *PS: Political Science and Politics* (March 1989), pp. 21–25.

8. Paul S. Herrnson, *Congressional Elections: Campaigning at Home and in Washington* (Washington, D.C.: CQ Press, 1995), p. 63, and table 3-1, pp. 66–68.

9. For example, at the congressional level, see Charlie Cook's *Cook Political Report,* Stuart Rothenberg's *Rothenberg Political Report,* and Brad O'Leary's *O'Leary Report.*

10. Steven K. Medvic, "Professionalization in Congressional Campaigns," chapter 6 in this volume.

11. These are 1994 figures from the Council of American Survey Research Organizations, reported in David Segal, "By the Numbers," *Washington Post,* March 4, 1996, p. B12. Well-known public pollsters, such as Louis Harris and Associates and the Gallup Organization, gain only a fraction of their income from political polling. The Gallup Poll, for example, generates less than 1 percent of the Gallup Organization's $60 million annual revenue from polling activities. Johnnie L. Roberts, "Pollsters Hope Commercial Clients Elect to Note Firm's Work during Campaign," *Wall Street Journal,* November 9, 1992, p. A5.

12. This study was conducted by Competitive Media Reporting, covering the seventy-five largest media markets in America. Reported in James Bennet, "Another Tally in '96 Race: Two Months of TV Ads," *New York Times,* November 13, 1996, p. D20. Years ago, V. O. Key Jr. observed: "The aggregate expended in the year of a presidential election may seem huge, yet it probably does not exceed the total of the annual advertising of the principal soap companies." *Politics, Parties and Pressure Groups,* 5th ed. (New York: Thomas Y. Crowell, 1964), pp. 487–88.

13. R. Craig Endicott, "National Ad Spending Up 11.4 Percent for '96," *Advertising Age,* March 24, 1997, p. 4.

14. From 1992–1996, more than $3 billion was spent by political candidates and committees on direct mail. A rough estimate is that $750 million was spent each year. *Campaigns & Elections,* May 1997, p. 23.

15. Barbara Whitaker, "Life of a Cold Caller: Riding on a Smile and a Thick Skin," *New York Times,* March 24, 1996, p. C1. The $385 billion figure, compiled by the Direct Marketing Association, comes from both outbound telemarketers—those firms conducting cold calls and business telemarketing to customers. Not included are fraudulent operators or the huge mail order business of inbound telemarketing.

16. Rosenbloom, *The Election Men,* p. 50.

17. Michael Clark, "Selling Issues: Political Consultants Are Shifting Their Business to Include Campaigns without Candidates," *Campaigns & Elections,* April–May 1993.

18. For example, Clinton reelection campaign and second-term pollsters Mark J. Penn and Douglas E. Schoen also have worked for AT&T, Texaco Inc., Chemical Banking Inc., Citibank, Control Data Corp., Eastman Kodak Co., Honeywell Inc., Major League Baseball, Nynex Corp., Procter and Gamble Co., Sony Corp., and the Trump Organization. They have also worked for candidates in Latin America, Israel, Greece, Turkey, and the Philippines. Peter Baker, "White House Isn't Asking Image Advisers to Reveal Assets or Disclose Other Clients," *Washington Post,* May 19, 1997, p. A8.

19. The partnership of Dick Morris and Richard Dresner, for example, ended in 1982 in bankruptcies, even though they had an extraordinary number of clients.

20. Stuart Rothenberg, "Change Is Good: The Consultant Soap Opera," *Roll Call,* March 13, 1995.

21. Hal Malchow, "The Targeting Revolution in Political Direct Contact," *Campaigns & Elections,* June 1997, pp. 36–39. See chapter 7 of this volume for a discussion of these new technologies.

22. Andrea L. Spring, "Seventy-four Women Who Are Changing American Politics," *Campaigns & Elections,* June–July 1993, p. 17. Among those and other successful consultants during the 1990s were pollsters Anna Bennett, Linda DiVall, KellyAnne Fitzpatrick, Celinda Lake, and Heidi von Szeliski; media and general strategy consultants Kim Alfano,

Cathy Allen, Kathy Ardleigh, Jill Buckley, Michelle Carrier, Jan Ziska Crawford, Mandy Grunwald, Anne Lewis, Donna Lucas, Marla Romash, Wendy Sherman, and Teresa Vilmain; fund-raising specialist Nancy Bosckor; telemarketers Liz Welch, Victoria Ellinger, and Linda Cherry; and direct-mail specialist Eva Campbell.

23. The most prominent was Democrat Ron Brown, a former head of the Democratic National Committee, fund-raiser, deal-maker, and Clinton's first secretary of commerce. But Brown was not really a political consultant. Of those who are political consultants, the most active African American is probably pollster Ron Lester. General consultant Kam Kawata and pollster Fred Yang represent the senior-level Asian American consultants, and Alex Castellanos and Armando Gutierrez are leading Hispanic communications consultants.

24. In its annual "Rising Stars" edition, *Campaigns & Elections* in 1991 listed consultants who quickly would be at the top of their profession: Paul Begala, then twenty-nine, helped elect Bill Clinton in 1992; Ed Goeas, then thirty-eight, became a top Republican pollster; Alan Secrest, then thirty-four, became a highly successful Democratic pollster; Richard Schlackman, then thirty-nine, headed a major Democratic direct-mail firm; and Peter Fenn, a relative oldster at forty-three, and his Democratic media firm dominated House races during the 1990s. Several relatively young political operatives have gone on to national elective office, including Senator Spencer Abraham (R-Mich.) and Representative Rosa DeLauro (D-Conn.). It is a profession where young, talented political consultants can attain a high level of responsibility very quickly in their careers. For example, Jason Linde, dubbed a "rising star" in 1996, managed his first race at age twenty, and by twenty-seven had significant campaign experience in seven elections. Another young professional, Jim Jonas, while still in his twenties was an award-winning political media producer for Republican candidates.

25. Margaret Scammell, "The Wisdom of the War Room: U.S. Campaigning and Americanization," Harvard University, Shorenstein Center on the Press, Politics and Public Policy Research Paper R–17, April 1997, p. 2.

26. Ibid., p. 16.

27. Chris Meyer, "Ten Years in the Making," *Campaigns & Elections,* April–May 1990, p. 39.

28. The AAPC for decades has had a code of professional conduct, but it is not enforced. In 1991 the AAPC held its first conference on political ethics, cosponsored by the Graduate School of Political Management and the Thomas Jefferson School in Public Policy of the College of William and Mary.

In 1997 pollster Frank I. Luntz was formally reprimanded by the American Association of Public Opinion Research—not the AAPC—for refusing to disclose wording of poll questions associated with the 1994 "Contract with America" campaign.

29. Adam Clymer, "Association of Political Handlers Attacks Ruse Polls as Unethical," *New York Times,* June 27, 1996, p. A20. See chapter 2 of this volume for a discussion of push polling.

CHAPTER FOUR

Lessons from the Field: A Journey into Political Consulting

MARTIN HAMBURGER

A s I type these words, it is the time between political campaigns—one cycle has just finished and the next is about to begin. It is also the time when out-of-work campaign staffers look for work. Many show up on my doorstep inquiring, "How can I become a political consultant?" That question rang in my ears when the editors of this volume asked me to recount my own path toward becoming a political consultant. My route was circuitous, but in a way this was typical, for it mirrors the quirky paths many of my colleagues also followed to their positions.

Most political party staffers I know had a similar start to their political activism. Most did not come from political families per se, but had just decided to get involved in a local campaign and continued to work for good Democrats (or, I assume, for good Republicans), one after another.

Editors' note: Martin Hamburger is a partner at Laguens, Hamburger, and Stone, a Democratic media consulting firm. Prior to becoming a professional consultant, he worked both as a campaign staffer on a series of political campaigns and as a professional staffer at the Democratic Congressional Campaign Committee (DCCC). Hamburger compares his experiences at the DCCC with his experiences as a political consultant and demonstrates the differing perspectives that committee staffers and political consultants bring to campaigns. Hamburger argues that he better serves his clients as a political consultant because of his experiences as a campaign staffer and, more important, as a party staffer. His journey to political consulting illustrates that the background consultants bring to campaigns can influence their effectiveness on those campaigns.

My path diverged a little from this one. Issue campaigning brought me to the world of politics and organizing. I became active in the nuclear freeze movement, where I first learned about organizing. I developed skills that I have called upon in every political campaign in which I have ever been involved; most important is an aptitude for organizing people to do things: write letters, call their friends, attend a rally, lobby, and so on.

This involvement in the freeze movement led me to Washington, D.C., and to politics. I felt that the best way to affect policy, particularly military policy, was through political action—lobbying, research, information gathering and dissemination, and education. I soon went to work for a public interest group called Council for a Livable World. Based in Washington, D.C., they are a lobbying organization and a political action committee (PAC). At first my job was mostly research and organizing—tracking the progress of legislation, informing grass-roots activists, and writing research reports that went to Congress (I dreamed of members of Congress falling asleep in bed with the lights on, with my reports folded over them).

At the time, I thought political campaigns were not for me. They seemed to lack substance and be populated by stress junkies and adrenaline mainliners (both observations turned out to be correct). While I was a faithful Democrat, I thought the issues were where my energies were best spent.

One experience changed my mind. I was sitting in the Senate gallery, watching a vote on an amendment to strike funds from the defense budget for production of new poison nerve gas weapons. We had worked hard on this amendment, organizing the grass-roots and supplying senators' officers with information. We believed we had at least fifty-one votes in our favor. Then-vice president George Bush was presiding over the Senate in case there was a tie that he could break, so tensions were high. We had whip-checked all our votes, and we knew they were present that day. As the secretary of the Senate called the roll, we were excited, but we knew anything could happen; just then, something did. Then-Senate minority leader Bob Dole strolled across the aisle and whispered in the ear of Republican senator James Exon of Nebraska, who was one of our solid votes—or so I thought. They nodded to each other, shook hands, and as Dole wandered back to the Republican side of the aisle, Exon changed his vote from "yea" to "nay." That made the vote a 50 to

50 tie, and Vice President Bush cast his vote to go ahead and begin production of new nerve gas weaponry.

The event taught me one thing. I could spend hours and hours working to change the minds of the politicians. But a politician's position can be fleeting. Perhaps it would be better to work on changing the politicians themselves. It was my resolution to begin working for candidates who I knew would stick to their beliefs, the beliefs I cared about. A campaign hack was born.

I immediately went to work for a Senate candidate, Representative Bob Edgar, who was running against Senator Arlen Specter in Pennsylvania. Specter was (and is) a clever politician, who was successful at coopting key segments of the Democratic vote in Pennsylvania; Edgar was a former minister with one of the most liberal voting records in Congress. It was a good cause that was fated from the beginning. But it was the first chance I had to apply all I had learned in issue organizing and advocacy to political organizing. I recruited volunteers, set up phone banks, organized election day activities, and steered clear of the press. On election day, we got thumped. I was hooked.

I embarked on the life of a political migrant worker, traveling from district to district, working on campaign after campaign. In my case, it was losing campaign after losing campaign. From 1986 through 1988 I racked up a surprisingly long record of campaigning, a record unblemished by success.

In 1989 I was hired as Michigan finance director for Senator Carl Levin's 1990 reelection campaign. It was in some ways the perfect campaign experience. Levin was thought to be vulnerable, had to raise tons of money, and the race would receive lots of visibility. I was the first campaign staffer hired. It was a true learning experience. For most of the first year, 1989, I traveled with the senator around the state whenever he had to do a campaign event. It seemed like that spring and summer I went to every festival in Michigan: the Shepherd Maple Syrup Festival, the Posin Potato Festival, the Holland Tulip Festival, the Yale Bologna Festival, and the Traverse City Cherry Festival, for example. I managed to endure both the festivals and the coming year of campaigning, raising about $3 million (in state) in the process. In November 1990 Levin was reelected to his third term, and I was again looking for work. However, not too long after the election, I got a call from a member of Congress who was thinking about running for the Senate and wanting to hire someone who had been through a Senate campaign to help him put things together. I jumped at the chance. I was excited to have the opportunity to help start a Senate campaign again—and possibly to run one.

I started work immediately. While the Senate campaign seemed far off, it was a chance to get back to Washington and reestablish connections with friends I had only been able to talk to by phone. I remember driving back into D.C. one evening, turning onto Maryland Avenue with its view of the Capitol, and hearing on the radio that the Persian Gulf War had started. It seemed a very dramatic time to be returning.

It was an opportunity for me to take some soundings—to see what I had learned and where it could take me. I sought out, in particular, pollsters. I met with them, engaged them at events and forums, asking always what they were seeing. Anytime a campaign was over, I would ask some questions about what had been done and why. When seeing campaign commercials, I would analyze them closely and, by figuring backwards, try to determine what the campaign's strategy was, who their electoral or demographic targets were, and what their message was. In short, it was a kind of secondary training experience to complement what I had experienced on the road. I think, in retrospect, that both sets of experiences were crucial for my development as a campaigner today.

In 1991 Representative Silvio Conte (R-Mass.) died. The Republican governor of Massachusetts, William Weld, called for a special election to be held about twelve weeks after Conte's death.

Doug Sosnick, then the political director of the DCCC, called me and asked if I would come talk with him about working for the DCCC on the upcoming special election in Massachusetts. Since it was the first special election of the new DCCC chairman's (Rep. Vic Fazio) tenure, they were planning on making an all-out effort on behalf of whomever the Democrats nominated. The experience would be quick, as the general election was scheduled for six weeks after the primary. Within a week, I was billeted in the law office of a sympathetic Democrat in Northampton, Massachusetts.

The experience was sublime for me. There was a ton of interest in the race, and I was the person most everybody called, at least to see what was what. With that interest, though, came pressure.

In the end, we were victorious, although we were not sure of victory even into election day. It was perhaps the sweetest win of my career. One week later I was hired by the DCCC as their deputy political director, which meant I did a lot of the things the political director did not really want to do.

I was in heaven. While it seems a little funny now, it was a thrill for me every morning to walk into a building that said "Democratic National Committee" over the door. I felt I had really made it somewhere.

What were the most exalting attributes of working for the party committee? I would learn them over time. The first was the way news traveled. Until then, I learned about news the way most everyone else did, by seeing it on the news that night or reading about it in the next morning's paper. At the DCCC, I discovered that committee people tended to find out about things right when they happened. When the story appeared on the news that evening, or in the paper the next morning, we were reading not to find out what happened but to see how it was "playing,"—that is, how everybody else was finding out how it happened.

The same was true, even more so, with political news in the races we were working on. Since someone at the DCCC was on the phone with all our campaigns sometime during the day, any little blip on the screen made it onto our radar immediately. We heard about campaign gaffes, fund-raising successes, political missteps, and endorsements well before anyone else in Washington did. It was fun to feel that we were operating in some sort of nerve center for political campaigns.

It was for this reason that I first started having closer interactions and communications with political consultants. Rather than me calling them and scraping for a piece of their time, I was suddenly finding my phone message box stuffed with pink slips from consultants wanting to "check in" with me and see what was up.

I was under no illusion that these experts were calling me to discuss political strategy on their races. They knew I knew things before others, and they were after me to drop tidbits of information useful to them in their efforts to secure clients. Consultants called looking for information—Who is running? What are their chances? How much money can they raise?—and my colleagues and I at the DCCC were some of the best sources for them.

And it was not just the consultants that called. PAC directors, political handicappers, and journalists all suddenly found the ramblings of this newly minted party apparatchik fascinating. Or so they led me to believe. I went along with the illusion. After all, how else would I see the inside of the city's finest lunch spots on my DCCC salary?

Yet this was (and is) one of the most visible intersections of political consultants and party staffers. "Marketing," as we call it, the elaborate mating ritual between consultants and campaigns, was one of the biggest reasons any consultant ever called me while I was at the DCCC. I tried to be obliging to everyone equally, but inevitably I would run afoul of one consultant who felt I was favoring another by giving him or her all the "good leads." The first time this happened, it was not pretty. Unbeknownst to me, someone complained about me to the political director, and, for the first time, I found out that when you take one of these higher visibility jobs you become someone people may have opinions about. Before, toiling in relative obscurity, no one disliked me, because no one knew me. Now, all of a sudden, just because of what I might be saying or not saying to some of these consultants, I was a person somebody out there did not like.

There were other surprises. When I had worked on campaigns, I made it a point to stay in touch with friends on other campaigns. Sometimes we would just talk to blow off steam, but often we would exchange ideas, try out strategies and tactics on each other, and help each other generally. So I was looking forward to my first road trip as a DCCC staffer, where I would get the chance to have that same kind of collegiality with the campaign I was visiting. I soon found that optimism misplaced.

Upon entering the campaign headquarters on this first trip, there was something wrong. The place was immaculate—no pizza boxes lying out, no overstuffed trash bags waiting by the door for someone to sling them into the dumpster. Everyone knew who I was and said "hello" to me. But it was not until I sat down with the campaign manager that I figured out what was bothering me.

I asked him, "How's it going?" or something equally innocuous. "Fantastic!" was the reply. What spewed forth for the next few minutes was the rosiest, most sunny discourse on how every aspect of the campaign was moving along ahead of schedule or under budget. The campaign office had been scrubbed and tidied. Nary a loose end was observable. Any ideas I had about making suggestions for action were met with: "We're already doing that." I had entered the Stepford campaign. At the end of my visit came the question: "So, when do we get our money?"

In that moment, I realized something about my new world. I had assumed, and had hoped, that the campaigns we were working on looked toward the DCCC, if not me, as some sort of bank of knowledge and support. I found out they perceived us only as a bank. The impending arrival of a DCCC staffer was like the impending arrival of a wealthy great aunt. You cleaned up, tried to make a great impression, and hoped you were still in her thoughts when it came time to hand out the money. You listened patiently to any advice offered, to make the offerer feel valued. But you almost never thought about it long enough to follow it.

As a staffer at the DCCC, I found this phenomenon most frustrating. While I was willing to believe that even I, the political genius that I was, might not have had all the answers, I was continually frustrated with the difficulty of working with campaigns and establishing a level of trust. I learned to spend a great deal of time on the phone with campaigns and campaign managers, developing a friendship, a strong relationship, and a bond of trust. Only then would I travel to a campaign, to work with them on a particular problem. Sometimes I was successful, sometimes I was not.

In many ways, the money we doled out to the campaigns complicated this. Often, when we went to visit a campaign, we were sent out with a check. The idea was that having the check would buy us a little credibility. Sometimes it helped, but often it was just the grain of salt rubbed in the open wound. By the time we were delivering contributions to the campaigns, it was July or August, and the campaigns had been begging us for them for quite a while already. We were making a big deal about giving them a "gift" they felt they had been deserving of for weeks or months already.

And for many campaigns, there would be no money. In the 1992 cycle, when Democrats had the majority but were deemed likely to lose seats, our goal was to win some open seats and hold our own among challengers, but above all to preserve incumbents. For the challenger candidates, with whom I identified, this was hard news. The House banking scandal only made this worse. Newt Gingrich and the Republicans were attacking our majority, and Congress as a whole, and we were fighting to preserve the reputations of both. Many Democratic challengers also wanted to run against Congress and use the bounced check scandal as a point of attack. Early on in the scandal, this caused great discomfort among the leaders of our party and their staffs. Most could be made to see that it would be hard to get candidates not to use an issue that was working for them, even if it made incumbent Democrats uncomfortable, but those who did run hard against Congress and Washington did not receive the same level of emotional welcome when they approached the DCCC for help.

As someone who had come from a background of working on lots of losing, longshot campaigns, I felt frustrated by this, too. Perhaps, in terms of an overall strategy of maximizing Democratic bottoms sitting in congressional seats, this was the right way to go. To me it seemed a violation of the spirit of what I thought our mission was—helping each campaign do the best it could.

Finally, the sheer volume of races we covered was a problem. Our "target list" in 1992 was dozens of races long. I was sent to some of the most important races (not all of them) and some we were watching to heat up at the end. I traveled to seventy-nine congressional districts in a space of about eleven months. I was on the road for stretches of ten days to two weeks at a time, often with only a few days in between. Those days were consumed with follow-up from the trip I had just done and preparation and planning for the trip to come. Needless to say, the interactions I had with these campaigns were not what anyone would call "quality time."

Election day came, and we "only" lost eleven seats. We called this a victory, which I guess it was. Immediately after the election, there were a number of recounts and other situations that needed to be settled, but soon the place that had been buzzing with excitement was merely humming, with the sound of résumés rolling off the laser printer. Mine was one of them.

I had been given the option of staying at the DCCC, in a different and better job, but, grateful though I was, I felt that it was time to move on. I had a few friends who were consultants, now offering me jobs with their firms; eventually, I took one of them. I was off on another adventure.

Two experiences stand out for me as examples of how my world had changed. The first was in my dealings with campaigns. Though it was just after an election, the firm I had joined had signed up with a campaign for whom election day was in February 1993. Early in my tenure at the firm, I joined conference calls with the campaign team. For the first three or four, I kept quiet and listened—an incredibly difficult posture for me to take. Finally, during the fifth call or so, I offered some minor contribution on strategy or tactics, bracing for the usual comments: "We're already doing that," or, "That may work in New Jersey, but we don't do things like that here." I was surprised. Instead, my idea was greeted with hosannas and plaudits. Suddenly, I had become a genius. After the call I mentioned this reaction to my friend and asked him why he thought I had gotten that reaction, when it was the same advice I would have given as a DCCC staffer, and it would have been met with skepticism. Why was the same advice being received so much better? "Easy," he said, "this time, they're paying for the advice. Of course they think you're a genius. Why would they be paying all this money to be taking advice from someone they thought was an idiot?" I thanked him, although I am still not sure if he was explaining me the new facts of life or insulting me. But the scenario was played out over and over again.

Life had changed in other ways as well. At the DCCC, campaign staff rarely asked me to do anything for them. If they did, they rarely followed up with me. As a consultant, suddenly our clients were always asking themselves if they were getting their money's worth, and I was always feeling the pressure to make sure they did. "Underpromise and over-perform" became my mantra, although I am sure I got it just the opposite most of the time.

Luckily, we had far fewer campaigns to deal with. Our firm probably only had a dozen campaigns with which we were actively involved at any given time. This was a far cry from the dozens of active files I had open at the DCCC. As a consequence, I had a far better handle on what was going on with my races than I did at the DCCC. Coming out of the DCCC, and knowing the load of the people there in my stead, I used this knowledge to my and my campaign's advantage. I called my counterparts at the DCCC and brought them up to speed on the races I cared about and pointed them to the tasks that needed attention. Sometimes I would go to a campaign and say, for instance, "You need to be raising more labor money." The campaign might disagree, and I would work with the relevant DCCC staffer to deliver the same message and perhaps even pitch in to help. I found that the DCCC staff liked working closely with the consultants and liked having the information they were not getting from the "Stepford campaigns"; I liked having more hands on deck to tackle the problems. Ultimately, I believe the campaigns were best served by this slight contrivance.

I also found that I knew how the committee made decisions about funding—what criteria would sway people making the decisions and how to get them the information that would help the tumblers fall into place and turn the key. I learned that throughout the campaign season I could be part of the information supply line that I so enjoyed while I was at the committee, to the benefit of my clients' bottom lines. To this day I work hard to keep the committee staff informed about important developments in my campaigns, with an eye toward the day when they make their funding decisions. I am told that many of my colleagues in the political consulting world do not devote as much attention to this effort.

One final irony occurred to me early on in my tenure as a DCCC staffer-turned-political-consultant: I was now the one on the phone to the DCCC staffers, pumping them for information about candidates. About this, too, I learned something that arose out of my tenure as a DCCC staffer.

As a consultant, marketing takes on supreme importance. Few political consultants are so well known that they can afford not to reach out and actively market themselves to campaigns and candidates. I certainly am not one of them. Our effort to reach new campaigns with our work, show them our stuff, and secure the opportunity to interview with them is high priority. Certainly, the DCCC staff was and continues to be a good source of leads. Early in a political season, the committee sends out staffers to districts, where they attempt to recruit quality candidates. Not long after a potential candidate begins to show interest, the consultants come along and send reels, packets of information, and proposals. The constant flow of information between consultants and party staffers only makes this more possible.

Having restarted this mating ritual election cycle after election cycle, I have learned that, while the leads from national party committees are helpful, they are usually not fresh. Just as I saved information for everyone who called, I find now that when I call a lead that came from a party staffer, some of my competition has inevitably been there before me or will be knocking on the door soon after. The party staffers who had come after me had evidently learned the same lessons I had.

Where I can, I try in my marketing efforts to get out ahead of the party committee, in part by using contacts I have in the states that I met and cemented while at the DCCC. Often I have found out about a person contemplating a run for office before the party committees discovered him or her. Getting there first is no guarantee of getting hired, but it usually does not hurt. And where you can make the party staffers' recruiting job easier, it only helps cement your relationship with them, and that can have benefits in the long run.

Party staffers and political consultants have the ability to help each other in numerous ways, but they also compete. Many assume that they come into conflict over money. As a consultant, I do much of what I did as a party staffer, only for more money. Hopefully, I have improved my skills and experience level as well. But in reality, rarely does money come into play as a point of conflict between consultants and party staffers. Most campaigns do not discuss their financial arrangements with their consultants with the party staff, and the consultants have every incentive to be discrete about them as well. When I was a party staffer, I never commented on individual financial arrangements, even when I knew about them, which was seldom. I often gave campaigns the advice to be good consumers and try to haggle over pricing and services with the consultants, to make sure the campaigns were getting the best deal. Now, as a consultant, I know campaigns get the same advice, and I have come to expect some bargaining from the campaigns as part of our negotiation process.

The truth of the matter is that most of the conflict comes over politics rather than money. In my own experience at the DCCC, around the aforementioned House bank scandal, I heard from consultants who disagreed with what they thought was the advice being distributed to the campaigns by the party staff. Yet therein lies the root of much of the conflict; it arises mostly out of second- and thirdhand perceptions of positions and rarely from the positions as articulated firsthand.

Recently I had the experience of urging a client to contrast his record on education with his opponent's record, using the issue of national testing standards as an issue. Testing had rated highly in our survey research as an issue, and I knew nationally that higher standards are an education solution on which voters placed a high priority. Yet the campaign reported that they had "checked with the DCCC, and their focus groups said the issue was a loser." I knew this could not be true, but I wanted to have the campaign make the decision to use the issue on their own, without extra prodding from me. I called the committee, explained what I had been told, and found that, yes, the campaign had heard the comment wrong and had oversimplified the response in quoting it back to me.

In the case of this example, the party staffer and the consultant had a potential conflict over the nature of political advice and the effect it would have had on the campaign. Sometimes it is a misunderstanding, sometimes it is not. Yet the potential for disagreement is there, and is significant, given that both party staffers and political consultants claim a degree of stewardship over the campaigns and seek to have their advice played out on the campaigns.

Conflict can also occur over questions of access. As a former party staffer, I may be more open to maintaining communications with, and taking advice from, current party staffers. But many consultants seek to block all communications with the party or even poison the relationships between the party staff and their campaigns. While I think this must be viewed as misguided in all cases, it does occur. Consultants who believe that the party staffers are criticizing them behind their back, or who feel that the committee may be exerting a negative influence on the campaign, may seek to limit the interaction between the campaign and the DCCC. The disagreements are almost always reciprocated and the loser is almost always the campaign.

As in my own case, many political consultants started out as party staffers. There are several reasons why this has become customary. First, political consulting firms looking to expand find a ready source of potential staff among party committee "graduates." From the consulting firm's perspective, these potential hirees know the districts, know how to deal with clients, and may have a range of contacts useful for marketing purposes. Naturally, they have the requisite political skills, or they would not have lasted through the cycle at the DCCC. So it is common to have party staffers move up the food chain into consulting.

Many political operatives choose to become consultants after having been at the party committees for other reasons as well. Like me, many come to the party committees after a period of life on the road. Their life while at the party committees is different in comparison—regular meals, a nice apartment, and a stable group of friends. Few choose to sacrifice these lifestyle comforts for life on the road again, and life as a consultant provides the opportunity to "get a life"—something many operatives mumble to themselves every morning after an election day, win or lose.

A few consultants came to their work originally out of issue advocacy communities, as I did. For them, or at least for me, political campaigning is the preferred venue for our personal political action. If we can do well by doing good, so much the better. I generally work for progressive candidates, although I have worked for some conservative Democrats—mostly people I have liked or admired personally. For me, political action has always been about trying to make things ever so slightly better than they were when you got there, and I have striven to make that principle the guiding one for all my actions. Where it will take me next, is anyone's guess.

CHAPTER FIVE

Hired Guns and House Races: Campaign Professionals in House Elections

PAUL S. HERRNSON

[Ronald] Reagan knew nothing about politics, but Spencer-Roberts did. They made a virtue out of Reagan's ignorance. They called him a "citizen politician" who should not be expected to know all the answers.... Reagan won the [California gubernatorial] election by a million votes and Spencer-Roberts got both cash and credit. Strong Reaganites say he would have won if Mickey Mouse ran his campaign, but prior to his race for governor, Reagan had no experience in politics; Spencer-Roberts did.

David Lee Rosenbloom, *The Election Men*[1]

Campaign professionals are frequently referred to as the "Great Houdinis" of the election world. Lore has it that all a candidate has to do is hire James Carville, Ed Rollins, or some other top-notch campaign consultants, allow these individuals to perform their wizardry, and watch the votes roll in. Of course, the folk wisdom of campaign managers and other political consultants is bound to over-estimate their influence. Consultants have an incentive to inflate their role in the electoral process. After all, many consultants spend nearly as much time marketing their services as they do working on political campaigns.

This study separates myth from reality as it relates to the impact of political consultants on congressional elections. Using data collected from candidates and campaign aides who competed in the 1992 House elections, I examine the staffing of contemporary House campaigns and analyze the impact that campaign professionals have on campaign fund-raising, strategy, communications, and electoral success. Campaign professionalism is operationalized as the number of major campaign activities that are performed by either political consultants or a paid campaign aide. This measure is designed to focus on the tasks that campaign professionals perform and their impact on campaigns. No distinctions are drawn between consultants and campaign aides or between consultants who work for nationally renowned firms and those who work for smaller, less well-known agencies.

There are many reasons to question whether such distinctions are important. First, many House incumbents hire congressional aides to work on their campaigns as managers or in other paid positions; some nonincumbents, especially state legislators and other elected officials, hire individuals employed in their offices to work on their campaigns. Candidates hire these and other paid staff because they believe that their political acumen, contacts, and knowledge of their districts are superior to the expertise that can be purchased from an out-of-town consulting firm. Some candidates also prefer to have political professionals working for them full time rather than part time. In some cases, paid staff are cheaper than consultants. Second, House candidates who hire nationally renowned firms usually receive their services from a firm employee, not the famous consultant for whom the firm is named, and this individual is not likely to have more experience or skill than the principal of a less renowned firm. Third, omitting paid campaign aides from the measure of campaign professionalism would seriously understate the level of professionalism of most incumbent campaigns; omitting lesser-known consulting firms would lead one to underestimate the professionalism of the campaigns of many nonincumbents who cannot afford to hire the services of one of the nation's premier consulting firms. Finally, the most important differences among campaign organizations are that some are comprised mainly of amateurs and others are comprised mainly of professionals. Individuals who toil behind the scenes at their firms and paid aides possess experience and institutional memory that make their contributions to a campaign more valuable than the contributions made by amateurs.[2]

The data on campaign professionalism were collected using a questionnaire that was mailed to all 1992 House campaigns involved in major-party contested elections. The questionnaire was timed to arrive two days after the election to ensure that the campaign was fresh in the mind of the respondents. It had a response rate of 42 percent and yielded 334 usable observations. The resulting sample is representative of the underlying population on such key variables as party affiliation, incumbency, and election outcome.[3] The data are used to demonstrate that campaign professionalism has a positive effect on congressional campaigns, particularly campaigns waged by challengers and open-seat contestants.

Campaign Organizations

For most of U.S. history, candidates for the House of Representatives, the Senate, and most state and local offices relied on state and local party committees to wage their campaigns. Although the separation of powers, federalism, and other institutional structures and laws laid out in the U.S. Constitution and in state statutes sowed the seeds for candidate-centered elections, party organizations were powerful enough to dominate the politics of many states and localities. The control they exercised over government jobs and contracts, and their influence over the social and economic lives of the largely poor, uneducated immigrants who comprised their constituents, made it relatively easy for party bosses to raise money, recruit campaign volunteers, and collect votes. Party committees, often referred to as old-fashioned political machines, were able to control virtually every facet of the election—from nominating candidates to mobilizing voters to cleaning up the remnants of the victory celebration.[4] During the late nineteenth century and the first half of the twentieth century, congressional campaign organizations often consisted of a candidate's loyal following within the party.

By the 1950s few congressional candidates could count on party committees to obtain their nominations or mount their campaigns. Election reforms, such as the Australian ballot and the direct primary and civil service laws that created merit requirements for government jobs and contracts, had their intended effect of crippling the political machines. Declining immigration, increased educational opportunities, suburbanization, and the rise of the middle class deprived the parties of the population groups that had formed their core constituencies.[5] The generational replacement of voters and the emergence of new issues that cut across the axis of conflict that divided Democrats and Republicans weakened voters' allegiances to the two major parties.[6] The introduction of the national press, the electronic media, and modern marketing and survey research provided candidates with techniques for learning about and communicating with voters that were independent of party committees.[7] Later, the Federal Election Campaign Act of 1974 and its amendments (collectively referred to as FECA) limited the sums that parties could contribute to or spend on behalf of federal candidates.

The legal, technological, and systemic changes in the political environment that led to the decline of party organizations and the introduction of new methods of campaigning hastened the development of the modern candidate-centered election system.[8] Under this system, candidates and the campaign organizations they assemble—not party committees—are the central actors in elections. Candidates, their campaign aides, and the consultants they hire are responsible for campaign management, communications, research, fund-raising, polling, voter mobilization, and the other activities that comprise a modern campaign.

Campaign professionals, including paid staff and consultants, play a prominent role in contemporary House campaigns.[9] Paid staff members manage 65 percent of all House campaigns, and political consultants are responsible for managing 19 percent (see table 5-1). Only 24 percent of all campaigns rely on a volunteer for campaign management—often a spouse, some other family member, or friend. Two percent rely on an interest group to provide a manager, and 4 percent do not have a manager, relying on the candidate to administer the campaign organization. Finally, only 1 percent of all House campaigns rely on a party committee for campaign management. Campaign professionals have clearly replaced party workers in the area of campaign management.

Campaign press relations, issue and opposition research, fund-raising, accounting, polling, and mass media advertising are also dominated by campaign professionals. House campaigns rely primarily on paid staff to carry out the first four activities, whereas polling and media tend to be carried out by consultants. The only areas of campaigning that are not dominated by campaign professionals are voter mobilization and legal compliance. House campaigns depend heavily on volunteers and parties for their get-out-the-vote (GOTV) and other mobilization activities and on volunteers for legal advice.

Significant variations exist across elections in the personnel who staff major campaign activities. Most incumbents hire paid staff to manage their campaigns. Very often incumbents rely on the chief of staff (COS) or administrative assistant (AA) from their congressional office to work as a full-time campaign manager. These individuals offer the candidate several advantages. They are familiar with the candidate's operating

Table 5-1. *Staffing Major Campaign Activities in the 1992 House Elections*[a]

Percent

Activity	All	Incumbents	Challengers	Open-seat candidates
Campaign management				
Paid staff	65	81	52	63
Consultant	19	18	15	27
Political party	1	...	1	1
Interest groups	2	2	3	1
Volunteer	24	11	34	25
Not used	4	2	7	3
Press relations				
Paid staff	61	74	47	52
Consultant	14	15	9	22
Political party	1	...	1	4
Interest groups	1	1	1	1
Volunteer	24	14	35	33
Not used	4	3	4	3
Issue and opposition research				
Paid staff	42	54	29	47
Consultant	22	28	12	28
Political party	15	4	25	15
Interest groups	7	7	8	7
Volunteer	31	16	41	40
Not used	7	10	7	3
Fund-raising				
Paid staff	53	71	36	62
Consultant	24	34	15	25
Political party	4	2	3	7
Interest groups	5	4	5	7
Volunteer	41	25	53	43
Not used	4	1	7	5
Accounting/FEC reporting				
Paid staff	64	82	52	62
Consultant	13	19	6	15
Political party	1	...	2	4
Interest groups	1	1	1	...
Volunteer	42	18	61	54
Not used	2	1	4	1
Polling				
Paid staff	8	8	7	6
Consultant	60	80	42	67
Political party	7	5	9	10
Interest groups	4	3	5	4
Volunteer	8	2	15	7
Not used	14	9	24	9

(*Continued next page*)

Table 5-1. *Continued*

Activity	All	Incumbents	Challengers	Open-seat candidates
Media advertising				
Paid staff	24	26	22	23
Consultant	61	76	42	71
Political party	2	1	1	3
Interest groups	1	...	2	...
Volunteer	15	3	29	11
Not used	5	3	8	4
Get-out-the vote drives				
Paid staff	39	80	25	36
Consultant	5	7	1	8
Political party	29	37	25	25
Interest groups	20	24	19	24
Volunteer	50	41	57	67
Not used	6	5	9	3
Legal advice				
Paid staff	11	14	8	11
Consultant	13	20	8	12
Political party	10	10	13	8
Interest groups	3	3	4	3
Volunteer	39	26	45	56
Not used	24	28	24	15
Summary Statistic				
Average number of activities performed by paid staff or consultants	5.5	6.9	4.1	5.8
N	331	120	137	74

Source: The 1992 Congressional Campaign Study, in Paul S. Herrnson, *Congressional Elections: Campaigning at Home and in Washington*, 2d ed. (Washington, D.C.: CQ Press, 1998).
... = *less than 0.5 percent.*
    a. Figures are percentages for general election candidates in major-party contested races, excluding a small number of atypical races. Figures for interest groups include labor unions. Columns may not add to 100 percent because some activities were performed by more than one person or group and because of rounding.

style, know the nuances of the congressional district, and have good relationships with local political activists. They also usually have contacts with individuals who contribute money to congressional campaigns, including local donors, political action committee (PAC) directors, members of the parties' congressional campaign committee, and other major contributors located in the nation's capital and other wealthy cities. Finally, it is easy for a COS, an AA, or other congressional aides to take a leave of absence from their current job to work on the campaign. When they leave their office on Capitol Hill to work for the campaign they are confident that their old job will be waiting for them when the election is over, as long as they performed their new task well and their candidate wins.

Open-seat candidates are somewhat less dependent on paid staff to manage their campaigns than are incumbents. They hire more paid consultants instead. Challengers hire the fewest campaign professionals to manage their campaigns. Paid staff manage 52 percent of all challenger races, and political consultants manage another 15 percent. More challengers rely on volunteers (34 percent) to manage their campaigns because their small campaign budgets preclude them from spending money to hire a professional manager. As a result, a substantial number of challenger campaigns are managed by individuals who can devote only some of their working hours to the election. This puts these campaigns at a tremendous disadvantage.

Press relations are an important part of any House campaign and are largely carried out by campaign professionals. As was the case with campaign management, most incumbent and open-seat candidates hire professionals to help them obtain free, frequently called "earned," media from electronic broadcasters and the press. Incumbents enjoy the advantage of being able to request that their congressional press secretary take a leave of absence to work on the campaign. Nonincumbents have to find a campaign press secretary using some other means. Open-seat candidates rely more on consultants than do incumbents. Approximately 40 percent of all challengers cannot afford to hire a press secretary or to pay a consultant to carry out press relations, which greatly handicaps their campaigns.

Issue and opposition research is often carried out by a combination of paid staff, consultants, party committees, interest groups, and volunteers. Paid staff and consultants carry out the research that is used by most incumbent campaigns. Four percent of all incumbents receive research support from a party committee. Many open-seat candidates also depend on the services of paid staff and consultants, but they also receive substantial amounts of research from volunteers, party committees, and interest groups. Comparatively few challengers can afford to have campaign professionals carry out policy and opposition research. Some of these candidates, mainly those in competitive contests, get some issue and opposition research from party committees and interest groups. Roughly 40 percent rely on research from volunteers.

Party committees have greatly increased the amount of issue and opposition research they carry out in recent years. The Democratic National Committee (DNC) and the Republican National Committee (RNC) have research divisions that mail or fax information on national issues to congressional, state, and local candidates and officeholders; to allied consultants and interest groups; and to political activists. The parties' congressional and senatorial campaign committees also disseminate "generic" issue research to House and Senate candidates and party activists. In addition, the two congressional campaign committees—the Democratic Congressional Campaign Committee (DCCC) and National Republican Congressional Committee (NRCC)—assemble highly detailed research packages for House candidates involved in competitive contests. These provide the candidates with facts and talking points about issues that are of importance to local voters. During the 1996 elections the DCCC provided fifty campaigns, mostly those waged by challengers and open-seat candidates, with detailed issue research about the impact that Republican House members' votes on Medicare, Medicaid, the budget, the environment, and other important issues would have on different groups of constituents. The NRCC, which is the wealthier of the two campaign committees, provided fifty challengers, fifty open-seat candidates, and nine incumbents with information that highlighted the impact that key pieces of Republican legislation would have on different constituent groups. These research packages included information on the balanced budget amendment, welfare reform, and the crime bill, including the votes that Democratic incumbents cast on these issues.[10]

Campaign fund-raising occurs in a variety of forms and places. Direct mail; large receptions that feature prominent politicians, athletes, or entertainers; and more intimate house parties are all used to raise money. Fund-raisers are usually held in the candidate's district; Washington, D.C.; New York City; Hollywood; and the other centers of government, commerce, and entertainment. Candidates go wherever the money is, and they use techniques that they believe will be effective to raise funds. Incumbents have the most professional fund-raising operations, with open-seat candidates following close behind. Challengers have the least professional fund-raising operations. Only about half are able to hire a professional fund-raiser. Parties and interest groups provide some challengers with fund-raising assistance, but they give considerably more help to open-seat candidates.

Virtually all candidates also depend on volunteers to help them raise funds. Private individuals who serve on finance committees solicit contributions on the candidate's behalf, help draw up lists of potential donors, and help organize fund-raising events. Many candidates, especially challengers and open-seat candidates, rely on volunteers to help them file the required disclosure reports with the Federal Election Commission.

Polling and advertising are highly technical campaign activities that require the involvement of individuals with specialized skills. As such, political consultants are often hired to carry out these activities. Substantial majorities of incumbents and open-seat candidates hire consultants to gauge public opinion in their districts and design and produce television and radio advertisements. Consultants conduct polling and media advertising in substantially fewer challenger campaigns.

Some candidates, including challengers, also receive polling and media services from their party and interest groups. However, 15 percent of all challengers are forced to depend on volunteers for their polling, and 24 percent take no polls. Volunteers also carry out the media advertising for 29 percent of the challengers, and 8 percent do not use the electronic media at all to communicate with voters.

Voter registration and GOTV drives and other voter mobilization activities require a great deal of manpower but few specialized skills. These grass-roots activities were traditionally the bailiwick of local parties, interest groups, and political activists. Parties, interest groups, and volunteers continue to make major contributions to voter mobilization in contemporary House campaigns. Incumbents depend as much, if not more, on individuals and organized groups, as do challengers and open-seat candidates. Most incumbents hire paid staff to plan and organize their GOTV operation, but fewer open-seat candidates, and especially challengers, are able to assign paid staff to carry out this task.

Similarly, most candidates rely on volunteers, party committees, and interest groups for legal advice. Incumbents are the most likely to keep an election-law expert on the payroll or on a retainer, followed by candidates for open seats. Nevertheless, substantial numbers of candidates of all types do not require the services of a salaried election lawyer.

The professionalism of House campaigns is reflected in the fact that the typical campaign uses paid staff or political consultants to carry out between five and six of the nine campaign activities previously discussed (see the bottom of table 5-1). Not surprisingly, incumbent campaigns are by far the most reliant on campaign professionals. The typical incumbent uses paid staff or consultants to carry out roughly seven of the nine campaign activities, as opposed to the typical challenger who relies on campaign professionals to carry out about four activities. The professionalism of campaigns for open seats lies between the two, scoring about six on the campaign professionalism scale. The major reason for the differences among campaigns, particularly the relative lack of professionalism of challenger efforts, is money. Challenger campaigns are often strapped for funds and cannot afford the luxury of hiring campaign professionals; they often marshal their resources for contacting voters instead.

Campaign Professionalism and Fund-Raising

Professional campaign fund-raisers bring a number of assets to a campaign. Direct-mail experts have contributor lists and a sense of the kinds of fund-raising appeals that work for different kinds of candidates. Event specialists know how to organize fund-raising committees and set up fund-raising events, and they are familiar with the strategies that guide the contribution decisions of individuals and the PACs that make large contributions. Campaign professionals involved in election activities besides fund-raising bring knowledge about the nuts and bolts of what generally does and does not work in campaigns or an understanding of the politics of individual congressional districts. These operatives' presence on a candidate's campaign team gives strategic contributors a sense that their donations will be spent wisely. The impact of campaign professionalism becomes evident when campaigns are divided into nine groups: first, on the basis of whether the candidate was an incumbent, challenger, or running for an open seat; and then, according to the number of activities listed in table 5-1 that were performed by paid staff or political consultants. Campaigns in which staffers or consultants performed between zero and two major campaign activities were classified as amateur, those where professionals performed between three and six activities were classified as moderately professional, and those where professionals performed between seven and nine activities were classified as highly professional.

Campaign professionalism has a significant impact on fund-raising (see table 5-2). Incumbents who assembled highly professional campaign

Table 5-2. *Impact of Campaign Professionalism on Fund-Raising in the 1992 House Elections*[a]

Average dollars

Type of funds	Incumbents			Challengers			Open-seat candidates		
	Amateur	Moderately professional	Highly professional	Amateur	Moderately professional	Highly professional	Amateur	Moderately professional	Highly professional
Total	276,348	485,940	644,270	48,504	173,498	334,714	176,998	465,153	555,191
PAC Contributions	147,898	246,289	278,918	6,795	29,480	52,743	39,420	92,620	136,176
Individual contributions of under $200	55,003	93,271	126,660	10,091	46,360	79,425	41,192	68,917	133,926
Individual contributions of $200 or more	48,484	103,477	169,037	12,178	40,500	72,511	53,111	170,453	153,040
Party money	3,856	7,181	17,052	5,404	27,672	26,959	17,624	29,844	18,791
Candidate contributions	...	6,014	19,874	11,548	22,104	91,374	20,815	82,847	96,817
Miscellaneous	21,107	29,708	32,729	2,488	7,382	11,702	4,836	20,472	16,441
N	9	21	89	44	47	42	13	25	35

Source: The Federal Election Commission and the 1992 Congressional Campaign Study. See Paul S. Herrnson, *Congressional Elections: Campaigning at Home and in Washington,* 2d ed. (Washington, D.C.: CQ Press, 1998).

a. Paid staff or political consultants performed between zero and two of the nine activities listed in table 5-1 in amateur campaigns. They performed between three and six of these activities in moderately professional campaigns and between seven and nine of these activities in highly professional campaigns. Party money includes party contributions and coordinated expenditures. Candidate contributions include loans the candidate made to the campaign. Miscellaneous includes interest from savings accounts and other investments. Total receipts include all contributions and party coordinated expenditures.

organizations raised $644,270 in 1992—almost 25 percent more money than the amount raised by incumbents who assembled moderately professional organizations ($485,940) and 57 percent more than incumbents who assembled amateur organizations ($276,348). The costs associated with putting together a professional campaign organization and the competitiveness of their elections clearly drove incumbents to raise more money. However, the positive causal relationship between campaign professionalism and fund-raising persists when statistical techniques are used to control for the effects that money and electoral competitiveness have on campaign professionalism.[11] This means that incumbents locked in tight elections may feel compelled to raise substantial amounts of money in order to hire more professional staff; the presence of additional staff helps incumbents raise more money than they would have collected otherwise, and they also benefit from the consultants' services. When incumbents assemble a highly professional campaign organization, they send a signal to potential contributors that they are involved in a competitive contest and will need a large war chest to mount their campaigns. Contributors clearly respond to the signals that incumbents present to them in their fund-raising requests.

Campaign professionalism has an even bigger impact on the fund-raising success of nonincumbents. The kind of campaign organization that a challenger or open-seat candidate assembles is a strong indicator of how well the candidate is going to do in the race. Challengers who assemble highly professional campaign organizations attract attention from Washington elites and from other individuals who routinely make political donations. They also gain more media coverage than challengers who mount amateur campaigns. Their heightened visibility also translates into a significant fund-raising advantage.

There is not much mystery to how consultants help nonincumbents raise money and attract media attention that they would not otherwise receive. Many consultants have worked for or with party committees, PACs, or the media in previous elections and understand how they operate. As Martin Hamburger points out in chapter 4, consultants know when party organizations make their contribution decisions, and they keep party officials appraised of the progress of the campaigns on which they are working in order to attract party support. The same holds true for raising contributions from PACs and individuals and for attracting media coverage; consultants use their experience and contacts to raise their candidates' visibility with individuals and organizations that are in a position to help their campaigns. This is especially important to non-incumbents who frequently begin the election season with little visibility among campaign contributors and the media. House challengers who assembled highly professional campaign organizations raised an average of $334,714 in 1992, nearly twice as much as those who assembled moderately professional campaigns ($173,498), and nearly seven times more than those who assembled amateur campaigns ($48,504). A similar pattern emerged for open-seat candidates.

Campaign contributors are influenced by many factors, and not all contributors respond equally to the same factors. The contribution figures for PACs and for individuals who make contributions of less than $200 demonstrate that these contributors are highly influenced by the professionalism of a candidate's campaign. Party committees and individuals who make contributions of $200 or more were also responsive to campaign professionalism, but their giving patterns were apparently influenced by other factors. On average, they donated somewhat more money to moderately professional open-seat campaigns than to highly professional campaigns.

Campaign Professionalism and Strategy

A campaign strategy is a plan that is designed to elect a candidate. Professional campaigns typically draw on a body of knowledge when designing campaign strategies. The four principles of campaign strategy that guide most professional strategists' understanding of elections are:

—Voters can be divided into your candidate's supporters, your opponent's supporters, and undecided voters—the majority of whom are uninterested in the election.

—Polling and other kinds of political research can be used to categorize voters into the preceding three groups.

—A winning coalition consists of your candidate's supporters and a subset of "persuadable" (sometimes called "undecided") voters that is large enough to ensure your candidate's election.

—The campaign's message, money, time, and other efforts should be directed to the voters who comprise the candidate's winning coalition. Resources should not be directed to anyone else.[12]

The four principles of campaign strategy seem simple, but designing a winning strategy is not an easy task. It requires specialized skills, knowledge, and more than an innate understanding of politics. In order to design a successful campaign strategy, one needs to understand the political behavior of voters in the election district, the nature of local politics from the voters' point of view, and the contrasting messages that the candidates are likely to present to the voters.

The first step in designing a successful campaign strategy is to define a target population—the groups of voters on which the campaign will focus its efforts. The target population is determined by first estimating the number of votes that will be cast and the number of votes that will be needed to win. The next step is to estimate the number of votes the candidate will receive from his or her supporters (often defined as voters who identify with the candidate's party) and from persuadable voters. Once campaign strategists determine the size and major components of the target population, they ascertain the geographic distribution of the candidate's supporters, the opponent's supporters, and persuadable voters. They usually get this information by analyzing the previous voting patterns in the district.[13]

The second step in formulating campaign strategy is to determine which population groups will comprise the candidate's winning coalition. Strategists use public opinion polls to learn about the attitudes of different voting groups. Polls enable campaigners to create a demographic and geographic map of the electorate. They help strategists identify the age, gender, marital status, race, ethnicity, income level, occupations, educational attainment, partisanship, and the ideology of the candidate's supporters, the opponent's supporters, and the persuadable voters. Polls also help campaigners learn about the concerns of these different groups of voters.[14]

The third step in campaign strategizing is to give the candidate's base and persuadable voters a reason to cast their ballot for the candidate. The candidate's status is a key factor in selecting a campaign message. Most elections that feature an incumbent are referendums on that candidate's performance. Incumbents seek to frame the election as a referendum on their successes in office. They claim credit for serving their constituents, for using government largess for the betterment of the district, and for pursuing popular policies in office.[15] Challengers, on the other hand, seek to blame the incumbent for the nation's or the district's problems and call for change.

In an open-seat election, where there is no incumbent, one or both of the campaigns will often attempt to claim the mantle of an incumbent, emphasizing their candidate's insider qualifications, such as experience and ties to the official who previously held the office. However, some non-incumbent campaigns will seek to attract votes by positioning their candidates as outsiders who are running to take on a corrupt or unresponsive political system. Some less frequently used campaign messages appeal to voters' ideology, views on one or two salient issues, or partisanship.[16]

Once campaign strategists have determined the where, who, and why of their strategy, they develop a campaign theme—a unifying overarching message that provides voters with a rationale for supporting the campaign's candidate or opposing its opposition. A good campaign theme is clear, concise, credible, compelling, and connected to voter perceptions about the election. It establishes clear contrasts between the candidates. A good campaign repeats its theme throughout all its communications, making it an important part of the candidate's image and the defining criteria that voters use when casting their ballots.[17]

As the preceding discussion demonstrates, the principles of campaign strategy are not complicated, but their application may require considerable expertise. This suggests that the strategies employed by House campaigns might differ according to their level of professionalism. Do more professional campaigns target different groups of voters or disseminate different kinds of messages to voters? Incumbents who assemble highly professional campaign organizations are less likely than others to use a shotgun approach to targeting than are others. Although few incumbent campaigns field amateur campaign organizations, seven of the nine (78 percent) of those that did so in 1992 targeted all voters in 1992, compared to only 43 percent of all moderately professional campaigns and 41 percent of all highly professional campaigns (see table 5-3). Incumbents who waged highly professional campaigns were somewhat more inclined than others to try to peel off pockets of support from the opposing party.

Challengers who waged highly professional campaigns were also less inclined to target all voters than were other challengers. Challengers with highly professional campaign staffs focused their efforts on members of their own party and independents instead. The results for campaigns for open seats are not as clear-cut. The percentage of moderately and highly professional open-seat campaigns that targeted voters who identified with their party and independents was greater than the percentage of amateur campaigns that did likewise. However, highly professional campaigns

Table 5-3. *Impact of Campaign Professionalism on Voter Targeting in the 1992 House Elections*[a]

Percent

Type of voter	Incumbents			Challengers			Open-seat candidates		
	Amateur	*Moderately professional*	*Highly professional*	*Amateur*	*Moderately professional*	*Highly professional*	*Amateur*	*Moderately professional*	*Highly professional*
Members of own party	...	10	11	5	4	10	15	13	3
Members of own party and independents	11	43	33	30	38	52	15	42	46
Independents	...	...	3	7	4	...	15	...	3
Members of opposing party and independents	...	...	5	9	6	2	5	4	6
Members of opposing party	...	...	3	5	4	5	...	...	3
Members of both parties	11	...	2	...	4	5	8	8	...
All voters	78	43	41	44	36	26	31	29	40
N	9	21	89	44	47	42	13	24	35

Source: The 1992 Congressional Campaign Study, in Paul S. Herrnson, *Congressional Elections: Campaigning at Home and in Washington*, 2d ed. (Washington, D.C.: CQ Press, 1998).

... = less than .05 percent.

a. Figures include responses from House general election candidates and campaign aides in major-party contested races, excluding a small number of atypical races. Columns may not add to 100 because of rounding.

were somewhat more likely to target all voters, but the differences among campaigns washes out when one considers the relatively large percentage of amateur and moderately professional campaigns that targeted members of both parties.

The messages that candidates communicate to voters also vary in accordance with the professionalism of their campaigns (see table 5-4). Roughly 44 percent of all incumbent campaigns focus on their candidate's issue positions. However, as incumbent campaigns become more professional, they concentrate less on their candidate's image and more on their opponent's image and issue positions. As one can well imagine, when incumbents make challengers the subjects of their campaign ads, they do not do so in a flattering way. This suggests that campaign professionals encourage greater negativity in elections.

Challengers conduct the most opposition-oriented campaigns. Highly professional and moderately professional challenger campaigns are more likely than amateur campaigns to focus on the incumbent's image and issue positions. This reflects the tendency of campaign professionals to turn challenger campaigns into a referendum on the incumbent. It also provides additional evidence for the belief that campaign professionals encourage candidates to wage negative campaigns.

Unlike incumbent and challenger campaigns, campaign professionalism does not have a systematic effect on the message focus of open-seat campaigns. There are no significant differences among the communications disseminated by open-seat campaigns that are staffed by amateurs, a moderate number of campaign professionals, or large number of professionals. This may be because of the relative freedom open-seat candidates have to choose an insider or an outsider strategy.

Campaign Professionalism and Communications

Campaigns communicate with voters using numerous media and approaches. Some media, such as television, radio, and direct mail, require a campaign to hire the services of highly specialized personnel— more often than not a political consulting firm. Press releases and other activities that are designed to attract free media require personnel who possess somewhat less technical expertise, but a professional press secretary is likely to have a bigger impact on a campaign than an amateur. Organizing literature drops, speeches and rallies, candidate visits to sites around the district, door-to-door canvasses, and debates requires some-

Table 5-4. *Impact of Campaign Professionalism on Message Focus in the 1992 House Elections*[a]

Percent

Message focus	Incumbents			Challengers			Open-seat candidates		
	Amateur	Moderately professional	Highly professional	Amateur	Moderately professional	Highly professional	Amateur	Moderately professional	Highly professional
Candidate's image	56	48	38	7	11	22	25	16	23
Candidate's issue positions	44	43	45	71	38	29	50	60	49
Candidate's image and issue positions	...	...	2	2	6	...	...	...	6
Opponent's image	...	5	5	3	23	17	17	12	20
Opponent's issue positions	...	5	8	16	15	22	8	12	...
Opponent's image and issue positions	...	...	...	...	4	7	...	...	3
All of the above	...	...	1	3	2	2	...	...	...
N	9	27	86	44	41	41	12	25	35

Source: The 1992 Congressional Campaign Study, in Paul S. Herrnson, *Congressional Elections: Campaigning at Home and in Washington*, 2d ed. (Washington, D.C.: CQ Press, 1998).

... = less than .05 percent.

a. Figures include responses from House general election candidates and campaign aides in major-party contested races, excluding a small number of atypical races. Columns may not add to 100 percent because of rounding.

what less skill than do the preceding communications methods. The same is true of placing newspaper ads, distributing billboards and buttons, and arranging speaking engagements for the candidate's spouse or other surrogate speakers.

Do campaign professionals have an impact on the mix of techniques that campaigns use to communicate with voters and an influence on the candidates' assessments of the importance of different communications techniques on their campaigns? The answer is "yes." Incumbents who assemble campaign committees comprised largely of amateurs, and who presumably are involved in noncompetitive elections, consider newsletters and direct mail to be their most important communications technique (see table 5-5). On a scale of 1 to 5, this rates 4.44, where 1 indicates they considered a communications technique unimportant and 5 indicates they considered it extremely important. They rank television next, followed by literature drops, press releases and free media, and speeches a nd rallies. Candidate visits in the district and other grass-roots activities are considered significantly less important. Incumbents who assemble moderately professional campaign committees also rank press releases and free media first, followed by newsletters and direct mail, television, and then radio. Speeches and rallies are ranked fifth, followed by candidate visits, and other grass-roots activities. Both sets of campaigns assign a great deal of importance to communication activities that require moderate skill levels. In fact, the typical amateur or moderately professional incumbent campaign assesses some of these communications methods as more important than methods that require considerable technical expertise. Highly professional incumbent campaigns, by contrast, reserve their highest evaluations for communications activities that require the greatest expertise. They rank television first, radio second, direct mail third, press releases and free media fourth. Literature drops, speeches and rallies, candidate visits, and other grass-roots efforts are considerably less important.

The patterns for challenger and open-seat campaigns, by and large, reflect those for incumbents. Amateur and moderately professional campaigns rank some aspects of campaigning that require little specialized skill or training among their four most important methods of reaching voters. They rank several methods that require significant campaign expertise as relatively unimportant. Highly professional challenger and open-seat campaigns, however, give high ratings to communications methods that require technical expertise or specialized skills.

Table 5-5. *Impact of Campaign Professionalism on the Techniques Used to Communicate with Voters in the 1992 House Elections*[a]

Score[b]

Type of communication	Incumbents			Challengers			Open-seat candidates		
	Amateur	Moderately professional	Highly professional	Amateur	Moderately professional	Highly professional	Amateur	Moderately professional	Highly professional
Television (paid or free)	4.33	3.55	4.23	3.51	3.87	4.30	4.15	4.88	4.66
Radio (paid or free)	3.89	3.33	3.81	3.49	3.49	4.14	3.54	3.96	3.85
Newsletters and direct mail	4.44	3.80	3.68	3.33	3.43	3.71	3.80	3.96	3.77
Press releases and free media	4.00	4.00	3.58	3.57	3.78	3.81	3.67	3.24	3.69
Literature drops	4.11	2.83	3.24	3.65	3.89	3.50	4.15	3.54	3.43
Speeches and rallies	4.00	3.20	3.19	3.98	3.52	3.24	4.08	3.72	3.20
Door-to-door canvassing	2.63	3.00	2.73	2.75	3.40	3.57	3.75	3.36	3.03
Debates	3.00	2.25	2.80	2.84	3.30	3.10	3.66	3.56	3.50
Newspaper ads	3.00	2.85	2.95	2.85	3.00	3.10	3.23	3.00	2.80
Billboards and buttons	2.78	2.24	2.50	2.63	2.66	2.79	3.00	2.84	2.38
Surrogate campaigning	2.50	2.24	2.27	2.60	2.80	2.68	3.00	2.28	2.55
Candidate visits to shopping centers, factories, etc.	3.50	2.95	3.23	2.80	3.23	3.10	3.17	3.00	2.89

Source: The 1992 Congressional Campaign Study, in Paul S. Herrnson, *Congressional Elections: Campaigning at Home and in Washington,* 2d ed. (Washington, D.C.: CQ Press, 1998).
a. Values listed are the arithmetic means of the scores. Figures include responses from House general election candidates and campaign aides in major-party contested races, excluding a small number of atypical races.
b. Candidates and campaign aides were asked to assess the importance of each technique on the following scale: 1 = not important, 2 = slightly important, 3 = moderately important, 4 = very important, 5 = extremely important.

Journalists also appear to respond to the professionalism of House campaigns, but in a way that might seem counterintuitive at first glance. When asked about the media coverage of their campaign and their opponents' campaign, most incumbents report receiving more free media and media endorsements than did their opponents (see table 5-6). Yet, incumbents who wage highly professional campaigns are less likely to respond that their campaign received the lion's share of press coverage and endorsements than are others. This reflects the fact that the strong challengers who opposed these incumbents, and encouraged them to assemble highly professional campaign staffs, were able to attract media coverage and endorsements that would have otherwise gone to the incumbent. Challengers and open-seat candidates who wage moderately or highly professional campaigns report receiving better treatment from the press than do challengers and open-seat candidates who assemble amateur campaign committees, both in terms of the amount of media coverage and the number of endorsements they receive. These candidates' campaign press secretaries and other staff undoubtedly helped them attract favorable media coverage, often at the expense of their opponents.

Campaign Professionalism and Electoral Success

Campaign professionalism clearly has an impact on House candidates' fund-raising, strategy, communications, and media relations. These are all means to an end—winning the election. The kind of campaign committee a candidate assembles also has an impact on his or her chances of electoral success. Incumbents who are involved in the most competitive elections usually put together the most professional campaign organizations, raise the most money, pay the closest attention to issues of strategy, make the most attacks on their opponents, and struggle the most to dominate election news coverage. Not surprisingly, their win-loss records are not as good as those of incumbents who face lower levels of competition and who do not feel the need to wage costly, highly professional campaigns.[18] In 1992 incumbents whose campaigns exhibited the highest levels of campaign professionalism won 92 percent of their elections, whereas incumbents who mounted less professional campaigns enjoyed a 100 percent success rate (see table 5-7). Of course, the number of incumbent defeats would probably have been larger if some of the incumbents who hired professional campaigners waged amateur campaigns instead.

Table 5-6. Impact of Campaign Professionalism on Earned Media Coverage and Endorsements in the 1992 House Elections[a]

Percent

	Incumbents			Challengers			Open-seat candidates		
	Amateur	Moderately professional	Highly professional	Amateur	Moderately professional	Highly professional	Amateur	Moderately professional	Highly professional
Respondents believing the media									
Gave own campaign more coverage	67	67	47	...	21	19	17	16	29
Gave opponent's campaign more coverage	...	10	11	72	38	47	83	32	27
Covered campaigns equally	33	24	42	28	40	33	...	52	44
N	9	21	88	43	47	42	12	25	34
Respondents reporting media endorsements									
Endorsed	78	76	63	2	9	5	15	24	34
Not endorsed	22	24	37	98	92	95	85	76	66
N	9	21	89	44	47	42	13	25	35

Source: The 1992 Congressional Campaign Study, in Paul S. Herrnson, *Congressional Elections: Campaigning at Home and in Washington*, 2nd ed. (Washington, D.C.: CQ Press, 1998).

... = less than .05 percent.

a. Figures include responses from House general election candidates and campaign aides in major-party contested races, excluding a small number of atypical races. Columns may not add to 100 because of rounding.

Table 5-7. *Impact of Campaign Professionalism on Electoral Success in the 1992 House Elections*[a]

Percent

Election outcome	Incumbents			Challengers			Open-seat candidates		
	Amateur	*Moderately professional*	*Highly professional*	*Amateur*	*Moderately professional*	*Highly professional*	*Amateur*	*Moderately professional*	*Highly professional*
Won	100	100	92	...	6	14	31	48	63
Lost	...	...	8	100	94	86	69	52	37
N	9	21	89	44	47	42	13	25	35

Source: The 1992 Congressional Campaign Study, in Paul S. Herrnson, *Congressional Elections: Campaigning at Home and in Washington,* 2d ed. (Washington, D.C.: CQ Press, 1998).

... = less than .05 percent.

a. Figures include responses from House general election candidates and campaign aides in major-party contested races, excluding a small number of atypical races.

The performance of challenger campaigns is also influenced by campaign professionalism. Challengers who waged amateur campaigns in 1992 had an abysmal record, whereas those who mounted moderately professional campaigns won 6 percent of their elections and those who mounted highly professional campaigns won 14 percent. Campaign professionalism is associated with even more favorable results in open-seat contests, which tend to be the most competitive of all elections. Open-seat candidates who waged amateur campaigns won 30 percent of their contests, those who waged moderately professional campaigns won 48 percent, and those who waged highly professional campaigns won 63 percent.[19]

Conclusion

Contemporary House campaigns are more professional than were their predecessors. The typical House incumbent campaign employs paid staff or political consultants for campaign management, fund-raising, polling, research, communications, and most other election activities. Open-seat campaigns are somewhat less professional than incumbent campaigns. Challenger campaigns are the least professional, but even most challenger campaigns are moderately professional. Campaign professionals perform many of the tasks that were once performed by political parties. They help candidates raise money, formulate strategy, and communicate with voters. They also have a significant impact on House candidates' prospects for success, especially the prospects of open-seat candidates and challengers. In many House races, campaign professionals have replaced local party organizations as the intermediaries between candidates and voters.

The "election men," as David Rosenbloom referred to campaign professionals, are involved in most congressional elections. Nevertheless, this study shows that campaign professionals are not as omnipotent as some members of their industry would have us believe, nor are they as inconsequential as some candidate loyalists argue. Rather, paid campaign staff and political consultants have an important but not an overwhelming impact on House races. Campaign professionals cannot eliminate the advantages of incumbency, nor can they turn an incompetent politician into one of presidential timber, but they can make the difference between victory and defeat in some House elections.

Notes

1. David Lee Rosenbloom, *The Election Men: Professional Campaign Managers and American Democracy* (New York: Quadrangle Books, 1973), p. 22.

2. On the role of institutional memory in election campaigns, see Marjorie Randon Hershey, *Running for Office: The Political Education of Campaigners* (Chatham, N.J.: Chatham House Publishers, 1984), pp. 60–73.

3. For more information on the data and the questionnaire, see Paul S. Herrnson, *Congressional Elections: Campaigning at Home and in Washington,* 2d ed. (Washington, D.C.: CQ Press, 1998) and *books.cq.com* (navigate to the "Free Resources" area).

4. See, for example, Frank J. Sorauf, "Political Parties and Political Action Committees: Two Life Cycles," *Arizona Law Review,* 22 (1980), pp. 445–64.

5. Jerrold B. Rusk, "The Effect of the Australian Ballot Reform on Split-Ticket Voting, 1876–1908," *American Political Science Review,* 64 (December 1970), pp. 1220–38; V. O. Key, *Politics, Parties, and Pressure Groups* (New York: Thomas Y. Crowell, 1964), p. 371; Nelson W. Polsby, *The Consequences of Party Reform* (Oxford University Press, 1983), pp. 72–74.

6. John Petrocik, *Party Coalitions: Realignments and the Decline of the New Deal Party System* (University of Chicago Press, 1981), chaps. 8 and 9; Paul Allen Beck, "A Socialization Theory of Partisan Realignment," in Richard G. Niemi and Herbert F. Weisberg, eds., *Controversies in American Voting Behavior* (Washington, D.C.: CQ Press, 1984), pp. 396–411.

7. Austin Ranney, *Channels of Power: The Impact of Television on American Politics* (Basic Books, 1983), p. 110; Doris Graber, *Mass Media and American Politics,* 4th ed. (Washington, D.C.: CQ Press, 1993), pp. 250–52.

8. Robert Agranoff, "Introduction: The New Style of Campaigning," in Robert Agranoff, ed., *The New Style in Election Campaigns* (Boston: Holbrook Press, 1972), pp. 3–50; Larry J. Sabato, *The Rise of the Political Consultants: New Ways of Winning Elections* (Basic Books, 1981).

9. This section draws from Herrnson, *Congressional Elections,* pp. 60–65.

10. Herrnson, *Congressional Elections,* pp. 88–89.

11. Paul S. Herrnson, "Campaign Professionalism and Fundraising in Congressional Elections," *Journal of Politics,* 54 (1992), pp. 859–70.

12. Joel Bradshaw, "Who Will Vote for You and Why: Designing Theme and Strategy," in James A. Thurber and Candice J. Nelson, eds., *Campaigns and Elections American Style* (Westview Press, 1995), pp. 31–32.

13. Bradshaw, "Who Will Vote for You," pp. 32–36.

14. Gary A. Mauser, "Marketing and Political Campaigning: Strategies and Limits," in Michael Margolis and Gary A Mauser, eds., *Manipulating Public Opinion: Essays on Public Opinion as a Dependent Variable* (Pacific Grove, Calif.: Brooks/Cole), pp. 19–46.

15. David R. Mayhew, *Congress: The Electoral Connection* (Yale University Press, 1974).

16. Bradshaw, "Who Will Vote for You," p. 39.

17. Ibid., pp. 43–44.

18. Herrnson, *Congressional Elections,* p. 205; Gary C. Jacobson, *Money in Congressional Elections* (Yale University Press, 1980), pp. 113–23.

19. These results are similar to those reported by studies that show that campaign professionalism does not have a positive impact on House incumbents' vote shares, is associated with small increases in the votes garnered by challengers and open-seat candidates, but does not have a big enough impact to make the difference between winning and los-

ing in most congressional elections. See Stephen K. Medvic and Silvo Lenart, "The Influence of Political Consultants in the 1992 Congressional Elections," *Legislative Studies Quarterly*, 22 (1997), pp. 61–77; Stephen K. Medvic, "The Effectiveness of Political Consultants as a Campaign Resource," *PS: Political Science and Politics*, 31 (1998), pp. 150–54; and Kristen la Cour Dabelko and Paul S. Herrnson, "Women's and Men's Campaigns for the U.S. House of Representatives," *Political Research Quarterly*, 50 (1997), pp. 121–35.

CHAPTER SIX

Professionalization in Congressional Campaigns

STEPHEN K. MEDVIC

The activities of professional political consultants are shrouded in mystery. While the average citizen has a general sense that consultants are "behind the scenes" in American elections, most have no idea what consultants do. Indeed, even political analysts are unclear about something as simple as the extent to which consultants are hired by candidates.

The purpose of this chapter is three-fold. First, it develops the notion of the consultant as a campaign resource. Because this conceptualization is somewhat unusual, a case must be made for using it to understand consultant activity. Second, it discusses the level of professionalization in House campaigns. Until recently, such a task would have been impossible given the lack of data on consultant hirings.[1] Finally, the impact of consultant use on electoral success is explored. Specifically, the question of whether the level of professionalization within a campaign contributes to electoral success is discussed. Of course, this is but one of the questions that need to be asked about consultant influence if we hope to determine the extent of that influence in American elections.

The Political Consultant as a Campaign Resource

A political consultant is a campaign resource. In many ways, consultants are similar to the most precious campaign resource of all—money.[2] Like money, consultants are thought to be crucial to electoral success and the more a candidate has (that is, the more "professionalized" the campaign), the more successful he or she is likely to be. Furthermore, as with other campaign resources, some candidates have an easier time acquiring the services of consultants than do others.[3] Yet consultant influence may be different for various types of candidates. Just as campaign spending seems to benefit challengers more than incumbents, consultants may help candidates at some sort of electoral disadvantage more than those not so hindered.[4]

The similarities between political consultants and money do not erase one important, and obvious, difference. Political consultants are human actors. As such, they are often thought of in individual terms. As Sidney Blumenthal suggests:

> Consultants each have their own political grammar, reflected in a particular campaign style. Although consultants dispense the same technique, politicians seek something unique that will permit them to win. Idiosyncratic expression becomes a precious commodity; it makes a campaign distinct, attracting voter attention.[5]

While the consulting industry's collective ability to work "magic" is taken for granted by politicians and the media, it is individual consultants who are deemed "kingmakers."[6] Political commentators routinely imply that campaign decisions made by specific consultants determine the outcome of elections.[7] During the 1993 New Jersey gubernatorial election, for example, the *New York Times* described the race as a clash of "two campaign titans."[8] That was not a reference to Democratic governor Jim Florio and Republican challenger Christine Todd Whitman, but to consultants James Carville and Ed Rollins.

Nevertheless, we know little about the impact of consultants on elections and we know even less about the effectiveness of individual handlers. In fact, there is good reason to believe that consultant talent does not vary much from one professional to the next.[9] Most consultants have vast experience running campaigns and have identified effective tactics on the job, through trial and error. Marjorie Randon Hershey explains this by applying social learning theory to campaigning.[10] According to Hershey, campaigners (including, and perhaps especially, consultants) "learn" which methods work and which do not as they act within various campaign environments.[11] In addition, there are common features of campaigns that campaigners will face in every setting (for example, two major party candidates, the media, voters with roughly similar levels of knowledge and interest, and so on). By generalizing from past experience, campaigners develop models that can be applied to future campaigns.[12] Consultants' learning is likely to be more complete than other types of campaigners' given the former's extensive experiences.

Professional consultants also share insights with one another through trade magazines (for example, *Campaigns & Elections*) and a national association (the American Association of Political Consultants [AAPC]). Finally, consultants increasingly learn skills during stints at the political parties or even at campaign "schools."[13]

Consequently, individual differences in consultants' talents are less fruitful in explaining the outcome of an election than is the use of consultants generally. In other words, a candidate's decision about whether or not to hire a consultant is more important than the decision about whether to hire Consultant A or Consultant B.

If it is true that consultants are more similar than different in terms of the skills they bring to a campaign, then it would be more useful to think of them, collectively, as a campaign resource than as individual handlers or firms. This conceptualization is most valid for "the relatively small and elite corps of interstate political consultants who usually work on many campaigns simultaneously and have served hundreds of campaigns in their careers."[14] For this group, differences in ability are particularly small.

For the systematic study of consultant influence, then, conceptualization of political consultants as a campaign resource is crucial. Without it, political scientists would be forced to examine the effectiveness of individual political consultants. With it, we can group consultants together and treat them like any other campaign factor. Their impact may vary from campaign to campaign, but some recognizable pattern of influence should appear. Before turning to an examination of that influence, the level of professionalization in congressional elections should be established.

The Level of Professionalization in House Elections

Unlike campaign funds, which the Federal Election Commission (FEC) has been tracking since 1976, political consultant activity has never been officially recorded. What Mark Petracca noted almost a decade ago remains true today—consultants have been understudied because there are insufficient data with which to systematically analyze their activities; the concept of "consulting" is unclear; and political scientists interested in elections prefer, for the most part, to focus on voters.[15]

While consulting remains conceptually vague and political scientists are still more taken with voting behavior than with campaign behavior, data now exist on consultant activity. Some of these data have been collected with surveys of candidates and their campaign staffs.[16] The data I use in the following analyses come from the biennial "Consultant Scorecard" gathered by *Campaigns & Elections* magazine (hereafter *C & E*). Specifically, I rely upon the scorecards for 1990 and 1992.[17] In their original form, the data in these scorecards are organized by consulting firm with the names of the candidates for whom each firm worked listed under the firm's name. In creating the data set to be used herein, the data were organized by candidate (as well as by congressional race) and consultant hirings were coded as 1 for "hired a consultant" and 0 for "did not hire a consultant." I also recorded the use of any of seven types of political consultants—pollsters; media handlers; fund-raisers; generalists; and fund-raising, persuasion, or direct-mail specialists.[18]

It should be noted that, beginning in 1990, *C & E* relied upon FEC reports on candidate expenditures as well as interviews with candidates and consultants to build their scorecards. This makes the scorecards more reliable than any data source yet established on consultant activity.

Following the operationalization of the Consultant Scorecards, consulting firms were included in my data set if they worked on at least two congressional or statewide races in a given election cycle. In addition, I included those consultants who were among the highest grossing professionals in their fields according to the *Handbook of Campaign Spending* for 1990 and 1992 or who were members of the AAPC.[19] Such requirements for inclusion in this data set ensure that only "professionals" are counted as consultants.[20]

In addition to the *Handbook of Campaign Spending,* data were gathered from the *Almanac of American Politics* and the FEC's "Report on Financial Activity" for 1990 and 1992.[21] Among other variables, these sources contain information on a candidate's share of the vote, campaign expenditures and receipts, and the electoral history of congressional districts.

Given the fact that, until recently, data on consultant activity in congressional elections were unavailable, estimates of consultant use have been rare. In his classic *The Costs of Democracy,* Alexander Heard claims that between 1952 and 1957 nineteen firms provided partial service to thirty-two general election campaigns for the House and ten additional firms gave full-service management to nineteen such efforts.[22] For the

1962 elections pollster Louis Harris estimated that 10 percent of all congressional candidates hired a professional pollster, and Robert Huckshorn and Robert Spencer found that professional "managers" were active in 4 percent of losing and 22 percent of marginal campaigns.[23] Furthermore, nearly 50 percent of the unsuccessful candidates and 61 percent of all marginals in 1962 hired public relations or advertising firms.[24]

Other estimates include Robert King and Martin Schnitzer's finding that 44 percent of members of Congress used pollsters in 1966 (and that Republicans used them more than Democrats), Rosenbloom's claim that as many as 150 House candidates hired professional management firms in 1970, and Goldenberg and Traugott's study of the 1978 congressional campaigns in which roughly 9 percent of House candidates employed a professional manager and 39 percent used a media handler.[25] In chapter 5 of this volume Paul Herrnson surveyed House candidates and their staffs and found that 19 percent relied on professional campaign managers, 22 percent used issue and opposition researchers, 24 percent employed fund-raisers, and 60 and 61 percent, respectively, hired pollsters and media consultants.[26]

While Herrnson's estimates are the best to date, they may be limited by a number of factors related to the nature of survey-based data. In questioning candidates and campaign staff, researchers are unable to control the campaigns' definitions of the terms used in the survey. In other words, what a researcher means by certain words may not be the same as what the candidate or staffer has in mind. It is not unreasonable for a candidate to believe, for example, that the attorney, and close personal friend, that he or she hired for strategic advise is a "consultant." Worse, surveys can be plagued by the short, or selective, memories of the candidates. Just as consultants tend to "forget" about the losing candidates for whom they worked, a candidate may be less willing to mention the use of a consultant when that candidate was successful than when he or she was unsuccessful. The explanation for such a response is that candidates appear to take credit for victories and shift responsibility for losses.[27] While Herrnson's survey included 334 respondents and was quite representative, most others present a limited number of cases, thus limiting the generalizability of the findings.

The data set used herein was compiled with these factors in mind.[28] Using these data, I have previously reported the level of consultant use in House elections.[29] In 1990 candidates in 46.3 percent of all House contests hired at least one consultant; in 1992 this figure rose to 63.7 percent.[30] Unlike Robert King and Martin Schnitzer's estimate for 1966, I found that Democrats were significantly more likely to hire consultants than were Republicans in both 1990 (52.5 percent versus 39.8 percent) and 1992 (71.4 percent versus 56 percent).[31] This may seem surprising given the general perception that Republicans are more sophisticated campaigners. Yet it is precisely that sophistication that explains the finding. The Republican party's "renewal" in the late 1970s and 1980s produced, among other things, "a full-service campaign consulting organization for Republican candidates" within the party.[32] In other words, the Republican party has been much more successful in providing professional services to its candidates than has the Democratic party. Thus, Democrats have had to acquire professional assistance on their own and, consequently, have been more likely to hire consultants than have Republicans.

Challengers were the least likely candidate type to hire consultants, while incumbents or open-seat candidates were the most likely, depending on the year. Seventy-five percent of open-seat candidates, 66.2 percent of incumbents, and 16.5 percent of challengers employed at least one consultant in 1990. For 1992 the numbers were 70.1 percent, 85.9 percent, and 36.4 percent, respectively. This is most likely due to the financial resources available to each candidate type. Because challengers typically have less money than incumbents or open-seat candidates, they are less able to hire consultants.

In terms of the mean number of different consultant types hired, what I call the "level of professionalization" of a campaign, House candidates hired an average of just under one (.95) specialist in 1990 (see table 6-1). On average, open-seat candidates hired the most consultant types (1.75), followed by incumbents (1.33) and challengers (.33). In addition, Democrats ran significantly more professionalized campaigns than did Republicans, with the former hiring an average of 1.13 consultant types to the latter's .76 ($t = -4.24$, $d.f. = 774$, $p = .000$). The level of professionalization, then, follows the pattern for basic consultant usage noted above.

Finally, candidates in competitive races hired more than twice as many consultant types, on average, than did those in noncompetitive districts. This is not surprising, considering that candidates in tough election battles raise more money than those with weak competition.

The overall mean for the number of different consultant types hired in 1992 was 1.45 (see table 6-2). This represents a significant increase over 1990's mean of .95 ($t = 7.64$, $d.f. = 1595$, $p = .000$) and may be the result

Table 6-1. *The Level of Professionalization in House Campaigns, 1990*[a]

Mean number of consultants

Type of candidate[b]	Democrats	Republicans	Total
Incumbents			
Competitive	2.11 (63)	1.92 (53)	2.03 (116)
Not competitive	1.12 (182)	.92 (101)	1.05 (283)
Overall	1.38 (245)	1.27 (154)	1.33 (399)
Challengers			
Competitive	1.11 (44)	.65 (51)	.86 (95)
Not competitive	.08 (77)	.11 (149)	.10 (226)
Overall	.45 (121)	.25 (200)	.33 (321)
Open seats			
Competitive	2.26 (19)	1.65 (17)	1.97 (36)
Not competitive	1.11 (9)	1.55 (11)	1.35 (20)
Overall	1.89 (28)	1.61 (28)	1.75 (56)
All			
Competitive	1.79 (126)	1.35 (121)	1.57 (247)
Not competitive	.82 (268)	.49 (261)	.66 (529)
Overall	1.13 (394)	.76 (382)	.95 (776)

a. The "level of professionalization" is the mean number of different consultant types hired: pollsters; media handlers; fund-raisers; generalists; and fund-raising, persuasion, or direct-mail specialists. Candidates from Louisiana were excluded because of that state's unique use of the "nonpartisan" primary (for details, see John C. Kuzenski, "The Four—Yes, Four—Types of State Primaries," *PS: Political Science & Politics*, 30 [1997], pp. 207–08). Bernie Sanders (I-Vt.) was also excluded from the data set (as was the Democratic House candidate in Vermont), although the Republican candidate (incumbent Peter Smith) was included. Sample sizes are in parentheses.

b. "Competitive" refers to those candidates who received between 40 and 60 percent of the vote; "not competitive" refers to those candidates who received over 60 or under 40 percent of the vote.

of House candidates' efforts to cut through the barrage of information about the presidential election (see note 29). The mean for 1992 House campaigns also differs from Herrnson's finding in chapter 5 that the average number of activities performed by campaign professionals was 5.5. It is quite possible, however, that this discrepancy is the result of the inclusion of "paid staff" as well as consultants in Herrnson's results.

In 1992 incumbents hired more types of consultants than did open-seat candidates or challengers. Members of Congress hired an average of 2.06 consultant types to open-seat candidates' 1.71 and challengers' .65. This general pattern (of incumbents using professionals to handle more aspects of their campaigns than open-seat candidates, who used them more than challengers) is confirmed by Herrnson's findings in table 5-1 of his chapter.

Once again, Democrats had significantly more aspects of their campaigns handled by consultants than did Republicans, although the

Table 6-2. *The Level of Professionalization*
in House Campaigns, 1992[a]

Mean number of consultants

Type of candidate[b]	Democrats	Republicans	Total
Incumbents			
Competitive	2.44 (88)	2.40 (47)	2.43 (135)
Not competitive	1.78 (116)	1.86 (83)	1.81 (199)
Overall	2.06 (204)	2.05 (130)	2.06 (334)
Challengers			
Competitive	1.67 (33)	1.07 (73)	1.25 (106)
Not competitive	.48 (87)	.24 (120)	.34 (207)
Overall	.81 (120)	.55 (193)	.65 (313)
Open seats			
Competitive	2.36 (53)	1.80 (49)	2.09 (102)
Not competitive	1.86 (35)	.54 (37)	1.18 (72)
Overall	2.16 (88)	1.26 (86)	1.71 (174)
All			
Competitive	2.27 (174)	1.65 (169)	1.97 (343)
Not competitive	1.32 (238)	.85 (240)	1.08 (478)
Overall	1.72 (412)	1.18 (409)	1.45 (821)

a. The "level of professionalization" is simply the mean number of different consultant types hired (see table 6-1). Candidates from Louisiana were excluded because of that state's unique use of the "nonpartisan" primary (for details see John C. Kuzenski, "The Four—Yes, Four—Types of State Primaries," *PS: Political Science & Politics*, 30 [1997], pp. 207–08). Furthermore, the candidates from Montana (which has an at-large representative), district 2 in Iowa, and district 1 in Maryland were excluded because two incumbents faced each other in those races. Finally, Bernie Sanders (I-Vt.) was also excluded from the data set (along with Democrat Lewis Young), although the Republican candidate for the House in Vermont (challenger Tim Philbin) was included. Sample sizes are in parentheses.
b. See table 6-1.

difference in means for candidates of the two parties does not appear large (1.72 for Democrats to 1.18 for Republicans; $t = 5.68$, $d.f. = 819$, $p = .000$). Finally, candidates in close races hired a greater number of consultant types, on average, than did candidates who were sure winners or losers (1.97 to 1.08).

With the level of professionalization in House campaigns established, I now turn to an analysis of the effect of these levels on electoral success. While previous work suggests that simple consultant use helps some candidates gain more of the vote than they otherwise would have, the impact of professionalization level has yet to be examined in any depth.

The Impact of Professionalization

Consultant influence in congressional elections has been explored by past research. One of the ways that influence has been studied seeks to establish the impact of the mere presence of consultants in a campaign.

According to this work, hiring a consultant does, indeed, have a positive effect on a candidate's share of the vote, although only for challengers and some open-seat candidates.[33]

The influence of a campaign's level of professionalization has also been examined previously. Herrnson, for instance, has explored campaign professionalism and its impact on fund-raising. He measured professionalism as "an index that records the number of specialized campaign activities performed by professional political consultants."[34] The results of Herrnson's investigation suggest that campaign professionalism has a positive impact on a candidate's ability to raise money from the party, political action committees, and individuals.[35]

In a cursory analysis, I have found that the level of professionalization in nonincumbent campaigns significantly adds to a candidate's percentage of the vote.[36] This was particularly true for open-seat candidates. In 1992 open-seat candidates stood to gain nearly five percentage points for each additional consultant type hired. Challengers, on the other hand, added just over one additional percentage point to their vote total per consultant.[37]

Before reexamining the influence of professionalization on candidates' vote shares, the theoretical reason for expecting a positive impact should be explored. As mentioned above, political analysts assume that professional consultants deliver what they claim. That is, political consultants are thought to be successful "vote catchers." This is probably a safe assumption, although as of now we have little theoretical reason to expect professional consultants to be more effective than other campaign staffers.[38]

We can, of course, rely on Hershey's application of "social-learning theory" to political campaigns.[39] Unfortunately, that theory takes us only so far. It explains that what consultants do is learned and refined over time, making them skilled at successfully handling various campaign situations. But it does not tell us what, *exactly*, consultants do.

I have attempted elsewhere to go a step further by suggesting that consultants assist campaigns in priming voters. They engage in what I call "deliberate priming," as opposed to the inadvertent priming that is the result of news reporting.[40] Shanto Iyengar and Donald Kinder explain what is generally thought of as priming—"*By calling attention to some matters while ignoring others, television news influences the standards by which governments, presidents, policies, and candidates for public office are judged.*"[41] To oversimplify a bit, I argue that consultants deliberately prime voters by finding those issues upon which a candidate has an electoral advantage, creating a message and strategy around those issues, and disseminating that message.[42] Of course, these issues can be image-related characteristics like trustworthiness, compassion, and so on. The point is that professional consultants, more than nonprofessional staffers, understand this process and are highly skilled at it, even if they do not have a name for it.[43]

Thus, consultants can be expected to help candidates garner more votes than they otherwise would have without professional assistance. Furthermore, the more consultants a candidate hires, the larger his or her vote total should be. Specifically, the more aspects of a campaign (for example, polling, general strategy, media, fund-raising, and so on) that are professionally handled, the better the candidate will do.

Using the data described above, I applied ordinary least squares regression to the following model to determine the relative influence of a campaign's level of professionalization on its vote total:

$Y = a_0 + b_1$ District partisanship $+ b_2$ Year $+ b_3$ Quality $+$
  b_4 Democratic spending $+ b_5$ Republican spending $+$
  b_6 Democratic professionalization $+ b_7$ Republican
  professionalization $+ e_i$,

where:

Y = the candidate's percentage of the vote;
a_0 = constant;
District
partisanship = the district's vote, in percentages, for the
                Democratic presidential nominee in the most recent
                election (that is, in 1990 the vote for Dukakis; in
                1992 the vote for Clinton);
Year = the election year, measured as 1 for 1992 and 0 for 1990
Quality = the nonincumbent's quality status measured as 1 if he or
            she had held prior elected office and 0 if not;[44]
Democratic
spending = the base 10 log transformation of the Democrat's total
             expenditures;[45]
Republican
spending = the base 10 log transformation of the Republican's
             total expenditures;

Democratic
professionalization = an index, ranging from 0 to 7, measuring the
number of consultant types hired by the
Democrat; and
Republican
professionalization = an index, ranging from 0 to 7, measuring the
number of consultant types hired by the
Republican.

Table 6-3 contains the results for the regression analysis for both
Democratic and Republican challengers. As expected, Democratic challengers gain votes by increasing the amount spent on their campaigns.
Furthermore, the level of professionalization proved a significant influence on a candidate's percent of the vote received. As suggested earlier,
campaigns run by professional consultants benefit not only from the
experience of the consultants but from the unique approach to campaigning that consultants bring to an organization. It stands to reason
that the more campaign activities handled by consultants, the greater the
candidate's share of the vote will be. The result, in this instance, is that for
each additional consultant type employed, a Democratic challenger

Table 6-3. *The Impact of Professionalization Level*
for House Challengers

Variable	Democratic challengers			Republican challengers		
	b	*beta*	α	*b*	*beta*	α
District partisanship	9.81E–02	0.090	0.110	–0.34	–0.409	0.000
Year	–3.73	–0.241	0.000	–2.12	–0.116	0.004
Challenger quality	1.59	0.080	0.158	2.25	0.096	0.022
Democratic spending	4.22	0.766	0.000	2.17	0.078	0.130
Republican spending	1.25	0.038	0.557	3.97	0.325	0.000
Professionalization (D)[a]	1.66	0.249	0.000	–0.29	–0.042	0.389
Professionalization (R)[a]	3.17E–02	0.005	0.934	1.35	0.127	0.006
Summary statistic						
Constant		6.60			21.38	
R^2		0.462			0.486	
Adjusted R^2		0.444			0.475	
N		214			348	

a. D = Democratic; R = Republican.

gained 1.66 percentage points. The only other significant factor was the year, suggesting that Democratic challengers did worse in 1992 than they did in the midterm elections of 1990, when Democrats were the "out" party.[46]

The table also indicates that, along with spending, Republican challengers also benefited from increasing levels of professionalization. Indeed, they picked up 1.35 percentage points per consultant type hired. Other significant factors included the positive influence of "quality" status and the negative effect of year (Republican challengers, too, did worse in 1992 than in 1990) and district partisanship (where the Democratic presidential nominee's performance and the incumbency advantage worked hand-in-hand).

The general finding here—that challengers benefit from increasing levels of professionalization—is also confirmed by Herrnson in chapter 5. He concludes that as challengers move from amateur to highly professionalized campaigns, their chances of winning increase dramatically. Yet the same is not true for incumbents. That is because, as Herrnson notes, those incumbents "in the most competitive elections usually put together the most professional campaign organizations" while those in safe seats mount far less professional campaigns.[47] Thus, while I am testing the impact of consultants on the percent of the vote candidates receive, Herrnson's examination of success rates mirrors my results.

The results of the analysis of open-seat races are provided in table 6-4. In this case, district partisanship had a significant influence on a Democratic open-seat candidate's vote. Without the incumbency advantage at play, Democratic congressional candidates faired better in districts where Democratic presidential nominees perform well. For each percentage point received by their presidential candidate, open-seat Democrats got an additional .38 percent of the vote. In the open-seat version of the regression model, candidate quality proved significant for the Democrats. Being an experienced candidate aided Democrats to the tune of 2.77 percentage points. Spending helped candidates of both parties in the expected ways.

The variable of most interest here, professionalization, proved significant only for Republicans.[48] For each additional consultant type employed by the Republican candidate, the Democratic open-seat contestant lost 1.35 percent of the vote. This finding presents us with something of a puzzle. Why would both Democratic and Republican

Table 6-4. *The Impact of Professionalization Level
for House Open-Seat Candidates*

Variable	Democratic open-seat candidates		
	b	*beta*	α
District partisanship	0.38	0.361	0.000
Year	–2.72	–0.089	0.082
Quality			
Democratic	2.77	0.106	0.032
Republican	–0.50	–0.020	0.714
Spending			
Democratic	6.34	0.169	0.005
Republican	–8.71	–0.470	0.000
Professionalization			
Democratic	6.03E-02	0.006	0.915
Republican	–1.35	–0.158	0.008
Summary Statistic			
Constant		49.51	
R^2		.777	
Adjusted R^2		.760	
N		110	

challengers, but only Republican open-seat candidates, benefit from an increased level of professionalization? The answer lies in the disadvantages faced by some candidates rather than others.

Challengers are clearly at a disadvantage when compared to incumbents. The former have far less money and far less name recognition, to highlight but two of their problems. This explains why campaign spending, for example, has more of an impact for challengers than incumbents (for whom it has virtually no impact).[49] In much the same way, level of professionalization, like consultant use generally, would also be expected to help challengers but not incumbents.

Yet this does not explain the positive influence of professionalization for one party's open-seat candidates but not its opposition's. Recall that the data used herein come from the 1990 and 1992 election cycles. Many scholars have argued that, prior to 1994, the Republican party confronted electoral obstacles not faced by the Democrats. Whether the result of structural circumstances, partisan loyalties in the electorate, party differentials in lower-level offices, or simply "interests, institutions, individuals, and ideas," Republicans found it difficult to overcome the factors stacked against them in open-seat races.[50] Thus, it should come as no surprise to find that open-seat Republicans benefit from a resource like "professionalization" while Democrats do not.

Implications

I have argued in this chapter that political consultants should be treated in the aggregate as a campaign resource not unlike money. While consultants themselves will surely resist such a conceptualization, political analysts must adopt it in order to draw conclusions about the industry as a whole rather than the abilities of individual consultants.

In addition, I have provided information on the level of professionalization in House campaigns. As with simple consultant use, incumbents and open-seat candidates have higher levels of professionalization than do challengers, and Democrats are more professionalized (at least in a candidate-centered way) than Republicans. Candidates in close races also use consultants for more campaign activities than do candidates in noncompetitive races.

In terms of the impact of professionalization levels on success in House races, the implications of the analysis are rather clear—the more types of consultants hired to assist with various aspects of the campaign, the better candidates will do at election time; those candidates who are at some sort of electoral disadvantage will benefit from campaign professionalism while candidates who are not so disadvantaged will not. Specifically, both Democratic and Republican challengers gained votes with higher levels of professionalization. In open-seat races, however, only Republican candidates could expect such a boost. The well-known disadvantages faced by Republicans in open-seat races prior to 1994 explain this potentially curious finding.

Unfortunately, disadvantaged candidates face a cycle of liabilities. In order to purchase professional assistance, candidates need money; yet money flows more freely to those candidates who are deemed viable; and viability can most easily be established by building a professionally run campaign. Needless to say, most candidates never find their way out of this cycle. To the extent that they can, however, the results of this analysis suggest that they can run significantly stronger campaigns.

Notes

1. Mark P. Petracca, "Political Consultants and Democratic Governance," *PS: Political Science and Politics*, 22 (1989), pp. 11–14.

2. Stephen K. Medvic, "The Effectiveness of the Political Consultant as a Campaign Resource," *PS: Political Science and Politics*, 31 (1998), pp. 150–54. See David A. Leuthold, *Electioneering in a Democracy: Campaigns for Congress* (Wiley, 1968), pp. 2, 87–89.

3. For example, just as incumbents have an easier time raising money than do challengers, the former are also more likely to be in a position to secure the services of professional handlers. This may be due to incumbents' superior fund-raising ability, their likelihood of victory, their knowledge of issues, and their ability to pay consulting bills. See Larry J. Sabato, *The Rise of Political Consultants: New Ways of Winning Elections* (Basic Books, 1981), p. 18; Frank I. Luntz, *Candidates, Consultants, and Campaigns: The Style and Substance of American Electioneering* (Basil Blackwell, 1988), p. 53. An advantage in attracting consultants may also exist for "quality" open-seat candidates, although the evidence here is mixed. See Stephen K. Medvic, "Is there a Spin Doctor in the House? The Impact of Political Consultants in Congressional Campaigns," Ph.D. dissertation, Purdue University, 1997, pp. 185–86.

4. Medvic, "The Effectiveness of the Political Consultant."

5. Sidney Blumenthal, *The Permanent Campaign*, rev. ed. (Simon and Schuster, 1982), p. 19.

6. Blumenthal, *The Permanent Campaign*, p. 19; David Chagall, *The New Kingmakers* (Harcourt Brace Jovanovich, 1981). A recent biography of Lee Atwater is an example of how specific consultants are mythologized. See John Brady, *Bad Boy: The Life and Politics of Lee Atwater* (Addison Wesley, 1997). Of course, as a quick glance through the advertisements in any issue of *Campaigns & Elections* magazine suggests, the "kingmaker" image is perpetuated by consultants themselves. See also Mary Matalin and James Carville, *All's Fair: Love, War, and Running for President* (Random House, 1994); Ed Rollins, *Bare Knuckles and Back Rooms: My Life in American Politics* (New York: Broadway Books, 1996); and Dick Morris, *Behind the Oval Office: Winning the Presidency in the Nineties* (Random House, 1997).

7. The "strategic" focus of so much of the media's election coverage, predicated as it is on the tactical moves of consultants, has been well documented. See, for example, Thomas E. Patterson, *Out of Order* (Knopf, 1993).

8. Richard L. Berke, "In Trenton, Echoes of Ali-Frazier as Two Campaign Titans Clash," *New York Times*, October 4, 1993, sec. A.

9. The question of who is, and who is not, a "professional" consultant is a complex one and is not addressed here in detail. I simply note that I consider a "professional" political consultant to be "someone whose income is derived, at least in part, from providing services to multiple political clients per election cycle, including but not exclusively a political party." Stephen K. Medvic, "Party Support and Consultant Use in Congressional Elections," paper presented at the annual meeting of the American Political Science Association, Washington, D.C., 1997; see also Medvic, "Is there a Spin Doctor in the House?" pp. 65–69.

10. Marjorie Randon Hershey, *Running for Office: The Political Education of Campaigners* (Chatham, N.J.: Chatham House Publishers, 1984).

11. Hershey, *Running for Office*, p. 39.

12. Ibid., pp. 60–73. These models should not be viewed as rigid structures within which all consultants operate. Hershey makes it clear that campaigners have flexibility

in drawing conclusions and are able to innovate in unique situations. Furthermore, consultants may not consciously develop or use these "models." Nevertheless, something resembling models in at least an informal sense can be articulated. For a discussion of the "implicit" models that political advertisers, for example, possess, see John Boiney and David L. Paletz, "In Search of the Model Model: Political Science versus Political Advertising Perspectives on Voter Decision Making," in Frank Biocca, ed., *Television and Political Advertising*, vol. 1: *Psychological Processes* (Hillsdale, N.J.: Lawrence Erlbaum Associates, 1991).

13. Angela Logan and Robin Kolodny, "Political Consultants and the Extension of Party Goals," paper presented at the annual meeting of the American Political Science Association, Washington, D.C., 1997; Bill Hamilton, "Studying Politics," *Campaigns & Elections* (December–January 1997), p. 52; F. Christopher Arterton, "Can Politics be Taught?" *Campaigns & Elections* (December–January 1997), pp. 53–54.

14. Sabato, *The Rise of Political Consultants*, p. 18.

15. Petracca, "Political Consultants and Democratic Governance," p. 11.

16. See Paul S. Herrnson, "Hired Guns and House Races: The Impact of Campaign Professionals," chapter 5 in this volume; Paul S. Herrnson, *Congressional Elections: Campaigning at Home and in Washington* (Washington, D.C.: CQ Press, 1995); Kirsten la Cour Dabelko and Paul S. Herrnson, "Women's and Men's Campaigns for the U.S. House of Representatives," *Political Research Quarterly*, 50 (1997).

17. David Beiler, "The 1990 Campaign Scorecard," *Campaigns & Elections* (December–January 1991), pp. 26–33; Robin Brown and Nancy Kruse, "Consultant Scorecard," *Campaigns & Elections* (January 1993), pp. 20–28.

18. Direct-mail specialists are those consultants who handle both fund-raising and persuasion mail. I have renamed the "persuasion mail" category "voter contact" in the tables and discussion that follows.

19. Sara Fritz and Dwight Morris, *Handbook of Campaign Spending: Money in the 1990 Congressional Races* (Washington, D.C.: CQ Press, 1992); Dwight Morris and Murielle E. Gamache, *Handbook of Campaign Spending: Money in the 1992 Congressional Races* (Washington, D.C.: CQ Press, 1994).

20. Medvic, "Is there a Spin Doctor in the House?" pp. 163–64.

21. Michael Barone and Grant Ujifusa, *The Almanac of American Politics* (Washington, D.C.: National Journal, 1990 and 1992); Federal Election Commission, "Report on Financial Activity" (Washington, D.C., 1990 and 1992).

22. Alexander Heard, *The Costs of Democracy* (University of North Carolina Press, 1960), p. 417. Heard surveyed only members of the Public Relations Society (PRS), but his results are reliable since, as Pitchell suggests, virtually all "political consultants" at that time were from public relations or advertising agencies, and we can safely assume that most of those were members of the PRS. Robert J. Pitchell, "The Influence of Professional Campaign Management Firms in Partisan Elections in California," *Western Political Quarterly*, 11 (1958), 280.

23. Louis Harris, "Polls and Politics in the United States," *Public Opinion Quarterly*, 27 (1963), p. 3. For their operationalization of "marginal" seats, see Robert J. Huckshorn and Robert C. Spencer, *The Politics of Defeat: Campaigning for Congress* (University of Massachusetts Press, 1971), p. 95.

24. Ibid., p. 106.

25. Robert King and Martin Schnitzer, "Contemporary Use of Private Political Polling," *Public Opinion Quarterly*, 32 (1968), pp. 434–35; David Lee Rosenbloom, *The Election Men: Professional Campaign Managers and American Democracy* (Quadrangle Books, 1973), p. 53; Edie N. Goldenberg and Michael W. Traugott, *Campaigning for Congress* (Washington, D.C.: CQ Press, 1984), p. 20.

26. Herrnson, "Hired Guns and House Races," chapter 5 in this volume, table 5-1.

27. Rationalizations of this sort have been demonstrated previously. See John W. Kingdon, *Candidates for Office: Beliefs and Strategies* (Random House, 1966); Marjorie Randon Hershey, *The Making of Campaign Strategy* (D.C. Heath, 1974). For instance, winning candidates are more likely than losing candidates to say issues were the determining factor in an election, whereas losers are more likely to point to party identification, a factor they cannot control. Hershey, *The Making of Campaign Strategy,* p. 71.

28. Yet, as with all data, there are limits to that reliability. There is the possibility, for example, that consultant hirings were missed or incorrectly included in the data set. Furthermore, Federal Election Commission reports do not indicate when subcontracting may have occurred in a campaign. Thus, if a generalist were hired directly by a candidate and that generalist, in turn, hired a pollster and a media handler, the latter two consultants would not be included in the data set (unless the interviews conducted by *C & E* revealed such information).

29. Medvic, "Is there a Spin Doctor in the House?"; Medvic, "Party Support and Consultant Use in Congressional Elections"; Stephen K. Medvic and Silvo Lenart, "The Influence of Political Consultants in the 1992 Congressional Elections," *Legislative Studies Quarterly,* 22 (1997), pp. 61–77.

30. I have suggested that the dramatic rise in consultant use from 1990 to 1992 could be the consequence of the presidential election year of 1992. In presidential years, congressional candidates have a more difficult time disseminating their messages. Thus, in order to cut through the "noise" of such an election cycle, congressional candidates may turn to professional consultants for help. Without data on House races in 1994 and subsequent elections, this thesis is impossible to verify.

An alternative explanation might be that election years ending in "2," which are the first elections following redistricting each decade, produce anxiety in incumbents who are unfamiliar with their new districts. In such a situation, candidates rely more heavily than usual on consultants in the hope that professional help will provide much needed information on the new electoral environment.

31. King and Schnitzer, "Contemporary Use of Private Political Polling."

32. L. Sandy Maisel, *Parties and Elections in America: The Electoral Process,* 2d ed. (McGraw-Hill, 1993), p. 69. See John F. Bibby, "Party Renewal in the National Republican Party," in Gerald Pomper, ed., *Party Renewal in America* (Praeger, 1981); Paul S. Herrnson, *Party Campaigning in the 1980s* (Harvard University Press, 1988).

33. Medvic and Lenart, "The Influence of Political Consultants in the 1992 Congressional Elections"; Medvic, "The Effectiveness of the Political Consultant as a Campaign Resource."

34. Paul S. Herrnson, "Campaign Professionalism and Fundraising in Congressional Elections," *Journal of Politics,* 54 (1992), p. 861.

35. Nonincumbents benefited from professionalism in terms of raising money from the parties and from political action committees, but not from individuals. Herrnson, "Campaign Professionalism and Fundraising in Congressional Elections," pp. 859–69. Only incumbents raised significantly more money from individuals as a result of increased professionalism (p. 867).

36. Medvic and Lenart, "The Influence of Political Consultants in the 1992 Congressional Elections." In their study of men's and women's campaigns for the House, Dabelko and Herrnson found that professionalism did not influence a candidate's likelihood of winning. Dabelko and Herrnson, "Women's and Men's Campaigns for the U.S. House of Representatives," pp. 121–35.

37. Medvic and Lenart, "The Influence of Political Consultants in the 1992 Congressional Elections," p. 72.

38. See James A. Thurber, "The Study of Campaign Consultants: A Subfield in Search of Theory," *PS: Political Science and Politics,* 31 (1998), pp. 145–49.

39. Hershey, *Running for Office.*

40. "Deliberate priming" is similar to what Jacobs and Shapiro call "intentional priming." Lawrence R. Jacobs and Robert Y. Shapiro, "Issues, Candidate Image, and Priming: The Use of Private Polls in Kennedy's 1960 Presidential Campaign," *American Political Science Review,* 88 (1994), p. 52; Stephen K. Medvic, "A Theory of Deliberate Priming," paper presented at the annual meeting of the Northeastern Political Science Association, Boston, Mass., 1996; Medvic, "Is there a Spin Doctor in the House?"

41. Shanto Iyengar and Donald R. Kinder, *News that Matters: Television and American Opinion* (University of Chicago Press, 1987), p. 63 (emphasis in original).

42. Ideally, all campaigns could operate according to such a plan. Nonprofessional campaigners, however, have usually not "learned" how to effectively prime voters. Instead, most campaigns start with an issue (or set of issues) they want to discuss whether or not those issues are ones upon which they have an advantage. For example, except in unusual circumstances, a Democratic candidate would have a difficult time convincing voters that he or she is "tougher on crime" than his or her Republican opponent; yet many try to do just that. Consultants help "focus" a candidate on issues that are potentially winning issues and, in the process, prime voters to vote on issues that are to their client's advantage.

43. Indeed, I am not arguing that consultants operate with these concepts in mind. I am simply offering an empirical theory about what they do. As such, this theory could be, but has not yet been, tested.

44. Jacobson and Kernell and Jacobson operationalize "quality" in this way. Gary C. Jacobson and Samuel Kernell, *Strategy and Choice in Congressional Elections,* 2d ed. (Yale University Press, 1983); Gary C. Jacobson, "Strategic Politicians and the Dynamics of House Elections, 1946–1986," *American Political Science Review,* 83 (1989), pp. 773–93. For a discussion of the various ways in which this concept has been measured, see Peverill Squire, "Candidates, Money, and Voters—Assessing the State of Congressional Elections Research," *Political Research Quarterly,* 48 (1995), pp. 891–97.

45. The log of a candidate's campaign expenditures accounts for the diminishing rate of return on each additional dollar spent by a candidate.

46. The failure of "district partisanship" to reach significance is not as surprising as it may at first appear. Although Democratic challengers would be expected to garner more of the vote in districts where their party's nominee ran well, the incumbency advantage clearly overcomes such an effect.

47. Herrnson, "Hired Guns and House Races," chapter 5 in this volume.

48. Herrnson's results in chapter 5 indicate, generally, that open-seat candidates with more professionalized campaigns win at higher rates than those with less professional or amateur campaigns.

49. Gary C. Jacobson, "The Effects of Campaign Spending in Congressional Elections," *American Political Science Review,* 72 (1978), pp. 769–83; Gary C. Jacobson, *Money in Congressional Elections* (Yale University Press, 1980); Gary C. Jacobson, "The Effect of Campaign Spending in House Elections: New Evidence for Old Arguments," *American Journal of Political Science,* 34 (1990), pp. 334–62; Stephen Ansolabehere and Alan Gerber. "The Mismeasure of Campaign Spending: Evidence from the 1990 U.S. House Elections," *Journal of Politics,* 56 (1994), pp. 1106–18. It should be noted that there are those who find a significant positive influence for incumbent spending. See Don Philip Green and Jonathan S. Krasno, "Salvation for the Spendthrift Incumbent: Reestimating the Effects of Campaign Spending in House Elections," *American Journal of Political Science,* 32 (1988), pp. 884–907; Don Philip Green and Jonathan S. Krasno, "Rebuttal to Jacobson's 'New Evidence for Old Arguments,'" *American Journal of Political Science,* 34 (1990), pp. 363–72;

Christopher Kenny and Michael McBurnett, "A Dynamic Model of the Effect of Campaign Spending on Congressional Vote Choice," *American Journal of Political Science*, 36 (1992), pp. 923–37; Robert K. Goidel and Donald A. Gross, "A Systems Approach to Campaign Finance in U.S. House Elections," *American Politics Quarterly*, 22 (1994), pp. 125–53.

50. William F. Connelly Jr. and John J. Pitney Jr., *Congress' Permanent Minority: Republicans in the U.S. House* (Lanham, Md.: Littlefield Adams, 1994), p. 153. See James E. Campbell, *Cheap Seats: The Democratic Party's Advantage in U.S. House Elections* (Ohio State University Press, 1996); Thomas E. Mann, "Is the House of Representatives Unresponsive to Political Change?" in A. James Reichley, ed., *Elections American Style* (Brookings, 1987); Gary C. Jacobson, "The 1994 House Elections in Perspective," in Philip A. Klinkner, ed., *Midterm: The Elections of 1994 in Context* (Westview Press, 1996); John J. Pitney Jr. and William F. Connelly Jr., "'Permanent Minority' No More: House Republicans in 1994," in Philip A. Klinkner, ed., *Midterm: The Elections of 1994 in Context* (Westview Press, 1996); Ronald Keith Gaddie, "Is there an Inherent Democratic Party Advantage in U.S. House Elections? Evidence from the Open Seats," *Social Science Quarterly*, 76 (1995), pp. 203–12.

CHAPTER SEVEN

Electoral Partnerships: Political Consultants and Political Parties

ROBIN KOLODNY

The political consulting industry is certainly multi-faceted and extremely complex. As a scholar of political parties, I ponder the question of the growth and evolution of the consulting industry from one central perspective: What does the political party have to do with any of it?

In one sense, this is the fundamental issue in the study of political consultants. If candidates and issue groups believed that their electoral needs could be entirely served by political parties, then there would be no market for a bevy of outside "vendors" such as our contemporary political consultants. This leads us back to the inevitable question of political party decline, which has consumed many party scholars and has lead some to suggest that party decline is the reason for political consultant growth and, in turn, that the rise of political consultants has further weakened the parties.

This chapter explores this party decline hypothesis but suggests another more provocative one to explain the relationship between parties and consultants. An alternative to the party decline argument is that modern campaigns demand specialized, technical services that are simply beyond the political parties' *institutional capacity* to deliver. If we consider that political parties were formed to make mass mobilization of voters occur efficiently for several levels of officeholders, then who is to say that parties still do not deliver on these promises?[1] In short, can parties reasonably be expected to respond fully to the demands of a candidate-centered campaign environment? Have the techniques of modern campaigning really been so transforming as to force parties to redefine their roles and call for the services of the consulting industry? My argument here is that modern campaigning has indeed exceeded the institutional capacity of political parties, a theme also implied by Shaun Bowler and David Farrell in chapter 9 of this volume.

We need only look to the phrase "candidate-centered campaigning" to see where parties went awry. American political parties have always suffered because of separation of powers and federalism. These features of our political system have made it difficult for parties to conduct centralized campaigns. What parties could do was provide a way to mobilize voters on election day—they could control the flow of people more than they could control a centralized party message. As modern campaign techniques became increasingly more sophisticated, individual candidates in marginal races took advantage of these methods to finely target their efforts. Political parties could not offer the specific information and persuasion techniques these candidates believed were vital to their chances for victory.

In the face of modern campaigning, parties had two options: provide the particular services candidates desired (and become different organizations than they currently are or have historically been) or rely on others to help them fulfill their mission. In order to become truly viable full-service campaign operations for all the candidates wearing their label, parties would have to change the rules of the electoral game in their favor. This is virtually impossible to envision in a single-member plurality electoral system, especially one where election dates are fixed and candidate selection is done through public primaries. Before the 1970s, American parties at least had the advantage of being seen as the central clearinghouse for fund-raising operations and giving direction on how to run general election campaigns. With the implementation of the Federal Election Campaign Act (FECA), the parties' role as central fund-raiser was undermined and new innovations such as direct mail emerged to help candidates raise money autonomously. The seeds for a private campaign industry explosion were thus sown and the parties had a choice of trying to beat it (they could not) or join it. As Paul Herrnson describes, the national parties began to use many of these new technologies themselves, and as the private industry continued to grow, parties positioned themselves as brokers between candidates and the private campaign industry.[2] Clearly, the change in campaign finance laws, the rise of new technologies, and the restrictions of the electoral system exceeded the parties' institutional capacity. Parties simply could not make both broad-based appeals and extremely narrow pitches simultaneously. As some were predicting the death of political parties, the parties instead found that forming alliances with consultants was a rational solution to the upheavals of modern campaigning. Indeed, we may even go as far as Frank Luntz when he states: "The national parties have also learned that today's skilled professional consultants are essential to modern electioneering, and moreover, that the campaign techniques they provide have not destroyed the parties but have strengthened them."[3]

Thinking about Political Parties

The central problem in the party decline/revitalization/resurgence debate is the lack of a clear consensus on the focus of the party. In other words, what is meant when we talk about political parties? Of course, there is the time-honored tripartite distinction to look to: party in the electorate, party in government, and party as organization. Although there are problems with this portrayal of parties, we are helped by viewing the role of consultants through these different lenses. It is quite clear that our discussion of parties and consultants differs dramatically when each of these three perspectives is taken as the central focus, although we necessarily focus on the party organization in the analytical section.

Party in the Electorate

The idea of defining political party as party in the electorate, or how the average voter feels about their party affiliation, voting habits, and the use of party labels to sort out political events and candidates, is hardly new. Electorate-centered party research began with the behavioralist explosion in the 1950s. With studies such as *The American Voter* and *The Decline of American Political Parties*, attention turned to the decline of party affiliation among voters.[4] Recently, John Coleman has argued that other indicators of party activity are meaningless if voters continue to ignore the shorthand value of political parties for voting cues.[5] There is no question that if the sole evaluator of party vitality is the strength of party identification (and by extension the use of party labels to guide voting behavior), political parties will fare poorly today. Though party identification is on the rise since the lows of the 1970s, so is split-ticket voting.[6] Any way you look at it, the party in the electorate concept is not favorable to political parties.

What does the party in the electorate perspective mean for political parties and political consultants? Clearly, American political parties need to have support from voters to remain viable. To increase the electorate's partisanship, parties try to promote positive messages about themselves, encourage or recruit promising candidates, and look to their staunchest supporters to continue turning out the vote and reaching out to potential new supporters. These activities are handled through the party organization (discussed below). So, how do consultants fit in? Consultants can assist parties in perfecting their message and outreach efforts to maximize voter turnout for the party's candidates on election day. Their efforts may or may not increase party affiliation among the electorate, but consultants mainly are hired to produce results for candidates or parties on election day. The important point here is that consultants' efforts are election cycle oriented and not geared for long-term party change. Viewed from the electorate's perspective, consultants are relatively unnoticed actors in the political game. When their "products" become controversial, it is the candidate who hired them—not the consultant or political party— who gets the electorate's blame. It may even be concluded that if voter allegiances are all that matter, then consultants are probably contributing to party decline by assisting candidates and parties in the formation of election day coalitions, rather than long-term allegiances.

Party in Government

Another set of scholars focuses on the power of party affiliation on political elites—that is, on the voting behavior of elected officeholders. At both the national and state levels, such scholarship has focused on voting cohesiveness in legislatures and the ability of the executive to exact loyalty out of members of his own party in the legislature. Most of these studies are postelectoral, meaning that they deal with events that happen after the elections have occurred and seemingly without consideration for the elections ahead. Elsewhere, I have argued that it is not possible to look to the behavior of the party in government without recognizing that every move it makes is motivated by electoral consequences.[7] Although the strength of the party in government has been criticized over time, its recent resurgence is in some measure due to assistance garnered from political consultants.[8] In the past officeholders formed party positions in caucus, though based largely on what they were hearing from their supportive constituents.[9] Today, party leaders seek the assistance of highly specialized consultants to help them focus their message and issue stands with the hope of shoring up their strength at election time. Famous recent examples of this are the use of consultants to help Republicans in the House of Representatives refine their "Contract with America" for the 1994 elections and by House Democrats to construct their "Families First" agenda for the 1996 elections. Party leaders clearly indicated that the traditional feedback loop in the political party branches (that is, the party organization knows what the party in the electorate wants and communicates it to the party in government) was no longer sufficient to meet their needs. Specialized pollsters and strategists were hired by the party in government directly to deal with their collective needs.

Consultants are clearly no surrogate for elected officeholders. They cannot and do not make the decisions party leaders need to make. However, consultants have been called upon by party leaders to provide polling information, research, and strategic advice directly to them, bypassing the party organization that might have provided such things in the past. Perhaps the reason for using consultants at this level has to do with the specialized attention and focus that consultants can provide to a particular section of the party (like the partisans of one chamber of a legislature) that a party organization with many demands upon it simply cannot.

Party as Organization

Many scholars who suggest that political parties are revitalized have looked at political parties from the lens of party organization.[10] Recently, John Frendreis argued that the activities of the party organization are the least understood of all facets of party and potentially the most important.[11] Though, as noted above, John Coleman and others are not impressed by party organization revitalization without concomitant revitalization of party identification in the electorate, it can be argued that only through observing the profound changes in party organization in the last twenty-five years can we truly appreciate the magnitude of change that campaigns and elections in the United States have undergone.[12] Though these changes in the campaign environment have effected all aspects of the party, it is clear that they pose the greatest challenge to the party organization, whose central mission is to be the front-line attack for the party and its candidates at election time. The question is whether it is reasonable to assume that party organization in the American context could cope with the myriad changes without assistance from specialized political consultants. In the parlance of business in the 1990s, political party organizations at the national and state levels have "outsourced" or "subcontracted" highly specialized needs to narrowly focused vendors—the political consultant industry—because they simply could not provide these services for themselves. This is not to say that political parties did not try to cope with the demands of modern campaigning by providing these services initially.[13] It is to say that political parties recognized that trying to serve all the new needs of candidates, especially needs that were highly particularized, would spread their resources too thin, leaving them unable to accomplish their broader goals.

Another way to look at the party organization dilemma is through John Aldrich's eyes. In *Why Parties?* Aldrich argues that political parties formed because of a feeling among ambitious politicians that joining forces in certain campaign tasks, such as mobilization of voters, would be more efficient and effective for each of them than having individual like-minded politicians (who were not direct competitors) conduct these activities separately and simultaneously.[14] Hence the political party, with its "brand name" and "economies of scale" for the use of politicians, was formed. The party organization, then, is merely an outgrowth of the ambitious politicians' personal goals and, as Frendreis would say, is not really distinct from either party in the electorate or party in government, but rather the culmination of all these facets of party.[15] Aldrich also argues that significant changes in campaigning since the 1960s have now modified the role party organizations play for ambitious politicians. With the weakening of party control over nominations, issues, and campaigns, candidates are now themselves the center of the campaign universe. Still, they see value in running as partisans (with a party affiliation) and have modified the party organizations to function as service providers rather than coordinators of election activity with real power.[16] Aldrich's analysis is slightly misleading as he makes it seem as though the parties *themselves* provide needed services to candidates. The reality is more akin to what Herrnson describes as "transactional" services, where parties efficiently and effectively match candidates to resource providers.[17] What has been lost in the attention paid to party organizational activity is that political parties were faced with a choice: stick with what they know (voter contact and message development) or develop new competencies (high-tech services such as polling and media production). After efforts in the late 1970s and early 1980s to do everything, political parties at the national and state levels decided to stay with what they did best and turn to loyal service providers—political consultants—to do the rest. This way, the parties remain relevant by acting as the middleman between candidates and consultants and retain focus on their strength—front-line work with the party in the electorate.

Why Parties Can Trust Consultants

Previously, I have argued that political consultants were *allied* with political parties rather than being their *adversaries*.[18] The adversarial view comes from early studies of the consulting industry that argued that consultants came from marketing or advertising backgrounds rather than political backgrounds (see chapter 1 of this volume for a discussion of this literature). This view assumes that consultants abandon party values, such as giving partisan candidates a consistent message, striving for control of a particular governmental institution (rather than just winning individual races), and being selective about clients based on their ability to do the job.

It can be argued that the contemporary consulting industry is more likely to have come from the parties than from Madison Avenue. If the parties train consultants, it is logical to assume that they take some party goals with them to private industry. Most consultants were found to be allied with parties, not competitors with them. Evidence that parties and consultants worked in allied partnerships came from a 1997 survey of political consultants.[19] Several interesting facts were discovered. First, 88.6 percent of these consultants said that their clientele belonged predominantly to one party. Only 11.4 percent said that they worked for clients affiliated with both parties or neither party. This gives great weight to the notion that consultants have strong ties to political parties. Second, the survey found that about half the consultants surveyed previously worked for political parties, a finding confirmed by James Thurber, Candice Nelson, and David Dulio in chapter 2 of this volume. The most common previous employer after political parties was individual candidate campaigns, not the private sector, as some of the consulting industry's critics typically charge. Third, the majority of political consultants claimed that political parties were clients of theirs. The likelihood of having a political party as a client increased if the consultant had a prior history of employment with a political party (76 percent) compared to those without such a history (44.4 percent). Fourth, a majority of consultants indicated that they coordinated regularly with political parties in the normal course of their work, and a majority of these said party activity enhanced their overall effectiveness as consultants. Each of these findings gives great credence to our *allied* view of consultants and parties and also confirms Martin Hamburger's experiences (see chapter 4 of this volume). Clearly, consultants do not see parties as competitors for their livelihood. On the contrary, consultants indicated that they fulfilled needs the parties could not serve.[20] Hamburger noted that consultants do try to drum up business from the parties, but that once the business is obtained, the parties' role beyond its monetary contributions fades for consultants and candidates. His experience confirms the interdependent relationship between parties and consultants explored in the next sections.

The Reality of Party-Consultant Relationships

The connection between the two national party committees (the Democratic National Committee and the Republican National Committee) and four Capitol Hill committees (the Democratic Congressional Campaign Committee, the Democratic Senatorial Campaign Committee, the National Republican Congressional Committee, and the National Republican Senatorial Committee) and political consultants is fairly well documented, although by no means comprehensive. We know that the national party committees routinely hire consultants themselves and have lists of preferred providers that they share with promising candidates.[21] Indeed, use of an approved consultant often is a prerequisite to receiving future party funding.[22] Additionally, consultants are well aware of the money parties have to spend on campaigns through coordinated expenditures and try to position themselves to work for certain campaigns at the national party's expense.[23]

What is less well understood is consultant use by state political parties. An examination of the use of consultants by state political parties can be even more revealing than looking at national party consultant use. For one thing, it is logical that the richer, higher profile national committees would use political consultants since they have more complex needs and are located right where most high-profile consultants are—in Washington, D.C. It is also likely that making inferences about parties based on only the experiences of the six national party committees could exaggerate the relationship between parties and consultants: it could just be a Washington community phenomenon. If, however, it is found that state parties use political consultants in ways similar to the national party committees, some broader statements can be made about party-consultant relationships. The activities of state and local parties account for the majority of direct voter contacts, making them an appropriate focus of study.

The State Party Survey

A survey was administered to executive directors of all one hundred state parties. Two party executive directors called to say they did not give out the information asked in the survey. Forty valid responses were received. The survey, which can be found in appendix B, asked about consultant use in broad terms. The respondents were fairly evenly split in party affiliation with nineteen Democratic parties and twenty Republican parties responding. One party would not reveal its affiliation.

The first question on the survey asked whether or not the party currently had a contract with a consultant or had plans to negotiate one in the 1998 election cycle. Of the forty respondents, thirty-five (or 87.5 percent) said they had such a contract or such plans. Only five (or 12.5 percent) of respondent parties said they had no such plans. Of the five parties who did not have contracts with consultants themselves, three of them said they advised candidates to hire consultants directly. Overall, thirty-eight of the forty (95 percent) respondents said they advised candidates to hire political consultants. It is significant then that only 5 percent of the respondents had an overall negative attitude toward political consultants (of these two, one was Democratic and one was Republican).

The thirty-five state parties that said they had contracts (or plans to enter into contracts) with consultants were asked to indicate which types of consultants these contracts would be with. The frequencies are listed in table 7-1. First, the number of consultant types each party said they would contract with should be noted. The range was a minimum of one consultant type and a maximum of seven, with a mean of 3.65 consultant types per party. Both the median and the mode for this measure were four. Table 7-1 shows the breakdown of consultant types preferred by parties.

Table 7-1. *Type of Consultants Parties Said They Would Hire*

Type of consultant	Number of parties that would	
	Hire	Mention as critical
Direct mail	27	19
Polling	27	13
Media production	18	3
Media buying	14	0
Fund-raising	15	11
Telemarketing	8	6
Voter file/get out the vote	7	5
General	5	1
Research	6	0

The two most popular types of consultants for state parties to contract with were direct-mail consultants and pollsters; both had twenty-seven parties mentioning their intention to hire these types of consultants. The next cluster consisted of media production consultants (with eighteen mentions), media-buying consultants (with fourteen), and fund-raising consultants (with fifteen).

The executive directors were then asked to indicate the one or two most critical types of consultants for their party's needs. The answers to this question (also in table 7-1) confirmed the centrality of direct-mail consultants to state parties, with nineteen mentions. The next most critical consultants named were polling (thirteen mentions) and fund-raising (eleven mentions) consultants. Interestingly, even though a significant number of parties said they intended to hire media consultants (for both production and buying), only three parties named media production consultants as critical and none named media buying. Telemarketing and voter file/get out the vote consultants surpassed the media consultants in importance (with six and five mentions respectively). The consultant types hired by state parties are consistent with our theory about the institutional capacity of parties—they hire consultants to provide assistance for their central task of voter mobilization and the fund-raising needed to make those efforts happen.

State parties were asked to indicate how much they intended to spend on consultant services during the 1998 (or in some cases the 1997) elec-

Table 7-2. *Range of Total Monies Spent on Consultants by Parties*[a]

Range	State parties
Nothing	5
$1–$9,999	5
$10,000–$24,999	8
$25,000–$49,999	3
$50,000–$74,999	6
$75,000–$100,000	2
Greater than $100,000	11

a. As reported by parties.

tion cycle. They were also asked to give a general sense of what proportion of their total budget would be spent on consultants. Let me say at the outset that based on most of the responses (and two telephone calls from state party executive directors saying they would not respond to the survey based on the "sensitive" nature of the money questions) that I am confident the self-estimates are entirely too low. Without easy means of independent verification, they must be taken at their word. Whenever a range of percentages was given by a state party for the proportion of their budget spent on consultants, the higher number in the range was used. The parties were asked to indicate the absolute amounts they would spend by broad categories. The spending categories and their frequencies are presented in table 7-2. Interestingly, 27.5 percent of the forty state parties reporting hiring consultants said they planned to spend more than $100,000 on them in the 1998 election cycle. The midway point in spending for all respondents (including those saying they would not be hiring consultants) is about $50,000 (with 52.5 percent planning to spend less than that and 47.5 percent planning to spend more). In terms of percentage of the total budget spent on consultants, the range was 0 to 50 percent, with a mean of 9.9 percent and a standard deviation of 11.6 percent (median and mode were both 10 percent). Looking at a breakdown of the percentages by amounts of money spent, we find that the higher the percentage of budget cited, the higher the absolute amount of money spent. Also, the more money spent, the larger the number of consultant types employed. It is important to note that although most state parties employ consultants directly, only a small proportion of their budget is invested in consultant services.

Advice to Candidates

More significant than state parties' direct spending on consultants are the referrals of consultants to candidates by the parties. As stated above, thirty-eight of the forty state party executive directors said they advised candidates to seek the services of political consultants. These respondents were asked to indicate how they introduced candidates to consultants. The choices, given in question 7 (which asked respondents to check all statements that applied), are:

—A. We have a list of preferred consultants/vendors that we give to candidates who pay for the services themselves (10 of 38).

—B. For certain candidates, we pay for the services of our preferred consultants/vendors (10 of 38).

—C. We recommend consultants informally, on a case-by-case basis (30 of 38).

There is a relationship between the amount of money the parties themselves spend on consultants and how they refer candidates to consultants. As expected, the parties that chose option B, where they pay for the services themselves, tended to spend more money on consultants (the correlation is .337 significant at the .03 level). More than half of the parties saying they spent greater than $100,000 on consultants chose this option. Also worth noting is that no party that spent less than $10,000 on consultants said they had a list of preferred consultants that they shared with candidates. Indeed, of the ten parties spending less than $10,000 on consultants, eight said they referred candidates to consultants informally (one did not recommend consultants under any circumstances). Clearly, parties spending less than $10,000 on consulting contracts have less institutionalized relationships with consultants than those spending more than $10,000.

Next, the parties were asked to indicate which types of consultants they referred to candidates most. Parties were asked to rank consultant types from most frequently recommended to least frequently recommended. For those respondents who did not rank consultant types but made check marks instead, each mark was coded as a one (biasing the results, but other options were less desirable). The frequencies are reported in tables 7-3 and 7-4. Here, the results are most intriguing as they demonstrate that the parties perceive their needs differently from the needs of their candidates as they indicated that they recommend different types of consultants from those they hire for themselves. The three

Table 7-3. *Ranking of Types of Consultants Recommended by Parties to Candidates*

Type of consultant	First	Second	Third	Fourth	Fifth	Sixth or lower
Direct mail	17	5	3	2	1	...
Polling	17	7	3	3	1	...
Media production	14	3	8	1	1	1
Media buying	3	2	4	4	3	2
Fund-raising	4	4	2	1	5	2
Telemarketing	1	1	0	0	0	0
Voter file/get out the vote	1	0	0	0	0	0
General	4	0	2	0	2	8
Research	4	0	0	4	0	8

most striking examples are with general consultants, research consultants, and media production consultants. General consultants were mentioned as being recommended to candidates by sixteen parties, but only five parties claim to have hired them for their own purposes. Research consultants had a similar endorsement with sixteen recommendations to candidates, but only six parties using them. Media production consul-

Table 7-4. *Comparing Tables 7-3 and 7-1*

	Number of parties that	
Type of consultant	Recommend this type to candidates[a]	Hire this type themselves[b]
Direct mail	28	27
Polling	31	27
Media production	28	18
Media buying	18	14
Fund-raising	18	15
Telemarketing	2	8
Voter file/get out the vote	1	7
General	16	5
Research	16	6

a. Table 7-3.
b. Table 7-1.

Table 7-5. *Functions that Parties Perform Better than Consultants, According to Parties*

Function	Number of mentions
Fund-raising	8
Grassroots organization	17
Information about local context, laws, and so on	21
Putting together overall campaign message, issues	9
Research	4
Voter file/get out the vote	13

tants were used by eighteen parties, but twenty-eight parties recommend them to their candidates. Conversely, more parties reported using tele-marketing consultants (phone banking for individual voter contact) than would recommend them to candidates (eight to two). The parties' two most preferred consultant types, polling and direct mail, were thought as useful (or more) to candidates as to parties. On the whole, these results suggest that the parties think that consultants can help candidates in different ways than they can help them themselves.

This discussion leads us to the last two substantive questions of the survey, where parties were asked to indicate what functions they perform better for candidates than consultants and which functions consultants perform better for candidates than parties. The findings here confirm the earlier discussion about the strengths and weaknesses of political parties in modern campaigning. The function most often cited by parties as their particular strength was their knowledge about the local political context, customs, and laws. This is coded under "information about local context" in table 7-5. The next two most cited functions also confirm this insight into the local context. "Grass-roots organization" refers to the parties' ability to recruit and deploy party activists to conduct a variety of campaign tasks: staffing party headquarters, organizing events, and mobilizing voters closer to election day. Next was the category of "voter files/ get out the vote." This category embodies the parties' efforts to get their rank-and-file supporters to the polls on election day by using detailed information on voters kept in their own files. The other three categories that were mentioned (putting together an overall campaign message, fund-raising , and research) were not mentioned nearly as often. Each of these three categories was also mentioned by other party executive directors as being under the purview of consultants' talents. But the local expertise categories (information, grass-roots organization, and voter files) are exclusively attached to the parties' bailiwick.

When parties were asked what consultants do better than they could themselves (table 7-6), the answers focused on highly technical services that have become standard in modern campaigning. The two top functions political parties said consultants performed better than they could were polling and media production. Polling was mentioned by seventeen parties and media production by sixteen. The next most frequently mentioned category was direct mail, with thirteen parties indicating this. Consultants were noted eight times for both their media buying talents and their ability to give individual attention to candidates. Two of these three categories overlapped with what some party executive directors said the parties did better themselves: fund-raising (six mentions), technical expertise (six mentions), and constructing the party's message (two mentions). This may reveal some fluidity in the changing nature of political parties. Some party executive directors believe that current fund-raising demands exceed their institutional capacity and find that an adequate party campaign message may require sophisticated techniques like polling to be perfected.

The 1997 survey of political consultants asked them the same two questions. The results were surprisingly similar, with the exception of fund-raising. Consultants were asked to comment on all levels of party,

Table 7-6. *Functions that Consultants Perform Better than Parties, According to Parties*

Function	Number of mentions
Fund-raising	6
Giving individual attention to candidates	8
Direct mail	13
Media buying	8
Media production	16
Constructing the party's message	2
Polling	17
Research	2
Technical expertise	6

Table 7-7. *Functions Parties Perform Better than Consultants,*
According to Consultants

Functions	Number of mentions
Fund-raising	40
Voter file/get out the vote	38
Information on local context	22
Grassroots organization	14
Research	14
Constructing the party's message	3

including national, and this tended to increase their opinion of the parties' fund-raising ability. Also, this survey revealed important distinctions in types of fund-raising. Political parties are often thought to do a better job of identifying "high-dollar" donors in the localities, while direct-mail consultants help the parties achieve a wider small donor base. National party committees are especially credited with cultivating political action committee donors for fund-raising success. With fund-raising aside, consultants said the top four functions parties performed better than consultants were voter contact/get out the vote, local information and candidate prospecting, grass-roots organization, and research (table 7-7). By far, consultants mentioned voter contact/get out the vote as the political parties' main strength with thirty-eight mentions. In many cases, these comments overlapped with grass-roots organization. The important point is that both parties and consultants think parties do a better job of mobilizing activists and rank-and-file voters than consultants could, a finding also confirmed by Herrnson in chapter 5 of this volume.

When consultants were asked to indicate which functions they performed better than political parties, the top three mentioned were giving individual attention to candidates, media production, and message development (table 7-8). Although various technical aspects of campaigning were also mentioned, only media production had repeated mentions. Media production and polling were the top two functions that parties thought consultants could do better than they could. Though parties also recognized the value of individual attention that consultants could give candidates, they thought this less important than the consultants themselves. This reflects a fundamental difference in the orientation of parties and consultants. More consultants work for candidates than for parties—

Table 7-8. *Functions Consultants Perform Better than Parties, According to Consultants*

Functions	Number of mentions
Giving individual attention to candidates	36
Media production	29
Constructing the party's message	20
Fund-raising	10
Get out the vote	9
Polling	7
Research	7
Direct mail	6
Technical expertise	4
Media buying	3

simply a supply-and-demand issue. In the consultant survey, several said that the party's problem was that it was not designed to deal with individual candidate fortunes apart from the overall party plan. This is obviously a perspective quite different from the perspective of those who contend that consultants can help construct the overall party message better than parties can; but again, much of that difference can be accounted for by the type of client a consultant has. Nevertheless, this tension between individual candidate interests and party interests does exist (and is what leads some to believe that the efforts of consultants weaken parties), but this does not necessarily mean that the two are at cross-purposes. As Aldrich argues, since the 1960s political parties have recognized the need to attend to individual candidates as the only way to achieve overall party goals.[24]

Insights into the Party-Consultant Relationship

While the survey questions give us much new data to interpret, they do not pick up the nuances of this relationship. To help with this, two open-ended questions were asked of parties. The first was, "How do consultants help fulfill your party's overall goals?" The second asked respondents to give any additional comments not covered by the survey. The most common answer to the question about goals was that consultants "round out our portfolio of services" or "plug holes in the total operation." The parties are acknowledging that they are not able to provide all the services modern campaigns require. In the words of a mid-Atlantic region Republican party executive director:

> Consultants help us in areas that we either lack the professional experience or the hardware to accomplish our goals. For example, polling and TV spot production. Consultants serve to broaden your perspective and give you a different view on how things should be done.

This statement acknowledges that using consultants enhances the party's overall performance in elections. The executive director of a southern Republican party explains how consultants complete the overall picture of the party's election strategy, often by choice:

> Consultants in certain areas—such as polling—serve as specialty subcontractors—just as a general contractor would recommend a brick mason. Consultants in general areas such as strategy and research serve to supplement the party's staff in peak demand periods (campaigns) much like contract workers in other words.

It is clear that the idea of using consultants as subcontractors for election needs is genuinely followed by the parties. The decision to go this route for the parties is not easy and comes at the expense of their own institutional autonomy. An executive director of a different southern Republican party said:

> The real question is what is better, full-time staff or consultants. It would cost more in the long run to hire full-time staff for projects that only take a month or two. General consultants are only hired when you can't afford to hire experienced staff. We usually only hire people who produce something (i.e., mail, TV, phone vendor).

This statement also reflects the idea that parties feel their strength lies in long-term political expertise about the local context, party activists, and mass mobilization. One cultivates staff for those functions and spares scarce resources for shorter-term technical "products" that consultants can provide. Not all consultants are viewed in such a positive light by parties. Often, parties see their role as adviser to candidates on how to use consultants. Two remarks demonstrate different approaches to advising candidates about consultants and about the use of consultants by parties:

Some consultants make money by having the candidate spend money in certain ways. The party must give the candidate objective advice on whether these expenditures are in the candidate's best interest. [Midwestern Republican party]

We are cautious about working with consultants. They are in business to make money, even your friends. It is best to negotiate aggressively with vendors on the front end of any deal instead of squabbling on the back end. Be specific as possible with vendors; if an item is not in the contract, there is no guarantee it will get done. [Southern Democratic party]

Here the parties voice their concern that consultants are more motivated by financial gain than the more obscure goals of victory for the party. These sentiments are a reminder that consultants are fundamentally self-sustaining businesses, and while their business is politics, they are still in business. In these cases, it is clear that while consultants can help candidates achieve their electoral goals, they cannot substitute for the role parties play in the overall campaign.

The consultants also had some interesting thoughts about parties in their responses to the open-ended questions. A common sentiment was that the strength of parties was also their biggest weakness. As one consultant put it:

Parties do good at seeing the big picture, but most [are] not very good at seeing the individual needs of candidates. Parties can provide for common needs of candidates or needs most and/or all candidates will have. It is the job of the consultant to see the specific individual needs of a particular candidate.

In an age of candidate-centered elections, when party in the electorate is in decline, the failure of parties to serve the individual needs of candidates can be very harmful. It can interfere with the parties' ability to stay relevant in elections. But other consultants take a more humble view of their contribution:

Parties play a larger role in politics than consultants. Our role usually begins with an acrimonious primary, which parties must then smooth over. In general elections, the "D" or "R" will ordinarily produce the vast majority of the votes a candidate receives. Candidate campaigns, guided by consultants, then add to that total,

through combinations of tactics. The margin of victory ... usually is
less than 10 percent or so.

But the margins mean the difference between winning and losing, being in
the majority or the minority. Still, this consultant is well aware that there
is a small attentive public in most election campaigns. Party identification
and party image still account for the bulk of votes in any given election.
But in competitive races, the efforts of consultants can sway a few voters, and that is often all that is needed to win—and for the candidate to
see the consultants' contribution as central.

Conclusions

The electoral partnership formed by political parties and political consultants is an understandable response to the increasing technological
sophistication of modern campaigns. In a political system that encourages
candidate independence from parties by design, it is hard to see how any
other option could have emerged without destroying any effectiveness
political parties may have. The survey evidence makes clear the willingness of political parties to enter into relationships with political consultants. Consultants are viewed by the parties as being complements to the
parties' overall strategy, not competitors to it.

This conclusion depends on a particular view of political party, however. If one defines political party as party in the electorate, they are
bound to see consultants as dangerous to party viability, since the efforts
of consultants encourage voters to come up with conclusions about candidates on their own, abandoning whatever party feeling they may have
if that would help the consultant's client. If one defines political party as
party in government, consultants may still be seen as troublemakers, since
they seemingly encourage a compartmentalization of interests by institution. If the presidential, senatorial, House, and state parties all hire different consultants to conduct different polls and different political
strategies, then we might conclude that consultants can help divide the
party among parochial institutional lines. This view assumes that American parties are not already so delineated (which I believe they are by
design). The other way to view the consultant-party in government relationship is to say that such partnerships prevent elected officeholders
from entirely abandoning party, as the consultants can show them the

degree of electoral utility their party label has and how to use collective tools to their personal advantage.

The final prong of party—party organization—is the most interesting. While the evidence presented here confirms that state party organizations have good relationships with political consultants, we can question the appropriateness of viewing party organization as a separate facet of party rather than the culmination of party itself. Several prominent party scholars have suggested scrapping the tripartite model of party and instead want to acknowledge that party organization is the true focal point for all activities of party. If this is so, then the party operatives have clearly shown how consultants help them compensate for the reality that modern campaigning techniques have exceeded their institutional capacity. That is, the party organization's historic and present purpose has been to bridge communications between the party in government and the party in the electorate. Party organizations have found that they could best accomplish this by creating extensive local networks of party activists who can tell them of political developments in their localities (information) and use this intelligence to form grass-roots organizations for election day. The parties are also seen as highly effective at direct voter communication. Indeed, parties indicate that they value direct-mail consultants most because they can help parties communicate with their constituencies quickly and efficiently. On the other hand, political parties clearly see candidates' needs for outside assistance differently than their own. When asked, parties say that candidates need assistance in general strategy and media production that is not really on point for the parties.

The responses of parties and consultants to questions about each others' strengths also confirm these conclusions. Both parties and consultants agree that parties have the advantage in local information, grass-roots organization, and get-out-the vote drives. On the other side, both parties and consultants agree that consultants are better able to provide technical expertise and individual attention to candidates. Parties are also appreciative of the polling and direct-mail capabilities consultants have that can help the parties' overall missions. The only two points parties and consultants did not agree upon were fund-raising and the development of the party's message. There were enough splits to indicate some competition or overlap between parties and consultants. However, differences in types of fund-raising account for much of this murkiness, and statements about party message were equally unspecified. We would be surprised to find perfect division of labor, but the amount of agreement over the strengths and weaknesses of parties and consultants is remarkable.

In the final analysis, scholars must reorient their approach to the party-consultant relationship. Consultants often have party backgrounds (or even go to work for the parties after having been on their own), share many goals with political parties, and often work harmoniously with political parties in productive electoral partnerships. The political parties may not have wanted to depend on consultants so much in the early stages of the modern campaign era, but they have come to acknowledge that the technological demands of modern campaigns have exceeded their institutional capacity to provide them. Both parties and consultants benefit from long-term electoral partnerships. The next step in this research area is to explore how durable these electoral partnerships are, how party officials and political consultants interact, and what candidates think of both party help and consultant help. Candidates might be expected to value consultant assistance more than party assistance, but since virtually all winning candidates run under a party label, I feel certain they attach some importance to political party organization in their campaigns. Lastly, the business of consulting will continue to depend on party coffers. With recent judicial decisions favoring unfettered spending by the parties (for independent expenditures and issue advocacy campaigns), consultants have lined up to help the parties exploit these loopholes to everyone's ultimate advantage.

Notes

1. John H. Aldrich, *Why Parties? The Origin and Transformation of Political Parties in America* (University of Chicago Press, 1995).

2. Paul S. Herrnson, *Party Campaigning in the 1980s* (Harvard University Press, 1988).

3. Frank I. Luntz, *Candidates, Consultants, and Campaigns: The Style and Substance of American Electioneering* (Basil Blackwell, 1988), p. 144.

4. Angus Campbell, Philip E. Converse, Warren E. Miller, and Donald E. Stokes, *The American Voter* (Wiley, 1960); Martin P. Wattenberg, *The Decline of American Political Parties, 1952–1994* (Harvard University Press, 1996).

5. John J. Coleman, "Resurgent or Just Busy? Party Organizations in Contemporary America," in John C. Green and Daniel M. Shea, eds., *The State of the Parties,* 2d ed. (Lanham, Md.: Rowman and Littlefield, 1996).

6. Wattenberg, *The Decline of American Political Parties.*

7. Robin Kolodny, *Pursuing Majorities: Congressional Campaign Committees in American Politics* (University of Oklahoma Press, 1998).

8. See, for example, David W. Rohde, *Parties and Leaders in the Postreform House* (University of Chicago Press, 1991).

9. R. Douglas Arnold, *The Logic of Congressional Action* (Yale University Press, 1990).

10. Herrnson, *Party Campaigning in the 1980s;* John F. Bibby, "Party Organization at the State Level," in L. Sandy Maisel, ed., *The Parties Respond* (Westview Press, 1990) pp. 21–40; James L. Gibson, Cornelius P. Cotter, John F. Bibby, and Robert J. Huckshorn, "Whither the Local Parties? A Cross-Sectional and Longitudinal Analysis of the Strength of Party Organizations," *American Journal of Political Science,* 29 (1985), pp. 139–60.

11. John Frendreis, "Voters, Government Officials, and Party Organizations: Connections and Distinctions," in John C. Green and Daniel M. Shea, eds., *The State of the Parties,* 2d ed. (Lanham, Md.: Rowman and Littlefield, 1996).

12. Coleman, "Resurgent or Just Busy?"

13. Luntz, *Candidates, Consultants, and Campaigns.*

14. Aldrich, *Why Parties?*

15. Frendreis, "Voters, Government Officials, and Party Organizations."

16. Aldrich, *Why Parties?*

17. Herrnson, *Party Campaigning in the 1980s;* Paul S. Herrnson, *Congressional Elections: Campaigning at Home and in Washington,* 2d ed. (Washington, D.C.: CQ Press, 1998).

18. Robin Kolodny and Angela Logan, "Political Consultants and the Extension of Party Goals," *PS: Political Science and Politics,* 31 (1998), pp. 155–159.

19. Ibid.

20. Ibid.

21. Ronald Brownstein, "The Long Green Line," *National Journal,* May 3, 1986, pp. 1038–42.

22. Herrnson, *Party Campaigning in the 1980s;* Luntz, *Candidates, Consultants, and Campaigns.*

23. Political Organizations and Parties Workshop, "Political Parties and Political Consultants: Allies or Adversaries?" Transcript (in possession of the author) of session delivered at the annual meeting of the American Political Science Association, Washington, D.C., August 27, 1998.

24. Aldrich, *Why Parties?*

CHAPTER EIGHT

Campaign Consultants and Direct Democracy: Politics of Citizen Control

DAVID B. MAGLEBY

KELLY D. PATTERSON

How citizens control government officials is an issue at the heart of democracy. During the early development of democracy, the citizens exercised direct control. Although the magistracies in Athenian democracy made a number of decisions for the city-state, the Popular Assembly remained the seat of power. Athenian citizens participated in decisions that, by today's standards, would be left to elected officials or technocrats.[1] The framers of the Constitution explicitly sought to remove citizens from direct participation in most of these decisions. By creating a republic, citizens were effectively barred from directly representing their own interests. Madison knew that the size of the nation-state, as opposed to the intimacy of the city-state, necessitated the selection and use of representatives. He spoke boldly in *Federalist 10* about the dangers of too much direct democracy: "Such democracies have ever been spectacles of turbulence and contention; have ever been found incompatible with personal security, or the rights of property; and have in general been as short in their lives, as they have been violent in

We would like to thank Carter Swift, Elizabeth Pipkin, and Marianne Holt for their work on this project. Funds for this study were provided by the College of Family, Home, and Social Sciences and the Department of Political Science at Brigham Young University. We would also like to thank the political consultants who graciously agreed to be interviewed and who participated in our survey. These consultants were eager to share their thoughts about the current state and practices in the consulting industry. We alone must bear the responsibility for any errors in the analysis.

their deaths." Today, citizens can be farther removed from decisions that affect their lives because of the rise of a global order. International organizations and corporations now make decisions that can affect the lives of millions of citizens without any mechanism to ensure that their interests are considered.[2]

The evolution of democracy from direct control by citizens to the exercise of control by elected representatives and unelected officials helps to explain why many view the increasing use of the initiative and popular referendum as a victory for the average citizen. Proponents of direct democracy argue that these procedures restore control to citizens and communities. Jack Citrin argues that what people like about the initiative process is not the control it gives them but that initiatives give "people a voice, a chance to express their opinion," concluding that "popular attitudes toward direct democracy are positive."[3] Yet people have no desire for "routine involvement in every policy choice at the state or national level" because they do not feel qualified to participate in all decision-making.[4] Although citizens do not want to become citizen lawmakers, they do feel that through the initiative process, the people can serve as a check on special interest groups and upon unresponsive legislators.[5]

Does the initiative and referendum process allow people to curb the power of interest groups and compel legislators to respond to the opinions of ordinary citizens? While the arguments for direct democracy appear to be rooted in a sincere desire to involve citizens directly in the decisions that governments make, it is important to consider whether or not the same ills that afflict representative democracy appear in the modern practice of direct democracy. If the process can be manipulated by special interests or relies on tactics that manipulate public opinion on initiatives, then many of the normative advantages claimed for the process disappear.

In this chapter, we examine the role played by political consultants in initiative campaigns. We begin by describing the characteristics of the political consultants who participate in these elections. We look at where initiative consultants do most of their business, the origins of the consultants' business, and what percentage of their time is spent on initiative campaigns. Consultants have different attitudes about candidate campaigns than they have about initiative campaigns. We show that many of these differences are rooted in the issue of control and in how the consultants view initiative campaigns. We examine the attitudes of the consultants toward this process and the extent to which they believe they are able to control the campaign. Initiative campaigns offer the prospect of more lucrative payoffs and more control than do candidate campaigns. Consultants play an important role in deciding what gets on the ballot in any particular state. These motivations can have deleterious effects on the democratic process if there is no method by which to hold consultants accountable for their activities. Finally, we examine the possible impact that the initiative consulting industry has on American democracy. The consultants themselves have mixed views about initiative campaigns. They realize that the process can be manipulated by themselves and their sponsoring special-interest groups. More broadly, our research on campaign consultants raises some questions about the current practice of direct democracy and the influence of political consultants.

Study Design

The data for this chapter come from two sources. First, we conducted extensive interviews with twenty-eight political consultants who work on initiative campaigns.[6] We originally obtained their names from a list of firms active in the industry from *Campaigns & Elections*.[7] We also searched the *New York Times, Washington Post,* and *Los Angeles Times* for stories on individuals involved in the referendum or initiative process. The list of people we interviewed includes consultants from signature collection, media, direct-mail, telecommunications, general campaign, strategy, polling, and initiative law firms. A list of all consultants in our sample is found in appendix C. Second, we followed up these interviews with a mail survey so that we could systematically organize and compare the responses of the consultants. The survey contains questions ranging from the types of services that each consultant's firm provides to his or her preferences between initiative and candidate campaigns. A copy of the questionnaire is found in appendix C. We obtained twenty-two responses to the survey from the original twenty-eight consultants that we interviewed. Finally, we sent the survey to all other political consultants who work on initiative campaigns. These individuals were listed in a subsequent edition of *Campaigns & Elections*.[8] We received twenty-nine responses to the second round of mailings. Overall, fifty-one consultants responded to the survey out of a total of sixty-nine who received it. While fifty-one responses may not be a large number, the responses are representative of the population of political consultants who work on initiative campaigns. There is a small number of consultants in this sector of the consulting industry. Therefore, by using both the interviews of the twenty-eight consultants and the survey responses from fifty-one of them, we believe we can make accurate inferences about the attitudes and motivations of the individuals who consult on initiative and referendum campaigns.

Growth of Initiative Consulting

There is little historical record of the activities of consultants in the initiative process. It is likely that even the earliest referendums had advisers involved on how to write the initiative, what the most persuasive arguments would be, and how to counter the opposition. The occasional local or state bond issue or constitutional change, to the extent that there was much professional campaign staff on either side, did not result in creating a cadre of initiative campaign professionals.

That changed in California in 1930 with the creation of Campaigns, Inc., the pioneering campaign consulting business for candidates as well as referendums. Clem Whitaker and his wife Leone Baxter worked in various referendum and gubernatorial campaigns. They found that by offering public relations representation they could maintain a campaign consulting business between election cycles.[9] As Stanley Kelley said, "It was a Whitaker and Baxter inspiration to conceive of political campaigning as a business."[10] Whitaker's first statewide campaign was to defend the 1933 Central Valley Project Act, which authorized $170 million in bonds for an irrigation and public power project. The powerful Pacific Gas and Electric (PG&E) Company sought repeal of the act through a popular referendum. Greg Mitchell summarizes the campaign as follows:

> It was David versus Goliath. PG&E had unlimited campaign funds; Whitaker had forty thousand dollars. [Whitaker and Baxter] tried out some new campaign tricks, bypassing the political parties and going directly to the voter—through the media. They coaxed their propaganda into practically every small-town newspaper in the state and made extensive use of radio, handling everything from the production of scripts to sound effects. Whitaker and Baxter defeated the referendum by thirty-three thousand votes.[11]

Whitaker and Baxter's win ratio was about 90 percent. Their ability to combine public relations with candidate and referendum campaign consulting was followed by later consultants like Stu Spencer of Spencer/Roberts. Spencer went on to be a prominent political adviser to Presidents Gerald Ford and Ronald Reagan.

The consulting industry has expanded and specialized to meet the needs of its clients. As V. O. Key and Winston W. Crouch argued in 1939, "the tremendous task of manipulating the attitudes of an electorate of over 2,000,000 with respect to numerous measures has led to the development of campaign organizations and expenditures rarely seen in states where the only issues voted on are constitutional amendments proposed by the legislature."[12] More recently, as we argue in this chapter, the model has been for greater specialization, including firms that focus solely on initiative campaigns while avoiding candidate campaigns or legislative representation.

Whitaker and Baxter's precepts about campaigning in the 1930s do not sound significantly different from what consultants say in the 1990s. In 1948 Whitaker told a meeting of public relations professionals, "we use campaign funds, not to dispense favors, but to *mold public sentiment,* to present our candidate, or our issue, in the most favorable light possible."[13] This attitude holds true today, although there is definitely a greater sense of specialization now than ever before. Bob Meadow reflected this attitude when he said that the initiative industry has specialization:

> For the same reason I think that there is professionalization in most professions, that you can go to a general practice attorney, but if you have civil litigation versus criminology, you have divorce proceeding versus corporate restructuring, you can again go to an attorney that specializes in that area.... There are media consultants, who will do TV and radio; there are direct mail consultants who develop direct mail in markets where television is not [fully] productive. There are fundraisers and there are pollsters. And there are a couple of others that are sometimes sprinkled in.[14]

Until recent years, the initiative process has been a distinctively western phenomenon.[15] While California may be a leader in the pervasive role the initiative plays in state politics, other states are seeing the process grow in importance. Virtually every state with the initiative process has seen a rise of activity in recent years. Figure 8-1 shows the rise and decline of initiatives and referendums throughout this century.

Figure 8-1. *Success of Initiatives and Popular Referendums in the United States, 1900–2000*

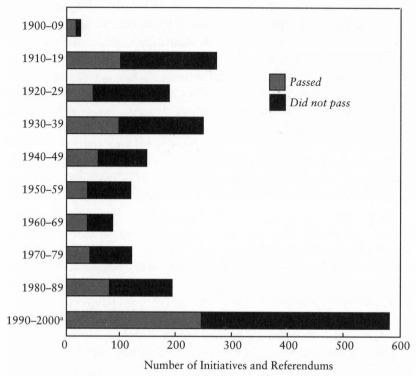

Number of Initiatives and Referendums

Source: For 1900–76, Virginia Graham, "A Compilation of Statewide Initiative Proposals Appearing on Ballots through 1976," Washington, D.C.: Congressional Research Service; for 1977–84, Sue Thomas, "A Comparison of Initiated Activity by State," *Initiative Quarterly,* 3 (1984), pp. 8–10; for 1985–96, state election officials.
a. Projected.

The Demographics of the Initiative Consulting Industry

A modern definition of a political consultant is "a campaign professional who is engaged primarily in the provision of advice and services (such as polling, media creation and production, and direct-mail fund raising) to candidates, their campaigns, and other political committees."[16] Specifically, the initiative and referendum consultants we have surveyed and interviewed are part of "the relatively small and elite corps of interstate political consultants who usually work on many campaigns simultaneously and have served hundreds of campaigns in their careers."[17]

The political consulting firms that are involved in the initiative process offer services that range from legal advice to fund-raising. A large percentage of the consultants surveyed stated that their firms offered polling, media production, media buying, direct mailing, and general campaign management, while a smaller percentage of the respondents provide legal advice, fund-raising, research, signature gathering, and telemarketing.

For the most part, the initiative consulting industry is concentrated in two locations: California and Washington, D.C. The concentration of business in California reflects the continued growth and popularity of initiative elections in that state. In 1994 more than $44 million was spent in California on ballot initiative contests. In 1996 the amount spent on all ballot measure campaigns was more than $141 million.[18]

The average consultant surveyed spends 36 percent of his or her time working on initiative campaigns and has been working in the consulting industry for an average of nineteen years. While a few of the survey respondents have worked in the consulting industry for only two or three years, the rest have been working for at least ten years. Initiative consultants are not political novices. The majority have spent at least a decade working in the political consulting industry.

Half of the respondents do most of their business in California. Firms with offices in Washington, D.C., tend to do a mixture of candidate and initiative work. The trend for firms with offices only in California has been toward specialization in initiatives. Nearly 60 percent of the California firms we interviewed derive less than 10 percent of their business from candidate campaigns. California firms rarely do work for political parties or wealthy individuals. When not doing initiative campaigns, California consulting firms are more likely to be working for interest groups. The connection between working for interest groups and on initiative campaigns is not new. Initiative consultancy has its roots in professionals who did public relations work generally and then would shift to initiative campaigns during election season.

Of the forty-eight respondents to our survey, nineteen have offices in Washington, D.C. Only three of the nineteen get more than half of their business from initiative campaigns. This means that those consultants with offices in Washington, D.C., tend to work on a mixture of candidate and initiative campaigns. Our impression is that consultants who occasionally work on an initiative in states like Arizona, Oregon, or Washington do so as part of a broader candidate and public relations practice. The growth of the initiative industry in Washington, D.C., is a fairly recent phenomenon. Those consultants who have spent the most time in the initiative consulting industry are less likely to have offices in

Washington, D.C., while those who have spent less time in the initiative consulting industry do have offices in the nation's capital.

There are two possible explanations for the growth of this industry in Washington, D.C. First, the initiative is now seen by many national interest groups as an important weapon. In the words of one consultant "if it's that much trouble to buy a lawmaker, it would be more fun just to buy a law, you know. And that you could fairly successfully spend your money in that arena probably as well as you could spend it giving donations to political candidates."[19] Many of the largest national groups have offices in the nation's capital, so there is ample opportunity for the political affairs offices of these interest groups and trade associations to consort with the consultants who can champion their cause. Of the twenty consultants with Washington, D.C., offices who worked on initiative campaigns, eight received the largest proportion of their business from special interest groups; three of them stated that they received more than 80 percent of their business from special interest groups. These three consultants who receive almost all their business from special interest groups indicated that they worked on initiative campaigns to the exclusion of candidate campaigns.

The second explanation for the large number of firms with offices in Washington, D.C., is the movement of some Washington firms from exclusive candidate work to a combination of initiative and candidate campaign projects. Many of the consultants cite the lucrative nature of initiative campaigns as a reason for engaging in both kinds of work. Seventy-three percent of the consultants we surveyed indicated that initiative campaigns pay better than candidate campaigns. One of the consultants interviewed, Kelly Kimball, said that she "never met a consultant who's in this because he believes in the causes.... There's some environmentalist groups.... But generally speaking, the professional consultant world is in this for the dough."[20] Therefore, given the rather substantial potential benefits of doing initiative campaigns, some candidate consultants might certainly be enticed into a mixture of candidate and initiative consulting.[21]

The majority of initiative work is concentrated in the western states that were strongly influenced by the Progressives, especially California. Initiative-prone states like Oregon, Washington, Ohio, and Michigan have pollsters or media firms that have handled campaigns in their own state and occasional measures in other states. Some of our respondents listed these states as places where they do a lot of business. However, the firms that become involved across ten states and in major battles tend to be from either Washington, D.C., or California.[22]

The growing popularity of initiative work among consultants may be due in part to the control that consultants have over the process. With the exception of nine consultants, the respondents agreed that initiative and referendum campaigns are easier to manage than candidate campaigns. Only six disagreed that initiative campaigns allow a consultant more freedom and control than candidate campaigns. We found these sentiments reflected in our earlier interviews with the consultants. Dawn Leguens stated that an initiative "allows for greater ability of message discipline."[23] Promoting a candidate leaves less room for consultants to persuade public opinion since a candidate brings with him or her a personality, appearance, and past that affects voters. Most initiatives possess no candidate appeal, and this gives the consultant more latitude to persuade voters to a point of view through media and through the writing of the initiative itself. Without the human dimension of candidate campaigns, voters in initiative campaigns have more of a "blank slate" and are more open to persuasion.[24]

Consultants' Clients

While the ordinary voters are extremely suspicious of the elected representatives and the organized interests that constitute the Washington establishment, many of the same special interests participate actively in the initiative process.[25] Some ballot initiatives result from grass-roots activity, but far more come from special interest groups or political candidates who have the resources to hire signature solicitors and campaign consultants. The average consultant who responded to the survey receives 33 percent of his or her initiative business from special interest groups, 28 percent from political candidates, 7 percent from political parties, 11 percent from grass-roots campaigns, 3 percent from wealthy individuals, and 18 percent from other sources, such as corporations.[26] With only 11 percent of a consultant's business coming from grass-roots campaigns, one can hardly make the argument that the initiative and popular referendum process returns democracy to the people. Indeed, the consultants realize that success in initiative campaigns usually demands professional services, and these services are becoming increasingly expensive to purchase. Consultant Bob Meadow says that there are two kinds of initiatives: initiatives that are truly from the citizens and those that come from groups with very deep pockets. The former are "typically underfunded," while the latter are "typically managed the way corporate enterprises are managed."[27] Another consultant, Mike Arno, echoes these sentiments when he says that "I think it is an accurate criticism [of the] initiative process that it's really only open to people with a lot of money."[28] With success in an initiative campaign linked to consultant involvement, a grass-roots campaign will falter without services such as signature solicitors and polling.

Effect on Democracy

Our respondents generally had a positive view of the initiative process's effect on democracy. Of the fifty-one consultants, thirty-seven (73 percent) said that initiatives have a "somewhat" or "very positive" effect on democracy, while nine (24 percent) said they have a "somewhat" or "very negative" effect. Furthermore, only two consultants indicated that initiatives have a negative impact on voter participation. Forty-one consultants (80 percent) thought that initiatives had a "positive effect" on voter participation. They also overwhelmingly stated that the initiative process had a "positive effect" on voter interest. Only ten consultants said that these campaigns negatively affected voter interest in politics. Therefore, most consultants believe that initiatives and referendums have a positive effect on voter activity and interest. They conclude that these campaigns strengthen democracy and do not alienate voters from the political process.

The support expressed by the consultants does not seem to vary based on the amount of time spent working on initiative campaigns. Consultants who do not spend the majority of their time working on initiative campaigns are not less likely to say that the initiative process has a positive effect on democracy. Conversely, when consultants spent more than 50 percent of their time working on initiatives, they were not more likely to say that the process is very positive or somewhat positive for democracy. The inclination of consultants to say that initiative campaigns have a positive effect on democracy probably emanates from two sources. First, consultants who have spent any time at all working on initiatives understand the process better and can more fully evaluate its strengths and weaknesses. Some initiative consultants argue that the process can correct flaws in representative government. Brad Bannon contends that "politicians are not receptive to public opinion, and the only way that you can execute public opinion is to get it on the ballot. I think a lot of times the only way the public can be heard is through the ballot process, as opposed to the legislative process."[29] Second, these consultants have a larger economic stake in the process. They might be reluctant to condemn a process that provides such large economic rewards. As Kimball says, "When you score the big pay days ... they generate more income than the presidential campaigns.... [A] consultant who tells you ... that money is not the issue ... [is] a liar."[30]

The initiative process is also less democratic than is sometimes believed because of the control that special interest groups have in the process. As stated earlier, initiative consultants receive the largest proportion of their business from special interest groups. Fifty-seven percent indicated that initiatives expand the power of special interest groups. Six of the respondents commented on the survey that the process can both expand and check the power of interest groups, depending upon the issue.

Those consultants who believe that the initiative process expands the power of special interest groups also believe that it has a negative effect on democracy. Even those individuals who believe the process has a positive effect on democracy maintain that the process expands the power of special interest groups. This should be an area of particular concern for the consultants. Americans have low levels of confidence in government and Washington, D.C., precisely because they perceive that special interest groups have too much power.[31] If and when citizens perceive that special interests drive the initiative process, popular support for the process will probably dissipate.

Some consultants recognize this eventuality. Ben Goddard states that "ballot initiatives have really become special interest wars."[32] He states that the "wars" between the special interest groups have "tended to diminish the people's attitude toward the initiative and referendum process. Simply because they see so many measures and the campaigns are so intense ... and the issues seemingly so small, that people tend to get turned off."[33]

One recent example of an initiative battle on a seemingly small issue that was waged mostly by interest groups and was heavily influenced by consultants was California Proposition 226, generally known as the "paycheck protection initiative." The initiative would have required annual written authorization from union members allowing their dues to be used for any political purpose. Similar measures were passed in 1992 by voters in Michigan and Washington. This tendency for issues to begin in one or two states and then move onto a national stage was also the case with such issues as property tax limitation and term limitation.

The June 1998 California vote on paycheck protection was seen by observers and involved interest groups as setting the stage for a series of state votes in November 1998 or for consideration of similar legislation in state legislatures. The roots of the California measure came from a battle between the California Teachers Association (CTA), which relies on paycheck deductions for its political funds, and Education Alliance, a group that supported seventy candidates in the 1994 and 1996 elections and relies on voluntary contributions. Mark Bucher, founder of the Education Alliance, knowing of the Washington initiative, started work on a California equivalent when one of his preferred candidates was defeated by a candidate to whom the CTA had donated $70,000.

But Bucher and his associates needed the help of the initiative industry to qualify for the ballot. Here the support of Grover Norquist, a conservative activist whose Washington, D.C.-based "Americans for Tax Reform," supplied $500,000 to help the measure qualify for the ballot and launch the campaign for its passage.[34] Another important early supporter who donated $49,000 to the campaign was J. Patrick Rooney, an Indiana businessman with close ties to House Speaker Newt Gingrich. The initiative also had distinctly partisan overtones, as California governor Pete Wilson chaired the "Yes on Proposition 226 Campaign" and "transferred more than $1.2 million from his gubernatorial campaign committee to the prop 226 battle."[35] Opposition to the campaign was largely funded by labor unions, who see paycheck protection as a direct threat to their political survival. The California Democratic Leadership Council strongly opposed the measure and reinforced the sense that this issue had strong partisan connotations. Just as support of the measure drew in money from outside the state, so did the opposition. It is estimated that together both sides spent in excess of $40 million in an effort to persuade voters to their point of view.[36]

Opinion shaping is where consultants again play the vital role. Consultants for the labor unions effectively redefined the measure as being about fairness and representation of a broader issue agenda, including social security, public education, and exporting American jobs. Their argument was that if paycheck protection passed, it would help conservative candidates and threaten public services. Knowing the unpopularity of labor unions, they downplayed the antiunion thrust of the initiative. Their message was that passage of the measure would impact large numbers of people and change the political balance of power. Fear of diminished support for public education, job security, and old-age benefits generated a much larger base of opposition to the proposition.

Opponents of the measure also sought to put the initiative in a negative light by criticizing those who were behind it. One of the television ads against Proposition 226 said: "When you take a closer look at Prop 226, you'll see that a foreign lobbyist [Norquist], multinational corporations, and an out-of-state insurance tycoon [Rooney] are behind it." This ad had all the markings of initiative campaign consultants who sought to redefine the initiative as emanating from such unpopular sponsors as foreign lobbyists, multinational corporations, or business tycoons with ties to Speaker Gingrich. Such redefinition can lead voters to reconsider their initial support and turn to being undecided or opposed to the initiative. They may still have favored the idea of paycheck protection, but they opposed this initiative because of its sponsors or their motives.

Supporters of the measure also understood the importance of defining the initiative in terms favorable to a "yes" vote. The title they chose, "Paycheck Protection," evokes a positive response. Moreover, their ads stressed individual freedom in deciding whether to give money for political purposes. The coalition of those pushing the initiative included Governor Wilson, Americans for Tax Reform, the Education Alliance and its primary sponsor Howard Ahmanson, the California Restaurant Association, and John Walton (Walmart).

Opponents tried to diffuse the impression that opposition was exclusively self-serving unions. Among those who came out in opposition to the measure were state chapters of the American Cancer Society, the American Lung Association, and the American Heart Association. These groups opposed the measure out of fear that the initiative would "dry up their paycheck deduction programs."[37] Having these respected groups oppose the initiative helped the "no" side create doubt among voters about the scope of the initiative.

As the campaign proceeded, the polls showed a dramatic opinion reversal from more than 70 percent supporting the measure in early polls to slight majorities opposing the initiative on the eve of the election.[38] On election day the measure was defeated with 53 percent voting against the measure and 47 percent voting for it. While losing on election day, the proponents of the measure were successful in forcing labor unions and their allies to focus on defeating the initiative rather than electing candidates.

Overall, the consensus among the consultants we surveyed and interviewed is that the initiative process expands interest groups' power. Special interest groups have an advantage in initiative campaigns, and this advantage comes from having organization and money. While initiative campaigns do not require the prolonged organization that candidate campaigns do, they do require an army of people to collect valid petition signatures or the resources to hire professional signature-gathering firms. Only a group with an organization already in place or with enough money to hire paid petition circulators can achieve this goal. This means that for an initiative or referendum to reach the ballot, it must be backed by someone with enough resources to put it there.[39] Even groups with enough organization to circulate petitions usually supplement their efforts with paid signature solicitors. Seventy-three percent of the consultants agreed that "virtually any issue could qualify for the ballot if its backers have sufficient funds."[40] Furthermore, those individuals who believe that the process expands the power of special interests also believe that any issue can qualify for the ballot as long as it has sufficient funds. Will Robinson reflects this idea when he states that "you could have someone literally write a $250,000 check to an initiative committee, in that many of these initiatives pop up when someone, an individual writes a substantial check to get the thing on the ballot."[41]

Qualifying initiatives for the ballot is a form of agenda setting. Because of the cost of getting a measure on the ballot, the power to set the agenda shifts from citizens to interest groups. The consultants realize that their participation is not representative of a mass movement. Max Besler states that "the problem is that these issues are almost exclusively put on by people who've got agendas to their own liking. And if those agendas happen to coincide with what's good [for] the people, then great, that's fine."[42] Indeed, in our earlier work, consultants stated that some issues that have often been "identified as mass protest issues, like legislative term limitation initiatives, were orchestrated by a national interest group out of its Washington, D.C., offices."[43]

Initiatives depend heavily upon money to win because of typically high media costs. A statewide initiative campaign requires extensive media coverage in order to reach all the voters. In our previous interviews, more than one consultant agreed that "almost all of the money that we spend is on media."[44] Consultants agreed that as a general rule more money is spent on media in statewide initiative and referendum campaigns than in statewide candidate contests, in part because candidate campaigns require more infrastructure. Well-funded campaigns, like those managed by Paul Mandabach, devote roughly "70 percent for communication—that's advertising, direct mail, materials; 20 percent for management fees, overhead expenses, offices, infrastructure; and 10 percent for research: survey research focus groups and testing of ads."[45] Even lower budget campaigns must find ways to use the mass media to communicate their message. Campaigns that rely on personal contacts and grass-roots organization to persuade voters are the exception, not the rule.

Consultants most frequently cite the California insurance-related initiatives of 1988 as examples of interest groups' deep pockets, the central role of consultants to the process, and strategic uses of counterinitiatives and ballot complexity. California voters on a single ballot faced five initiatives relating to the single topic of automobile insurance reform. Prior to the election, a legislative compromise between the principal antagonists—insurance companies and trial lawyers—broke down. Instead, a group that labeled itself "Access to Justice" placed a measure on the ballot (Proposition 103) that rolled back insurance rates. Activist Ralph Nader later joined in supporting this measure.

Trial lawyers, again with the assistance of consultants and the collaboration of Attorney General John Van de Kamp, sponsored a measure that reduced auto insurance rates and gave an insurance commissioner rate-regulating authority. Insurance companies, upon the advice of their consultant Clint Reilly, believed they not only needed to oppose Propositions 100 and 103 but also placed three countermeasures on the ballot—Proposition 101, which would reduce premiums by cutting back on accident damage claims; Proposition 104, which would have implemented no-fault insurance; and Proposition 106, which would have restricted trial lawyers' fees.

How were ordinary voters to traverse this maze of overlapping and conflicting measures? Part of the strategy of Clint Reilly, whose firm spent more than $60 million on the campaign, was to force the trial lawyers to oppose Propositions 101, 104, and 106, thereby diverting resources from persuading voters to vote for Proposition 100. Alternatively, voters might decide that the whole bundle of initiatives was too confusing and rather than risk enacting a mistake, they would vote against all five initiatives. In the end, voters narrowly enacted Proposition 103, the Ralph Nader-backed initiative, and the outcome has been interpreted as a setback for insurance companies.

The large amount of money spent on media initiative campaigns most likely contributes to consultants' willingness to handle such campaigns. Consultants receive a percentage of the media buys in their campaign, and initiative media buys can be highly lucrative. Consultants who seem to have "cashed out" include William Butler and Arnold Forde, who ran a direct-mail fund-raising and petition circulation effort for several Howard Jarvis initiatives following passage of Jarvis's California Proposition 13 in June 1978. Clint Reilly also seems to have "cashed out" after his participation in the 1988 California insurance propositions. Most consultants we surveyed state that initiative campaigns pay better than candidate campaigns.

With the important role of resources both to qualify an issue for the ballot and to advertise an issue to voters, the democracy of "direct democracy" is highly dubious. In the process's first stage of qualifying an issue for the ballot, the average voter has little control over the agenda put before him by special interest groups. The voter can decide to vote "yes" or "no," but he or she has little or no input on what issues are on the agenda. Furthermore, groups that cannot afford to invest substantial sums promoting their measure are likely to be discouraged from becoming involved in the process.

Consultants, Initiatives, and the Issue of Control

We began this chapter by briefly tracing the evolution of democracy from direct citizen control of public policy to indirect control through representatives. In some modern examples of governance citizens do not even have the benefit of representatives. We also reviewed the history of the debate surrounding the use of initiatives and other forms of citizen control of public policy. Proponents of direct democracy have long argued that initiatives and referendums could return a measure of control back to the citizens. However, even before the advent of professional campaigns, there were strong reasons to suspect that methods of direct democracy would greatly benefit powerful interests. As V. O. Key and Winston W. Crouch stated in 1939, initiatives are prone to be the "instruments of the turbulent few."[46]

The survey responses and interviews with the consultants confirm the suspicions of the earliest opponents of methods of direct democracy. Special interests have significant advantages in ballot campaigns that ordinary citizens cannot replicate. The consultants themselves exercise a tremendous amount of control in these campaigns They define the message, construct the ballot wording, and in some cases suggest issues to be placed on the ballot. This power is most often exercised without the mediation of political parties or candidates.

The indirect control that citizens can exercise through a party's or candidate's anticipation of voter reaction is lost in the current system of direct democracy. First, initiatives are rarely defined in partisan terms and, except for measures expressly sponsored by candidates, parties and candidates often avoid becoming identified with initiatives. In the most comprehensive examination of ballot proposition voting, Magleby found that "voting on ballot propositions appears to be more structured by party and ideology than other factors, but each measure has a marked random and ad hoc nature."[47] Therefore, predicting initiative voting across issues is very difficult, even when measures such as party and ideology are included; it is even more difficult in the case of noninitiative ballot measures.

Second, the money needed to craft and disseminate the message of an initiative campaign comes largely from sources barely, if at all, discernible to voters. This issue is compounded by the widespread agreement on the decisive role that money plays in these kinds of campaigns. Consultants have generally agreed that spending is more important in initiative campaigns than candidate races. When asked about the importance of campaign spending, one consultant replied, "I think it is an accurate criticism [of the] initiative process that it's really only open to people with a lot of money."[48]

As discussed earlier, most campaign consultants are supporters of the initiative process. They point to the expressive quality of the process and the ability of citizens to bypass deadlocked institutions at the state or local levels. Pollster Bob Meadow points out that the process is good for groups that cannot get what they want from legislatures, like trial lawyers, teachers, or fundamentalists. Some consultants take a more mixed view; as one put it, the process has "more good than bad in it."[49] Another consultant added that initiative campaigns are free from some of the funding restrictions present in candidate campaigns. "You can't corrupt the electorate, per se, as opposed to being able to corrupt a person by giving him money, or how much money he gets."[50]

In previous work, we concluded that "rather than reducing the power of interest groups, the functioning of the initiative and popular referendum in contemporary American politics has enhanced the power of some interest groups while excluding issues from the ballot box agenda which are of concern to less well-organized or affluent groups."[51] The results of our survey and interviews prompt us to add that a great deal of control in this process is exercised by the consultants themselves. This power is exercised normally in concert with interest groups. The relationship between the interest groups and the consultants cannot be checked by a formal party structure that is concerned with its electoral record. Nor is the relationship controlled by a candidate concerned with reelection. In both of these instances the anticipation of voter reaction acts as a restraint on what parties and candidates can do. Without such restraints, the consultant–interest group relation effectively nullifies most of the significant input that citizens can have on a process that is supposed to represent their interests.

Notes

1. Bernard Manin, *The Principles of Representative Government* (Cambridge University Press, 1997).

2. Robert A. Dahl, "A Democratic Dilemma: System Effectiveness versus Citizen Participation," *Political Science Quarterly,* 109 (Spring 1994), pp. 23–34.

3. Jack Citrin, "Who's the Boss? Direct Democracy and Popular Control of Government," in Stephen C. Craig, ed., *Broken Contract: Changing Relationships between Americans and Their Government* (Westview Press, 1996), pp. 268–93.

4. Ibid.

5. Ibid., pp. 272–73.

6. For a detailed discussion of these interviews see David B. Magleby and Kelly D. Patterson, "Consultants and Direct Democracy," paper presented at the annual meeting of the American Political Science Association, Washington, D.C., August 27–31, 1997.

7. We interviewed twenty-eight consultants from lists of consultants involved in initiative and referendum campaigns, including those identified as "winners," published in *Campaigns & Elections* magazine's postelection issues for 1994 and 1996.

8. We ultimately sent surveys to sixty-nine consultants. For a previous study, we interviewed twenty-eight consultants from lists of consultants involved in initiative and referendum campaigns, including those identified as "winners," published in *Campaigns & Elections* magazine's postelection issues for 1994 and 1996. After the initial interview, we sent these twenty-eight consultants the questionnaire that was sent to all other consultants. Therefore, our questionnaire was distributed in two waves: first to the twenty-eight consultants previously interviewed; and second to the forty-one consultants listed in *Campaigns & Elections* as working in the initiative and consulting industry to whom we had not already sent the survey.

9. Richard Rapaport, "In the Beginning: A History of California Political Consulting," *California Journal,* 22 (1991), pp. 418–24.

10. Stanley Kelley Jr., *Professional Public Relations and Political Power* (Johns Hopkins University Press, 1956), p. 39.

11. Greg Mitchell, *The Campaign of the Century: Upton Sinclair's Race for Governor of California and the Birth of Media Politics* (Random House, 1992), p. 130.

12. V. O. Key and Winston W. Crouch, *The Initiative and Referendum in California* (Cambridge University Press, 1939).

13. Kelley, *Professional Public Relations and Political Power*, p. 39, emphasis ours.

14. Bob Meadow, interview by David B. Magleby, Washington, D.C., tape recording, May 1, 1997.

15. Charles M. Price, "The Initiative: A Comparative State Analysis and Reassessment of a Western Phenomenon," *Western Political Quarterly*, 28 (1975), pp. 243–62.

16. Larry J. Sabato, *The Rise of Political Consultants: New Ways of Winning Elections* (Basic Books, 1981), p. 8.

17. Ibid.

18. Center for Governmental Studies Project, memorandum re: total expenditures for and against California initiatives, facsimile to Kelly D. Patterson from Craig B. Holman, May 28, 1998.

19. Dawn Leguens, interview by David B. Magleby, Washington, D.C., tape recording, June 17, 1997.

20. Kelly Kimball, interview by David B. Magleby, Riverside, Calif., tape recording, June 26, 1997.

21. Magleby and Patterson, "Consultants and Direct Democracy."

22. Ibid., pp. 9–10.

23. Leguens, interview by David B. Magleby.

24. Magleby and Patterson, "Consultants and Direct Democracy."

25. John R. Hibbing and Elizabeth Theiss-Morse, *Congress as Public Enemy: Public Attitudes toward American Political Institutions* (Cambridge University Press, 1995); Kelly D. Patterson and David B. Magleby, "Trends: Public Support for Congress," *Public Opinion Quarterly*, 56 (Winter 1992), pp. 539–51; David B. Magleby and Kelly D. Patterson, "Trends: Congressional Reform," *Public Opinion Quarterly*, 58 (Fall 1994), pp. 419–27.

26. These averages are estimates from our survey of initiative consultants. Because each consultant gave his or her own estimates and because not all consultants indicated work in the same categories, our original average of their percent estimates yielded a total of 108 percent. We converted the percentages into a scale that would sum to 100 percent.

27. Meadow, interview by David B. Magleby.

28. Mike Arno, telephone interview by David B. Magleby, tape recording, July 9, 1997.

29. Brad Bannon, telephone interview by David B. Magleby, tape recording, July 9, 1997.

30. Ibid.

31. Hibbing and Theiss-Morse, *Congress as Public Enemy*; Patterson and Magleby, "Trends: Public Support for Congress"; Magleby and Patterson, "Trends: Congressional Reform."

32. Ben Goddard, telephone interview by David B. Magleby, tape recording, July 8, 1997.

33. Ibid.

34. David Corn, "Union Dues, Political Don'ts," *Nation*, 266, 18 (1998), pp. 16–20.

35. Eric Bailey and Carl Ingram, "Labor, Wilson Clash over Use of Union Dues," *Los Angeles Times*, May 25, 1998, p. A3.

36. Frederick Rose, "A Special News Report about Life on the Job—and Trends Taking Shape There," *Wall Street Journal*, May 12, 1998, p. A1.

37. Bailey and Ingram, "Labor, Wilson Clash over Use of Union Dues," p. A30.

38. "Trend of Voter Opinions about Prop 226 Requiring Permission before Withholding Wages or Union Dues for Political Contributions," field poll, May 29, 1998, table 1.

39. David B. Magleby, "Campaign Spending and Referendum Voting," paper presented at the annual meeting of the Western Political Science Association, Albuquerque, N.M., March 10–12, 1994.

40. Appendix B, this volume.

41. Will Robinson, interview by David B. Magleby, Washington, D.C., tape recording, May 1, 1997.

42. Max Besler, telephone interview by David B. Magleby, tape recording, July 9, 1997.

43. Magleby and Patterson, "Consultants and Direct Democracy," p. 8.

44. Goddard, telephone interview by David B. Magleby; Magleby and Patterson, "Consultants and Direct Democracy."

45. Paul Mandabach, telephone interview by David B. Magleby, tape recording, July 14, 1997.

46. Key and Crouch, *The Initiative and Referendum in California,* p. 439.

47. David B. Magleby, *Direct Legislation: Voting on Ballot Propositions in the United States* (Johns Hopkins University Press, 1984), pp. 178–79.

48. Arno, telephone interview by David B. Magleby.

49. Meadow, interview by David B. Magleby.

50. Stu Mollrich, interview by David B. Magleby, Irvine, Calif., tape recording, June 26, 1997.

51. Magleby and Patterson, "Consultants and Direct Democracy," p. 24.

CHAPTER NINE

The Internationalization of Campaign Consultancy

SHAUN BOWLER

DAVID M. FARRELL

Political campaign consultancy, in its various manifesta-
tions, has been a fact of U.S. political life for quite some
time.[1] How much has this political consultancy been exported to other
nations? There has been little systematic evidence available on the extent
of international links between campaign organizations across national
boundaries. There is plenty of anecdotal evidence about the "moonlight-
ing" activities of political consultants from the United States in "overseas" markets, and there is also some reference to the phenomenon in
the earlier academic works on U.S. political consultants. But so far no systematic research has been carried out.[2] In this chapter we make a preliminary assessment, starting in the second section, with an outline of
some of the conditions that may help facilitate or dampen the spread of
such consulting services across borders. We then analyze the actual pattern of consulting internationally, relying on evidence gathered from a
mail survey of consultants administrated during the spring of 1998.

We are extremely grateful to the political consultants who responded to our mail survey.
In addition we wish to thank the following for providing very useful background material
on their countries of expertise: Barry Ames, Attila Ágh, David Altman, Ernesto Cabrera, Ali
Çarkoglu, Raymond Christensen, Rosario Espinal, Reuven Hazan, Gabriella Ilonszki,
Charles D. Kenney, Petr Kopecky, Tatiana Kostadinova, Jonathan Mendilow, Esteban
Montes, Charles Polidano, Steven Reed, Jeffrey Ryan, Taka Sakamoto, and Manuel Sánchez
de Dios. The usual disclaimer applies.

Modern means of mass communication were adapted for political use almost as soon as they were used in commercial settings. Radio broadcasts in the 1920s and evidence of other activities stretch back even further, including the use of newspaper advertisements, cinema advertising, and opinion polls.[3] Other countries have not been immune to the spread of political consultancy, a fact which, of itself, could be seen as one possible indicator of the "Americanization" of politics.[4]

Research has already shown how campaign styles across the developed world (and also many of the wealthier countries of the developing world) have been professionalizing.[5] For the most part, the scholarly debate has revolved around the extent to which this convergence is due to a process of Americanization, or the adoption of the latest tools, strategies, and techniques of professionally run campaigns in the United States.[6] This term, often seen as one of abuse, has been tied to a wide variety of trends within European politics, such as poll-driven campaigns and negative advertising.

To see an illustration of this general phenomenon, we have to look no further than the 1999 Israeli elections. In the most publicized instance of U.S. consultants going overseas to wage an election campaign, three of the most well-known U.S. electioneers—Stanley Greenberg, Bob Shrum, and James Carville—helped elect the new Israeli prime minister, Ehud Barak. And while he did not win the election, Binyamin Netanyahu was not without U.S. representation, as Arthur Finkelstein was part of his campaign team.

Consultants, and their marketing techniques adapted from the commercial world, have formed a familiar part of elections for a long time in the United States and now in many other nations. Needless to say, their spread has mirrored technological advances in new media. For instance, there was no use for video consultants and webmasters in the 1950s because they did not exist, but there were other kinds of advisers and advice that could be given to candidates and parties. By the 1990s technological advances—many of which originated in the United States— necessitated the hiring of different kinds of experts.[7] To call both the presence and use of all these techniques "American" seems to be an overstated use of the phrase. Yet the emphasis upon the technology of campaigning necessarily pushes us in that direction and leads us to label most aspects of modern campaigning "American," even though they may simply reflect the technology of modern electronics.

A related distortion can come from the very term *Americanization*. While for some this may be a pejorative term (and hence something to be hidden), for others the term may be one of pride. To the extent that "American" is linked with positive connotations of modernity and efficiency, then being American-trained or being influenced by American ideas may be seen to be a good thing in and of itself. Evidence from a recent study based on survey data of international political consultants by Fritz Plasser, Christian Scheucher, and Christian Senft shows that knowledge of the latest U.S. campaign literature was judged important by 64 percent of European consultants; these consultants also judged regular observations of U.S. campaigns (63 percent) and personal contact with U.S. consultants (39 percent) to be important.[8] This would lead one to conclude that the spread of U.S. ideas is important in international political consulting.

Rather than examine the spread of ideas and technologies, we focus on a more concrete expression of the American model, namely the use of outside consultants themselves. That is, we distinguish between campaign technique and campaign organization. The latter influence is where Americanization may be most deeply felt, since it marks the "contracting out" of one of the central purposes of party organizational life. Rather than having strong parties that provide campaigning advice (and possibly constraints), candidates can simply hire professional consultants. The fact that these consultants use the latest video equipment for television advertising or the Internet for soliciting campaign support is neither here nor there when compared to the fact that they exist as organizations outside of the party. To use an economic analogy: U.S. parties have gone past the model of vertical integration (of doing everything from start to finish) and have gone to the contracting out stage, where certain functions of the party are performed by outsiders commissioned to do the task.[9] In fact, some argue that they have contracted out all of the basic campaign functions.[10]

This is not only a different way of "doing politics," it is also one that is more distinctively American than the use of sound bites, direct mailers, videos, focus groups, or any one of a thousand other techniques that are also part and parcel of today's election campaigns outside the United States. Moreover, it is an organizational development that threatens the traditional notions of party.[11] (However, according to the findings of Plasser, Scheucher, and Senft, twice as many European consultants compared to U.S. consultants view parties as having a valuable contribution to make to candidates' campaigns.) This reaches an extreme form in the hiring of U.S. consultants to wage elections not on U.S. soil. Here, not only are campaigns run by people outside the party, but by foreigners, too. Once a polity has arrived at this stage, there is a different model of political activity in which politics is conducted by nonparty actors. This can be seen as doubly American. First and foremost it represents an important organizational model distinctively familiar to the United States, where party organizations in the traditional sense of the term are weak. Second, and less important, it can literally represent the Americanization of politics to the extent that U.S. firms are among those traveling overseas to carry out this work.

Two aspects of campaigns—technological and organizational—are linked at some level. Cable and satellite programming, web technology, and direct-mail videos all provide new avenues for campaigning that are technologically driven; this means that someone somewhere in a campaign is being paid to handle them. Furthermore, as the number of campaign firms grows, competition between candidates intensifies and the will to win drives consultants to introduce new techniques with more promise of luring voters. It is too easy to confuse the medium and the message. Despite all the hype, it is not yet clear if these new technologies have changed what campaigns are about or simply how campaign messages are delivered. There is a large difference between providing consulting services in-house (from within a political party and its own officials and experts) and contracting services to stand-alone consultants. Whether these consultants set up web pages or handbills would seem less important than the question of whether they are part of a political party and its philosophy or just some outside (albeit, perhaps, sympathetic) contractor trying to win an election using any means necessary.

The politically relevant issue is the hiring of consultants, rather than the changing of technology. We seek to address whether this occurs across national borders on a regular basis. To the extent that it does, we can see a sign of the increasing Americanization of electoral politics. U.S. elections can be said (at least for the purposes of our argument) to represent an ideal type of democratic politics where parties are weak, candidates are strong, and seemingly every kind of electoral expertise is available for hire on a contract basis. Campaign consultants exist as distinct, stand-alone entities, hired by parties and candidates but, at the same time, distinct from them.[12] To the extent that the Americanization of politics proceeds apace, we should see evidence of this elsewhere in the world. It will be given physical expression by the presence of foreign—and especially U.S.-based—consultants in elections outside the United States. In short, then, we take the Americanization of electoral politics as our theme in order to examine the extent to which campaign consultants have spread across the world, a process in which the dominant U.S. model of electioneering is adopted by other campaign organizations.[13] Our empirical question, then, is how much of this U.S. *organizational* model is being exported overseas? In examining this, we describe the way in which the Americanization of politics spreads.

Electoral Environments

The electoral environment fundamentally affects the nature of consulting. After all, there is not much point in chasing overseas work if the market the consultant is chasing has a very unfamiliar environment or if there are serious restrictions on the kinds of campaign practices the consultant might be accustomed to. At its most extreme, some governments simply do not allow elections or they hold what are little more than acclamatory ballots in which only one party contests for power. The last ten years have seen a flowering of democratic elections in the Americas, in central and eastern Europe, and in the former Soviet Union, providing a minimum condition for growth in cross-national consulting. Associated with these democratizing trends have been a series of sponsored efforts aimed explicitly at exporting political expertise, electoral help, and democratization.[14] The Soros Foundation across central and eastern Europe and the Swedish-based International Institute for Democracy and Electoral Assistance are two examples of key nongovernmental actors engaged in this kind of behavior.

More "official" and long-standing examples can be seen not just in the actions of U.S. government agencies such as the United States Information Agency (USIA) and the U.S. Agency for International Development (USAID), but also in the prominent work of the German party foundations. To speed the rebuilding of political parties after the Nazi period, the German government established party foundations, one for each of the main parties, and endowed them with substantial amounts of public money. Anxious to further the development of democracy in other countries, these foundations started funding overseas political activities from the late 1950s onward. By the end of the 1980s the estimated total amount involved was more than $170 million.[15] Despite conducting most of their work in underdeveloped countries, the foundations have also established offices in industrialized countries. In recent years their

efforts have increasingly centered on the newly emerging democracies
of east and central Europe and the former Soviet Union. In 1989, for
instance, the Social Democrats' Friedrich Ebert Foundation had projects
in at least one hundred countries. The Christian Democrats' Konrad
Adenauer Foundation has focused its attentions on Latin America, while
the Bavarian-based Christian Social Union's Hanns Seidel Foundation
concentrates its activities in Africa.

U.S. government support from USIA and USAID, for example, is
routed through a series of nongovernment agencies, such as the National
Endowment for Democracy, the International Department of the AFL-
CIO, and the Human Rights and Democratic Initiatives Program and
Democracy Program for Latin America and the newly independent states
of the former Soviet Union. Pinto-Duschinsky estimates that the total cost
of the U.S. government's political aid program in 1989 was just under
$100 million.[16] The National Endowment for Democracy's funds are for
the most part channeled through the U.S. equivalent of party founda-
tions, for example, the National Republican Institute for International
Affairs, the National Democratic Institute for International Affairs, the
Free Trade Union Institute (affiliated with the AFL-CIO), and the Center
for International Private Enterprise (affiliated with the U.S. Chamber of
Commerce).

An important determinant of the level of activity of consultants and
their supporting international benefactors is the electoral environment
in each recipient country. National conditions, such as campaign finance,
the presence of debates among leaders, or the permissibility of television
advertising, may allow greater or lesser scope for consultants to become
involved in a country's elections. Table 9-1 displays some information
about the campaign environment in thirty-two countries. In twenty-one
of the countries paid TV spots (as opposed to or in addition to state-
sponsored public advertising) are allowed, and in many cases these are
subject to few or no restrictions.[17] This in itself would suggest some role
for political consulting in making advertisements and in media buying.
In addition, other contextual factors, such as television debates between
leaders, open the door for other kinds of specialization. For example,
speech writers and media coaches would all seem to have job opportunities in the twenty-six states that allow them. Finally, it would seem that
many of the parties in these countries should have little difficulty raising
the necessary cash to pay for professional expertise. In twenty of the
countries under investigation, the state provides public funding in support

of the campaign activities of political parties. Overall, table 9-1 suggests that there is moderately fertile ground for the role of consultants in election campaigns around the world.

Distinct geographical patterns appear in the table. For instance, it is interesting to note how the campaign process of the developed democracies (such as the North American and western European nations) has tended to become more open in recent years. In the early 1980s Anthony Smith revealed that there was little access to private TV spots (only in Australia, Canada, Japan, and the United States) and far less use of leaders' debates.[18] The newer democracies of eastern and central Europe and Latin America have more liberal regimes in terms of the right to buy TV spots, and they have well-financed campaign organizations in terms of public funding of the parties. Against this, however, it is interesting to note the tendency to set legal limits on the reporting of poll results in the final two days before elections in many of these newer democracies. Uruguay even goes so far as to ban alcohol in the final forty-eight hours.[19]

An example of restrictions in the electoral context can be found in the May 1998 Hungarian elections, where Gallup-Hungary posted the results of an opinion poll on their website and was accused of violating the country's ban on publishing poll results in the last eight days of a campaign. The Hungarian National Election Committee threatened to prosecute them unless they removed it. When news of this appeared on the World Association of Public Opinion Research (WAPOR) e-mail listserv, it prompted a furious reaction from the managing director of the London-based MORI polling agency, Robert Worcester:

> Should anyone wish to let the light in to their election period by conducting surveys during their election poll publication ban period, we stand ready, able and willing to post them on www.mori.com, and welcome the opportunity to strike a small blow for freedom of information and the right of people to know what others are thinking, in the most systematic and objective way we know how to measure public opinion.[20]

The 1995 Turkish election provides an interesting example of the limitations in practice of enforcing some of these campaign restrictions. As Çarkoglu points out, in a new law passed only weeks before the election, "publication or distribution, in any form, of election forecasts or polling results of any kind in a way that could affect voters' decisions was

Table 9-1. *Variations in Election Campaign "Environments" in Thirty-two Countries*

Region and country	TV spots[a]	Leaders' debates[b]	Restrictions on TV access[c]	Other campaign restrictions	State campaign finance
Latin America					
Argentina	Yes	Yes	Equal	48-hour ban on campaigning and on polls	Yes
Brazil	No	Yes	Proportionate		No
Chile	Yes	Yes	Proportionate	Public rallies must be authorized; campaigning only in 30-day period before election	No
Dominican Republic	Yes	No	No		Yes (since 1997)
Peru	Yes	Yes	No		No
El Salvador	Yes	No	No		Yes
Uruguay	Yes	Yes	Proportionate	48-hour ban on campaigning and alcohol	Yes
Eastern Europe					
Bulgaria	Yes	Yes	Proportionate	48-hour ban on campaigning; 14-day ban on polls	Yes
Czech Republic	Yes	Yes	Equal	48-hour ban on campaigning; 7-day ban on polls	Yes
Hungary	Yes	Yes	Equal (if >1% vote)	48-hour ban on campaigning; 8-day ban on polls; limits on candidate expenditure	Yes (just introduced)
Mediterranean (southern) Europe					
Israel	Yes	Yes	Proportionate	None since 1996	Yes
Malta	No	n.a.	Proportionate		No
Spain	No	Yes[d]	Proportionate	Maximum 20% of budget can be spent on all advertising; 48-hour ban on polls	Yes
Turkey	Yes	Yes	Equal	Since 1995 no election forecasts can be broadcast	Yes

Australasia and Japan					
Australia	Yes	Yes	Proportionate		Yes
Japan	Yes	Yes	Proportionate	Limits on expend.; candidate restrictions[e]	Yes (since 1995)
New Zealand	Yes	Yes	Proportionate	Limits on candidates' expenditure	No
North America					
Canada	Yes	Yes	n.a.	Limits on expenditure; 48-hour ban on polls	Yes
United States	Yes	Yes	No	Limits on president's expenditure	Yes (for president)
Western Europe					
Austria	Yes	Yes	Proportionate		Yes
Belgium	No	Yes	n.a.		No
Denmark	No	Yes	Equal		No
Finland	No	Yes	Equal		No
France	No	Yes	Equal	Limits on expenditure; 7-day ban on polls	Yes (for president)
Germany	Yes	Yes	Proportionate		Yes
Ireland	No	Yes	Proportionate	Limits on expenditure	Yes
Italy	Yes	Yes	No	7-day ban on polls	Yes
Netherlands	Yes	No	No		No
Norway	No	Yes	No		Yes
Sweden	Yes	Yes	Equal		No
Switzerland	No	No	n.a.		No
United Kingdom	No	No	Proportionate	Limits on local expenditure	No

n.a. = not available.

a. "Paid" spots, as opposed to free TV advertising.

b. In some cases (notably Scandinavia), there is little actual debate between the candidates, who are instead quizzed by a panel of journalists.

c. In some cases by law; in others, rules set by broadcasters. For the most part, this relates only to state-owned networks.

d. Party leaders have only consented to debate on TV in 1993.

e. Most of the restrictions are focused on candidates (not parties); among them are a ban on campaigning until the final fifteen days, no doorstep canvassing, and restrictions on speechmaking and on distribution of written materials.

forbidden."[21] Despite this law, however, the largest daily newspaper, *Milliyet*, went ahead and published poll results three days before the election. Soon after, other newspapers followed suit.

Who Are the Overseas Consultants and Where Do They Work?

Over time, international political consultancy has developed into a profession with its own norms, standards, and associations. The International Association of Political Consultants (IAPC) was founded in Paris in 1968 by Joe Napolitan and the French political consultant Michel Bongrand. Its current membership is about one hundred members.[22] In its *1997 Register of Members*, the breakdown of the ninety-nine listed members was as follows: forty-five U.S. consultants, ten from Germany, seven from Sweden, four from Australia, three each from France, Italy and Venezuela, and the remainder are from Argentina, Austria, Canada, Costa Rica, Israel, Japan, Puerto Rica, Russia, South Africa, Spain, Switzerland, and Turkey. Thirty-three of the IAPC's members claimed to have worked on campaigns in countries other than their own. In nineteen of these cases (58 percent), the consultants are United States–based; of the remainder, only three consultants each from Germany, Sweden, and Venezuela showed any kind of proclivity for foreign work.

Despite a strong American flavor to its composition, not all members of the IAPC are United States–based. There are a number of non-U.S. firms willing to offer their services. Two questions follow from this: Which countries provide work for these firms? And, can we say anything about the conditions under which they work?

Our answers at this stage are, admittedly, preliminary. In the spring of 1998 we conducted a mail survey of campaign specialists and consultants, using the membership lists of the IAPC and WAPOR. We sent out 171 surveys and received 61 responses (for a response rate of 35.7 percent). Of these, 35 (21 percent) confirmed that they were involved in election campaign work in countries outside their main base (hereafter we will refer to these as "overseas consultants"). The remainder were a mix of people who said they did no overseas work and others (mostly from the WAPOR list) who said they did no political work.[23]

We make no grandiose claims of representativeness here since no one knows what a representative sample looks like. However, as this research (like much of the other research in this volume) is new and preliminary, we are not bothered by these results. As noted above, the number of consultants who do overseas consulting is unknown at this time. With this beginning, we hope to provide a springboard for other research.

Table 9-2 provides some details on the countries of origin and the locations of overseas work of our respondents (although not all provided full details). Just as the IAPC's membership has a distinctly American flavor, 51 percent of the respondents represented U.S.-based agencies.

The fact that so many consultants claim to work on campaigns overseas is significant, because this indicates that there is a sizable market for election campaign services over and above any work supplied to home-based firms. In light of this, a surprising finding is that a significant number of the countries listed as locations for overseas work already have domestic consultants in their own right; the most striking example is the United States.

A glance at the reported locations of overseas work in table 9-2 indicates certain tendencies that might influence the choice of areas in which to work, notably: (1) neighboring (or at least reasonably adjacent) countries, (2) countries with some kind of historical connection (such as former colonies), and (3) countries linked on the basis of overseas aid (Sweden looks particularly interesting in this respect).

It is clear from tables 9-2 and 9-3 that at least as far as politicians are concerned, political consultants are a transportable commodity across national boundaries. The most significant point, however, to draw from table 9-2 is the astounding list of countries in which overseas firms have worked.[24] Table 9-3 provides more details by listing alphabetically (arranged by region) the sixty-nine countries in which consultants have worked and indicating how often each country was mentioned by a respondent. Even if we ignore those countries that only show up once, we still see a large number of countries mentioned. Again, it is interesting to see the prominence of the Americas as a location for overseas work, comprising a plurality of our cases (37 percent; 34 percent if Canada and the United States are excluded).

Not all respondents were able or willing to name the countries in which they had worked. However, in another part of the survey they were invited to indicate the number of overseas elections in which they had worked. Table 9-4 summarizes these responses (see also the last column of table 9-2). There seems to be a set of "super consultants" who run elections everywhere. Almost one-third of the respondents (31 percent) claim to have worked on more than twenty-one overseas campaigns. The

Table 9-2. *Survey Respondents and the Location of their Overseas Work*

Country of origin	Number of consultants	Number of countries[a]	Locations of overseas work
Australia	1	4	Japan, New Guinea, New Zealand, "several Pacific countries"
Costa Rica	1	5	El Salvador, Guatemala, Honduras, Nicaragua, Panama
France	3	4.5[b]	Belgium, Hungary, Mauritius, Portugal, Spain, Rhodesia, Vietnam, French-speaking West Africa, Central and South America, United States
Germany	3	6.7	Austria, Brazil, Chile, Costa Rica, Ecuador, Guatemala, Hungary, Israel, Kenya, Nicaragua, Peru, Poland, Portugal, Spain, Sweden, Turkey, Venezuela
Italy	1	n.a.	n.a.
South Africa	2	3.5	Czech R., Chile, Malawi, Namibia, Zambia, United Kingdom (Northern Ireland)
Spain	1	9	Bolivia, Columbia, Dominican Republic, Ecuador, France, Guatemala, Peru, Portugal, United States
Sweden	1	16	Argentina, Bosnia, Czech Republic, Denmark, Estonia, Finland, Hungary, Latvia, Lithuania, Malta, Mozambique, Namibia, Norway, Philippines, Poland, South Africa, European Union
United Kingdom	3	6.5[b]	Bulgaria, Gibraltar, Hungary, Lithuania, Malaysia, Malta, Mexico, Russia, S. Africa, Taiwan, Turkey, United States
United States	18	5.8[b]	Argentina, Albania, Australia, Belgium, Bolivia, Bosnia, Brazil, Canada, Chile, Costa Rica, Cyprus, Czech Republic, Denmark, Dominican Republic, Ecuador, El Salvador, Estonia, France, Germany, Greece, Guam, Hungary, Italy, Latvia, Lithuania, Macedonia, Malta, Mauritius, Mexico, Netherlands, New Zealand, Nicaragua, Nigeria, Panama, Philippines, Poland, Slovakia, South Africa, St. Marten, Spain, Sudan, Sweden, Russia, United Kingdom, Ukraine, Venezuela, European Union (Party of European Socialists)
Venezuela	1	3	Costa Rica, Dominican Republic, Peru

n.a. = not available.
a. Average number of named locations for overseas work.
b. Some respondents did not divulge any countries.

Table 9-3. *Destinations of the "Overseas Consultants"*

Region/country	No. of mentions	Region/country	No. of mentions
Asia-Pacific (8 percent)	14	Zambia	1
Australia	4	Eastern Europe/former	32
Guam	1	Soviet Union (18 percent)	
Japan	1	Albania	1
Malaysia	1	Bosnia	2
New Guinea	1	Bulgaria	1
New Zealand	2	Czech Republic	4
Philippines	3	Estonia	3
Taiwan	1	Hungary	5
Vietnam	1	Latvia	2
Americas (37 percent)	65	Lithuania	3
Argentina	3	Macedonia	1
Bolivia	3	Poland	3
Brazil	4	Russia	3
Canada	2	Slovakia	2
Caribbean	2	Ukraine	2
Chile	3	Western/southern Europe	45
Costa Rica	5	(26 percent)	
Dominica	4	Austria	2
Ecuador	5	Belgium	3
El Salvador	2	Cyprus	1
Guatamala	2	Denmark	2
Honduras	1	Finland	1
Mexico	5	France	2
Nicaragua	7	Germany	2
Panama	3	Gibraltar	1
Peru	2	Greece	2
United States	3	Israel	1
Venezuala	9	Italy	4
Africa (11 percent)	19	Malta	2
Kenya	1	Netherlands	1
Malawi	2	Norway	1
Mauritius	3	Portugal	2
Mozambique	1	Spain	3
Namibia	3	Sweden	5
Nigeria	2	Turkey	3
Rhodesia (pre Zimbabwe)	1	UK	7
South Africa	4		
Sudan	1	Total (100 percent)	175

Table 9-4. *Number of Overseas Election Campaigns*
on which Consultants Claimed to Have Worked

Number of campaigns	N	Percent
1 to 5	12	34
6 to 10	4	11
11 to 15	4	11
16 to 20	4	11
More than 21	11	31
Total	35	...

average number of *countries* these consultant have worked in (which is different from the average number of campaigns) is 6.1, and the standard deviation is 5.1. The overall message is clear: there is a wide range of talent taking up work in a large number of countries.

This is confirmed by country experts who we contacted in a separate survey in the spring of 1998. There were fifteen countries for which we received responses to our survey: in thirteen of them there was clear evidence of election work being carried out by foreign consultants, in addition to the work of indigenous consultants.[25] The countries involved—and, where known, the origin of the overseas consultants— were as follows: in Latin America—Argentina, Brazil, Chile, Dominican Republic (overseas consultants from Chile and Spain), El Salvador (United States), Peru (United States); in Europe—Bulgaria (Germany), Czech Republic (Germany), Hungary (Germany and France), Malta (United States), Spain, Turkey (United States and France); and in the new prime-ministerial system of Israel (United States and France).

Nature and Origins of Overseas Consultancy Work

Consultants' responses to our survey provide important insights into the kind of work in which they are engaged. Respondents' firms provide general advice, rather than more narrow specialist services. In a sense this could reflect a role as "consultants' consultants"—providing general tactical advice (and some more specialist advice), but having little input into the more strategic aspects of the campaign. This is also consistent with the theory that overseas consultancy is a relatively new growth industry. In his seminal study of U.S. political consultancy, Larry Sabato suggests that in the early phase of the work political consultants tended to operate at a rather general level, providing an overall package of ser-

Table 9-5. *Work of the Overseas Consultants*

Type of work	N	Percent
Nature of work[a]		
General advice/consultancy	24	47
Polling and market research	16	31
Advertising	8	16
Other	3	6
Total	51	...
Role in campaigns[b]		
Political consultant	26	74
Party staff member	0	0
Representative of a specialist agency	7	20
Other	2	6
Total	35	...

a. "How would you best categorize the nature of your work" (multiple answers possible).
b. "Which of the following best describes your role in election campaigns?"

vices for the client.[26] In more recent years this picture changed as more and more consultants entered the fray and as campaigns sought to become ever more professional: consultants increasingly became more specialized in terms of the services they provided.[27] The responses to the first question posed in table 9-5 are consistent with this: almost half of our respondents (47 percent) felt the service they provided for their overseas client was general in nature, covering more than one field of expertise; of the remainder, 31 percent provided polling and market research and 16 percent helped with campaign advertising.[28]

There is no evidence in our data of party campaign professionals being sent over to work on the election campaigns of sister parties. As we see in the second question posed in table 9-5, these hired guns classify themselves as political consultants first and foremost: 74 percent of the respondents categorized themselves as "political consultants," and the bulk of the remainder (20 percent) indicated that they were the representative of a specialized campaign agency. Finally, no respondent reported acting as the agent of a party.

Most of the consultants were brought into other countries by invitation. As table 9-6 shows, 41 percent of the consultants were recruited directly by the client, 26 percent were brought in on the coattails of another consulting firm, and 12 percent were brought in on the basis of arrangements between sister parties. This evidence is an important illustration of the "demand-driven" presence of consultants in campaigns. To some extent, both the conventional image of consultants and the real-

Table 9-6. *Why Consultants Worked on an Overseas Campaign*[a]

Reason	N	Percent
Direct approach by the client	27	41
Initiated by the consultant	14	21
Contacted by another consultant	17	26
Support for a sister party	8	12
Total	66	...

a. Multiple answers were possible.

ities of doing business would tend to suggest that political consultants are pushing themselves on politicians and that the whole process is supply-pushed. This might seem to be especially true for recent democracies where politicians—perhaps looking to the west for guidance on how elections should be fought—might be easy prey. However, our survey shows that only 21 percent of the sample admitted to having successfully developed business for themselves in the overseas market.

Another expectation about the origins of overseas consultancy relates to the institutional features of the target country. For instance, candidate-centered campaign systems (usually, though not exclusively, associated with presidential political systems) will likely produce more work for consultants.[29] To measure this, we asked our respondents whether, on the whole, they tended to work for political parties or for individual candidates. Only 14 percent of the respondents claimed to be working exclusively for candidates; by contrast, 34 percent indicated that they worked for parties and 51 percent said they worked both for parties and candidates. To an extent, this finding could well be representing the fact that certain other institutional features, such as the level of freedom of the campaign market or the degree of campaign finance given to political *parties*, are providing a stronger effect than candidate-centeredness on the proclivity to use overseas consultants.

Having outlined some aspects of the extent to which consultants travel to foreign countries to do business, it is worth noting some of the differences between national and international contexts. Campaign consultants cannot randomly apply their trade across international borders. A number of contextual factors limit the applicability of techniques that are relied upon in one country or another. As Napolitan observes, "there are some delicate areas in campaigning abroad, because politicians in many countries are fearful of the reaction in their own countries to the use of American consultants. This is not true in some countries—but in others the feeling is strong indeed."[30] A much cited case in point is the United Kingdom. Despite its suitability in terms of common culture, language, and economic wealth, for a long time it appeared resistant both to use U.S. campaign techniques and, more particularly, to employ U.S. campaign consultants. For instance, Napolitan cites his difficulties in attracting any kind of British interest in the activities of the IAPC in the early 1970s.[31] By the end of the 1970s an opening appeared when the Conservative party's 1979 campaign made extensive use of techniques and personnel from the United States. This prompted Sabato to remark that the "aloof and skeptical British politicians [were] coming around."[32]

There seems to be a mixed picture regarding the willingness of parties or candidates in the host country to acknowledge the presence of overseas consultants. We asked our respondents: "On the whole, have you found that your clients are happy to reveal that you are working for them, or are they more prone to try and hide your presence?" For 51 percent of the respondents, the answer was "it depends." But 34 percent said that most clients prefer to hide their presence, and only 14 percent said that their clients were "happy to reveal" them. In some open-ended comments, there is a suggestion of a geographical dimension to this, as best summarized by the comment of one consultant: "In Europe we hide. In the Caribbean and Latin America we're ballyhooed." Recently, in Ecuador, Argentina, and Columbia, the fact that American political consultants were assisting candidates was prominently advertised and considered a positive for the campaigns.

In sum, even though overseas consultants are spreading everywhere across the democratic world, and even though most of them are being invited in by the locals, they are not that popular in many places. Nevertheless, there is some evidence to suggest that the amount of overseas work is on the increase: twelve of our respondents said that their overseas workload was increasing; only six said it was decreasing.

Finally, we asked a series of questions designed to measure how, and in what respects, overseas work might be different from the consultants' work in their native country. As the data in table 9-7 show, the bulk of our respondents (69 percent) view overseas elections as quite different from what they are used to in their home territory. Open-ended responses to this question revealed a range of reasons for the difference. On one hand, overseas elections are both stimulating—"the variety of things we do is greater and more interesting"; "more interesting, larger role; the only consultant"—and, on occasions, financially rewarding—"less

Table 9-7. *Consultants' Roles and the Importance
of Ideology in Home and Overseas Campaigns*

Issue	N	Percent
Consultants' role at home and overseas[a]		
About the same	9	31
Different	20	69
Importance of ideology[b]		
Prefer to work for candidates with ideological tendency		
close to mine	23	72
Ideology is not so important. What matters more are	9	28
qualities and abilities		
Importance of ideology overseas versus at home[c]		
More important	4	12
Less important	13	39
About the same	16	49

a. "Is your role in overseas campaigns about the same as in home campaigns?"
b. "We want to know if the ideological tendency of the party/candidate is important?"
c. "Is ideological tendency of a party/candidate in an overseas campaign more or less important than in home campaigns?"

involvement, less time, better fees." Some of the consultants claimed not to be "emotionally affected" and to find the experience "less intensive." But on the other hand, there were negative points as well. Many reported feeling "greater distance from the original decisionmakers" and in "less control of activities." One consultant commented: "Because of distance, the advising role is concentrated into less days. The biggest frustration in working overseas is people don't call you to chat or explore ideas."

The last two questions in table 9-7 are, in part, designed to test whether the ideological tendency of a client matters to a greater or lesser extent in overseas elections than it might at home. Sabato, for instance, has suggested that "crossing ... borders seems to [be] ideologically liberating" for many consultants.[33] Almost 75 percent of our respondents had a clear preference for working with candidates who had a similar ideological tendency. This result is more interesting when juxtaposed with those of James Thurber, Candice Nelson, and David Dulio in chapter 2 of this volume. Recall that in their survey of U.S. consultants, ideology and political beliefs were cited as a motivation for becoming a political consultant by only just over 26 percent of the respondents. More important to the U.S. consultants was the thrill of the competition that comes along with the campaign, and on par with consultants' political beliefs as a motivation was the money one could earn. Needless to say, the notion of "ideology" is an ambiguous term, and some of our consultants simply ignored these questions. One commented: "It is often very difficult to determine 'ideology' in many parties, especially in nonindustrialized countries." This might explain why 39 percent of our sample indicated that ideology is *less* important in overseas elections compared to campaigns in their native land. Additional comments indicated a tendency to heighten the importance of candidates being "committed to democracy." As one consultant stressed, he wanted a candidate who was "consistent, ethical, and who could stand up to scrutiny." Only one consultant stressed the importance of a candidate's or party's "ability to pay their bills." This anecdotal evidence of concern about ethical behavior is again bolstered by the findings of the Thurber, Nelson, and Dulio survey that found that contrary to the conventional wisdom, U.S. consultants are not as dastardly as some would like us to think. Thurber and his colleagues point out that U.S. consultants find some of the most deplorable campaign practices—such as push polling, suppressing voter turnout, and making false statements—to be clearly unethical.[34] While we do not try to draw comparisons between U.S. and other political consultants, we believe that the combination of evidence points to a concern on the part of consultants about democracy and the way in which campaigns are waged.

Conclusion

This chapter has presented a preliminary analysis of overseas political consulting. As we have seen, the extent of overseas work is impressive, both in terms of the number of companies engaged in this work as well as the numbers of countries using foreign consultants. The Americanization of electoral politics seems to be quite thoroughgoing; though perhaps, instead of Americanization, a better term might be *modernization*, since it is not simply U.S.-based consultants who engage in overseas work. In other words, not only the clients are worldwide; so are the companies that service them. Moreover, since this is a process that seems to be demand-driven—national politicians and parties are inviting relevant expertise—and since the number and kind of elections held around the world continue to grow, so, too, will this activity.

It seems reasonable to suppose that parties that can rely on contracted services have little need to develop such services for themselves. This, in turn, suggests a possible weakness in the electioneering functions of parties. It may be especially true for new democracies where party organizations are in their infancy.[35] Whether such trends matter or not in a wider political sense is a topic for conjecture. It also seems to be a topic for greater study within the literature on political consultants.[36] For, while documentation of the new technological innovations and approaches has tended to preoccupy the bulk of analysis on political campaigning, it is the organizational consequences that have remained less well studied. Unfortunately, then, the long-term political consequences of these trends are not quite as clear as the trends themselves.

Notes

1. See Dennis Johnson, "The Business of Political Consulting," chapter 3 in this volume.

2. Joe Napolitan, *The Election Game: And How to Win It* (Doubleday, 1972); Larry Sabato, *The Rise of Political Consultants: New Ways of Winning Elections* (Basic Books, 1981).

3. See James Thurber, "Introduction to the Study of Campaign Consultants," chapter 1 in this volume; S. Bowler, T. Donovan, and K. Fernandez, "The Growth of the Political Marketing Industry and the California Initiative Process," *European Journal of Marketing,* 30, 10–11 (1996), pp. 173–85; and Robert Friedenberg, *Communication Consultants in Political Campaigns* (Praeger, 1997).

4. David Farrell, "Political Consultancy Overseas: The Internationalization of Campaign Consultancy," *PS: Political Science & Politics,* 30 (1998), pp. 171–76; Margaret Scammell, "The Wisdom of the War Room: U.S. Campaigning and Americanization," Harvard University, Shorenstein Center on the Press, Politics and Public Policy Research Paper R–17, April 1997.

5. S. Bowler, and D. Farrell, eds. *Electoral Strategies and Political Marketing* (St. Martin's, 1992); D. Butler and A. Ranney, eds. *Electioneering* (Oxford University Press, 1992); David Farrell, "Campaign Strategies and Tactics," in Larry LeDuc, Richard Niemi, Pippa Norris, eds., *Comparing Democracies: Elections and Voting in Comparative Perspective* (Sage, 1996); and David Swanson and Paolo Mancini, "Patterns of Modern Electoral Campaigning and their Consequences," in D. Swanson and P. Mancini, eds., *Politics, Media, and Modern Democracy: An International Study of Innovations in Electoral Campaigning and Their Consequences* (Praeger, 1996).

6. Swanson and Mancini, "Patterns of Modern Electoral Campaigning and their Consequences."

7. Thurber, "Introduction to the Study of Campaign Consultants."

8. Fritz Plasser, Christian Scheucher, and Christian Senft, "Is There a European Style of Political Marketing? A Survey of Political Managers and Consultants," in Bruce Newman, ed., *The Handbook of Political Marketing* (Sage, 1999).

9. David Farrell, Robin Kolodny, and Stephen Medvic, "The Political Consultant/Political Party Relationship: A Health Warning for Representative Democracy or a Welcome Advance?" paper presented at the annual meeting of the American Political Science Association, Boston, September 3–6, 1998.

10. See Thurber, "Introduction to the Study of Campaign Consultants."

11. Plasser, Scheucher, and Senft, "Is There a European Style of Political Marketing?" See also Farrell, Kolodny, and Medvic, "The Political Consultant/Political Party Relationship."

12. Contrast this with the party-centered scenario in western Europe where parties have tended to professionalize their own staff. Angelo Panebianco, *Political Parties: Organization and Power* (Cambridge University Press, 1988); David Farrell and Paul Webb, "Political Parties as Campaign Organizations," paper presented at the conference on Unthinkable Democracy, University of California at Irvine, Newport Beach, California, March 13–14, 1998. See Robin Kolodny, "Electoral Partnerships: Political Consultants and Political Parties," chapter 7 in this volume.

13. There is some debate in the literature over the utility of the term "Americanization." Some suggest that the converging trends may simply reflect a general process of "modernization," driven by socioeconomic and technological development, to which all systems in some way or another are inevitably susceptible. R. Negrine and S. Papathanassopoulos, "The Americanization of Political Communication: A Critique," *Harvard International Journal of Press/Politics*, 1, 2 (1996), pp. 45–62; Swanson and Mancini, "Patterns of Modern Electoral Campaigning and their Consequences." We follow Scammell's line on this: "The key point ... is that there is some consensus that 'Americanization' is useful as a shorthand description of global trends and that the U.S. is the leading exporter and role model of campaigning." Scammell, "The Wisdom of the War Room," p. 4.

14. Geoffrey Pridham, "Transnational Party Links and Transition to Democracy: Eastern Europe in Comparative Perspective," in Paul Lewis, ed., *Party Structure and Organization in East-Central Europe* (Brookfield, Vt.: Edward Elgar, 1996).

15. Michael Pinto-Duschinsky, "Foreign Political Aid: The German Political Foundations and their U.S. Counterparts," *International Affairs*, 67, 1 (1991), pp. 33–63.

16. Ibid.

17. Interestingly, there are few cases outside of the United States in which there are no rules regarding the rights of parties to broadcast media access.

18. Anthony Smith, "Mass Communications," in D. Butler, H. Penniman, A. Ranney, eds., *Democracy at the Polls* (American Enterprise Institute, 1981). See also Valentine Herman and F. Mendel, *Parliaments of the World* (Berlin and New York: de Gruyter, 1976).

19. Another interesting case is Singapore, where TV spots have recently been banned, having been reclassified "in the same category as obscene movies." Party Developments, "Singapore Political Ads and Pornography under Same Classification," *Party Developments*, 3, 5 (1998), p. 11.

20. E-mail from Robert Worcester, posted on the wapornet-listserv, May 13, 1998.

21. In addition, candidates were forbidden from distributing prizes or presents during the campaign. Ali Çarkoglu, "The Turkish General Election of 24 December 1995," *Electoral Studies*, 16 (1997), p. 80.

22. *IAPC Newsletter*, April 1999.

23. A few surveys were returned as undeliverable to the addressee.

24. In a survey such as this we have no means of distinguishing cases of real campaign "work" from those cases where the consultant may simply have given a lecture or perhaps gone on a political "vacation." Therefore, the trends reported in these tables can only be treated as *indicators* of the phenomenon of overseas consultancy.

25. The two exceptions were Japan and Uruguay. In the latter case, our national expert indicated that Uruguay was an "exporter," not an "importer," of campaign talent.

26. Sabato, *The Rise of Political Consultants*.

27. See Thurber, "Introduction to the Study of Campaign Consultants"; Farrell, "Campaign Strategies and Tactics."

28. The rather high figure we report for polling and market research might in part be an artifact of our sample, given that a large number of our respondents were contacted via the WAPOR list of members.

29. Farrell, "Campaign Strategies and Tactics"; Farrell, "Political Consultancy Overseas."

30. Napolitan, *The Election Game*, p. 244.

31. Ibid., p. 255.

32. Sabato, *The Rise of Political Consultants*, p. 61.

33. Ibid., p. 59.

34. See David A. Dulio, "'Just Win, Baby!' Campaign Consultants, Ethical Standards and Practices, and Campaign Reform," paper presented at the annual meeting of the Midwest Political Science Association, Chicago, 1999.

35. Paul Lewis, "Introduction and Theoretical Overview," in Paul Lewis, ed., *Party Structure and Organization in East-Central Europe* (Brookfield, Vt.: Edward Elgar, 1996).

36. Farrell, Kolodny, and Medvic, "The Political Consultant/Political Party Relationship."

Measuring Campaign Consultants' Attitudes and Beliefs

The sample for the survey discussed in chapter 2 of this volume was drawn by Princeton Survey Research Associates, under contract with American University's Center for Congressional and Presidential Studies and the Pew Research Center for the People and the Press, and funded by a grant from the Pew Charitable Trusts. It was a stratified sample, drawing on experienced firms in four major sectors of the industry (survey research, media, fund-raising, and general consulting).

The results are based on 200 in-depth telephone interviews with principals in major consulting firms, completed between November 1997 and March 1998.[1] The firms and individuals were selected through a two-stage process. First, a list of 302 political consulting firms (including general consulting, media, survey research, and fund-raising firms) was created by searching *Campaigns & Elections* magazine's postelection reports from 1992, 1994, and 1996. These firms were identified as being associated with one or more campaigns for president or Congress in any of the three preceding election cycles.

Second, the 302 firms were divided into two groups. The first group consisted of firms that had been involved in one or more presidential campaigns, five or more Senate campaigns, or thirty or more congressional campaigns during the last three election cycles. All other firms made up the second group. Each firm in the first group was contacted for an interview. In addition, a subset of firms from the second group was randomly selected for interviews.

Individual consultants were selected from firms in the groups outlined above and were identified from the 1996 *Political Resource Directory's* list of principals or partners. For firms of two or more principals, one of the principals was selected at random to be interviewed first. When an interview was completed with the first principal at each firm, that person was asked for the names of the firm's other principals or senior associates who work on political campaigns. These individuals were then contacted for interviews. Therefore, even though firms were used to create the initial list, the unit of analysis is the individual.

Each individual selected for an interview was sent a letter requesting their participation in the study. Subsequently, every person was contacted (several times, if necessary) to complete an interview.

Table A-1 presents the distribution of sampled individuals in the survey.

Table A-1. *Distribution of Survey Participants*

Item	N	Percentage
Total individuals selected	339	
Ineligible individuals[a]	25	
Net total	314	
Completed interviews	200	64
Incomplete interviews	1	0
Refused	19	6
No answer[b]	40	13
Could not be contacted	54	17
Total	314	100

a. These were individuals who were no longer employed at that firm or screened out (they did not work on a campaign in 1992, 1994, or 1996, or were not a principal or senior associate).
b. These individuals were left messages (with a secretary or on an answering machine or voice mail) more than ten times.

SCREEN QUESTION 1

About how many congressional, Senate, or presidential races did you personally work on in the 1996 election cycle? Would you say fewer than five, five to 10, 10 to 15, or more than 15?

	N	Percent
Fewer than five	70	35.0
Five to 10	74	37.0
10 to 15	25	12.5
More than 15	29	14.5
Didn't work on any 1996 races	2	1.0

SCREEN QUESTION 2

Was your role in these races primarily as a pollster, a media consultant, a fund-raiser, or a general consultant?

	N	Percent
Pollster	57	28.5
Media consultant	80	40.0
Fund-raiser	22	11.0
General consultant	38	19.0
Direct mail consultant	1	0.5
Other	1	0.5
Don't know/refused	1	0.5

SCREEN QUESTION 3

In your firm, are you currently a principal, a senior associate, or a junior associate?

	N	Percent
Principal	178	89.0
Senior associate	22	11.0
Junior associate	0	0.0
Other	0	0.0
Don't know/refused	0	0.0

QUESTION 1

In what year was your first paid campaign job?

	N	Percent
1958–73	41	20.5
1974–83	80	40.0
1984–96	78	39.0
Don't know/refused	1	0.5

QUESTION 2

In that job, were you part of the campaign staff or were you a consultant?

	N	Percent
Campaign staff	131	65.5
Consultant	59	29.5
Both	5	2.5
Party member	3	1.5
Other	2	1.0

QUESTION 3

What type of campaign was it? Local, state, national House or Senate, or presidential?

	N	Percent
Local	43	21.5
State	48	24.0
National House or Senate	64	32.0
Presidential	28	14.0
Congressional	5	2.5
Gubernatorial	6	3.0
Other	4	2.0
Don't know/refused	2	1.0

QUESTION 4

All things considered, how satisfied are you with your current job overall? Very satisfied, mostly satisfied, mostly dissatisfied, or very dissatisfied?

	N	Percent
Very satisfied	121	60.5
Mostly satisfied	69	34.5
Mostly dissatisfied	8	4.0
Very dissatisfied	0	0.0
Don't know/refused	2	1.0

QUESTION 5

Thinking now about political consultants as a group, that is, general campaign managers, pollsters, media consultants, and fund-raisers, which of the following to you think most motivates professional consultants?

	N	Percent
Political beliefs	52	26.0
The thrill of competition	65	32.5
Money	53	26.5
Political power and influence	17	8.5
All of the above	3	1.5
Don't know/refused	9	4.5
Other	1	0.5

QUESTION 6A

When you consider taking on a race, how important are the political beliefs of the candidate?

	N	Percent
Very important	117	58.5
Somewhat important	73	36.5
Not too important	5	2.5
Not at all important	2	1.0
Don't know/refused	3	1.5

QUESTION 6B

When you consider taking on a race, how important is the candidate's ability to raise money and pay bills?

	N	Percent
Very important	110	55.0
Somewhat important	83	41.5
Not too important	6	3.0
Not at all important	0	0.0
Don't know/refused	1	0.5

QUESTION 6C

When you consider taking on a race, how important are the candidate's chances of winning?

	N	Percent
Very important	32	16.0
Somewhat important	122	61.0
Not too important	31	15.5
Not at all important	12	6.0
Don't know/refused	3	1.5

QUESTION 6D

When you consider taking on a race, how important is the candidate's ability to govern?

	N	Percent
Very important	79	39.5
Somewhat important	80	40.0
Not too important	24	12.0
Not at all important	11	5.5
Don't know/refused	6	3.0

QUESTION 7A

How much impact to you think political consultants have on the public policy agenda in the United States?

	N	Percent
A great deal	24	12.0
A fair amount	83	41.5
Not very much	87	43.5
None at all	4	2.0
Don't know/refused	2	1.0

QUESTION 7B

How much impact to you think political consultants have on the way political leaders conduct themselves once in office?

	N	Percent
A great deal	21	10.5
A fair amount	78	39.0
Not very much	86	43.0
None at all	8	4.0
Don't know/refused	7	3.5

QUESTION 8A

From your perspective, how would you rate the quality of the candidates running for the House and Senate?

	N	Percent
Excellent	11	5.5
Good	93	46.5
Fair	84	42.0
Poor	11	5.5
Don't know/refused	1	0.5

QUESTION 8B

From your perspective, how would you rate the quality of professional political consultants?

	N	Percent
Excellent	13	6.5
Good	99	49.5
Fair	74	37.0
Poor	10	5.0
Don't know/refused	4	2.0

QUESTION 8C

From your perspective, how would you rate the quality of political journalists?

	N	Percent
Excellent	3	1.5
Good	60	30.0
Fair	98	49.0
Poor	37	18.5
Don't know/refused	2	1.0

QUESTION 9A

In the time that you have worked in politics, has the quality of the candidates running for the House and Senate . . .

	N	Percent
Gotten better	33	16.5
Gotten worse	83	41.5
Stayed the same	83	41.5
Don't know/refused	1	0.5

QUESTION 9B

In the time that you have worked in politics, has the quality of professional political consultants . . .

	N	Percent
Gotten better	71	35.5
Gotten worse	65	32.5
Stayed the same	62	31.0
Don't know/refused	2	1.0

QUESTION 9C

In the time that you have worked in politics, has the quality of political journalists . . .

	N	Percent
Gotten better	20	10.0
Gotten worse	98	49.0
Stayed the same	80	40.0
Don't know/refused	2	1.0

QUESTION 10

Have you ever helped elect a candidate who you were eventually sorry to see serve in office, or not?

	N	Percent
Yes	89	44.5
No	111	55.5

QUESTION 11A

Turning now to the specifics of political campaigns, on a scale from 1 to 10, where 10 represents a factor that is most important to winning an election and 1 represents a factor that is least important to winning, where would you place the amount of money available to a campaign?

	N	Percent
1–4	2	1.0
5–7	49	24.5
8–10	149	74.5

QUESTION 11B

. . . where would you place the quality of the candidate's message?

	N	Percent
1–4	2	1.0
5–7	33	16.5
8–10	165	82.5

QUESTION 11C

. . . where would you place the candidate's abilities to campaign?

	N	Percent
1–4	4	2.0
5–7	104	52.0
8–10	92	46.0

QUESTION 11D

. . . where would you place the partisan makeup of a state or a House district?

	N	Percent
1–4	5	2.5
5–7	88	44.0
8–10	105	52.5
Don't know/refused	2	1.0

QUESTION 12

In your experience, generally, which is the more serious problem for a campaign: a candidate with a weak message or a candidate who is a poor campaigner?

	N	Percent
Weak message	150	75.0
Poor campaigner	44	22.0
Neither [volunteered]	4	2.0
Don't know/refused	2	1.0

QUESTION 13

Generally speaking, if you have enough campaign resources, how difficult is it to sell a mediocre candidate to voters? Is it very easy, somewhat easy, somewhat difficult, or very difficult?

	N	Percent
Very easy	17	8.5
Somewhat easy	68	34.0
Somewhat difficult	95	47.5
Very difficult	17	8.5
Don't know/refused	3	1.5

QUESTION 14

And if you have enough campaign resources, how difficult is it to handle a candidate's unpopular stands on issues? Is it very easy, somewhat easy, somewhat difficult, or very difficult?

	N	Percent
Very easy	9	4.5
Somewhat easy	65	32.5
Somewhat difficult	112	56.0
Very difficult	13	6.5
Don't know/refused	1	0.5

QUESTION 15

Now thinking about the role that candidates play in deciding campaign strategy, in what percentage of the campaigns you've worked on did the candidates play the leading role in deciding campaign strategy?

	N	Percent
0 to 25 percent	63	31.5
26 to 50 percent	54	27.0
51 to 75 percent	38	19.0
76 to 100 percent	42	21.0
Don't know/refused	3	1.5

Question 16

In your experience, does the campaign of an independent issue advocacy group on behalf of a candidate help or hinder his or her campaign?

	N	Percent
Help	131	65.5
Hinder	23	11.5
Depends [volunteered]	39	19.5
No effect [volunteered]	3	1.5
Don't know/refused	4	2.0

Question 17

To what extent do you think ad watches—that is, the press coverage focusing on the accuracy of political ads—have made campaigns more careful about the content of their ads? A great deal, a fair amount, not very much, or not at all?

	N	Percent
A great deal	47	23.5
A fair amount	64	32.0
Not very much	63	31.5
None at all	24	12.0
Don't know/refused	2	1.0

Question 18

Thinking back to the 1996 election cycle, how many campaigns, if any, do you know of that used push polling, that is disseminating false or misleading information about a candidate under the pretense of taking a poll? Would you say many, some, a few, or none?

	N	Percent
Many	15	7.5
Some	26	13.0
A few	97	48.5
None	57	28.5
Don't know/refused	5	2.5

There was no Question 19

QUESTION 20A

I'd like your opinion on some possible problems that might keep the national political system from working as well as it should. First, what about elected officials caring more about getting reelected than doing what's best for the country?

	N	Percent
Major problem	75	37.5
Somewhat of a problem	71	35.5
Not much of a problem	54	27.0

QUESTION 20B

. . . how about good people being discouraged from running for office by the amount of media attention given to candidates' personal lives?

	N	Percent
Major problem	110	55.0
Somewhat of a problem	70	35.0
Not much of a problem	20	10.0

QUESTION 20C

. . . how about political contributions having too much influence on government policy?

	N	Percent
Major problem	48	24.0
Somewhat of a problem	70	35.0
Not much of a problem	82	41.0

QUESTION 20D

. . . how about a decline in moral and ethical standards among people in politics and government?

	N	Percent
Major problem	28	14.0
Somewhat of a problem	63	31.5
Not much of a problem	104	52.0
Don't know/refused	5	2.5

QUESTION 21

How much trust and confidence do you have in the wisdom of the American people when it comes to making choices on election day? A great deal, a fair amount, not very much, or none at all?

	N	Percent
A great deal	84	42.0
A fair amount	84	42.0
Not very much	25	12.5
None at all	4	2.0
Don't know/refused	3	1.5

QUESTION 22

What about on domestic policy issues? How much confidence do you have in the judgment of the American people about major domestic policy issues? A great deal, a fair amount, not very much, or none at all?

	N	Percent
A great deal	59	29.5
A fair amount	98	49.0
Not very much	36	18.0
None at all	5	2.5
Don't know/refused	2	1.0

QUESTION 23

In your opinion, how well informed or poorly informed are voters about major policy issues? Very well informed, somewhat well informed, somewhat poorly informed, or very poorly informed?

	N	Percent
Very well informed	3	1.5
Somewhat well informed	61	30.5
Somewhat poorly informed	96	48.0
Very poorly informed	36	18.0
Don't know/refused	4	2.0

QUESTION 24A

Now a few questions about the causes of voter cynicism. To what extent do you think negative campaigning affects voter cynicism?

	N	Percent
A great deal	49	24.5
A fair amount	86	43.0
Not very much	59	29.5
None at all	6	3.0

QUESTION 24B

To what extent do you think politicians' poor performance while in office affects voter cynicism?

	N	Percent
A great deal	54	27.0
A fair amount	93	46.5
Not very much	52	26.0
None at all	0	0.0
Don't know/refused	1	0.5

QUESTION 24C

To what extent do you think the way the news media report on politics affects voter cynicism?

	N	Percent
A great deal	127	63.5
A fair amount	55	27.5
Not very much	14	7.0
None at all	3	1.5
Don't know/refused	1	0.5

QUESTION 24D

To what extent do you think the way money is raised in campaigns affects voter cynicism?

	N	Percent
A great deal	49	24.5
A fair amount	73	36.5
Not very much	65	32.5
None at all	12	6.0
Don't know/refused	1	0.5

QUESTION 25A

As I read you some changes that have been proposed to reform the way political campaigns are financed, please tell me how you would rate each in terms of benefit to the country. First how would you rate providing public financing to pay the costs of campaigns of candidates that accept spending limits?

	N	Percent
Excellent	51	25.5
Good	33	16.5
Fair	23	11.5
Poor	93	46.5

QUESTION 25B

And how would you rate providing free TV time to candidates?

	N	Percent
Excellent	58	29.0
Good	43	21.5
Fair	38	19.0
Poor	60	30.0
Don't know/refused	1	0.5

QUESTION 25C

And how would you rate eliminating soft money?

	N	Percent
Excellent	31	15.5
Good	34	17.0
Fair	68	34.0
Poor	66	33.0
Don't know/refused	1	0.5

QUESTION 25D

And how would you rate increasing individual contribution limits?

	N	Percent
Excellent	77	38.5
Good	54	27.0
Fair	28	14.0
Poor	39	19.5
Don't know/refused	2	1.0

QUESTION 25E

And how would you rate limiting spending by issue advocacy groups?

	N	Percent
Excellent	27	13.5
Good	28	14.0
Fair	46	23.0
Poor	95	47.5
Don't know/refused	4	2.0

QUESTION 26

How common are unethical practices in the political consulting business? Do unethical practices happen very often, sometimes, not very often, or rarely?

	N	Percent
Very often	19	9.5
Sometimes	83	41.5
Not very often	71	35.5
Rarely	24	12.0
Never [volunteered]	1	0.5
Don't know/refused	2	1.0

QUESTION 27[2]

In your own words, what are the most common unethical campaign practices?

QUESTION 28A

Please tell me whether, in your opinion, each of the following campaign practices is something you feel is acceptable, questionable, or clearly unethical. First, how about focusing primarily on criticism of the opponent.

	N	Percent
Acceptable	163	81.5
Questionable	35	17.5
Clearly unethical	1	0.5
Don't know/refused	1	0.5

QUESTION 28B

. . . focusing primarily on the kind of person a candidate is, rather than on issues.

	N	Percent
Acceptable	145	72.5
Questionable	50	25.0
Clearly unethical	1	0.5
Don't know/refused	4	2.0

QUESTION 28C

. . . making statements that are factually untrue.

	N	Percent
Acceptable	1	0.5
Questionable	4	2.0
Clearly unethical	195	97.5

QUESTION 28D

. . . making statements that are factually true but are taken out of context.

	N	Percent
Acceptable	26	13.0
Questionable	121	60.5
Clearly unethical	51	25.5
Don't know/refused	2	1.0

QUESTION 28E

. . . using scare tactics about a candidate's issue positions.

	N	Percent
Acceptable	73	36.5
Questionable	91	45.5
Clearly unethical	28	14.0
Don't know/refused	8	4.0

QUESTION 28F

. . . using push polls.

	N	Percent
Acceptable	14	7.0
Questionable	41	20.5
Clearly unethical	140	70.0
Don't know/refused	5	2.5

QUESTION 28G

... trying to suppress voter turnout.

	N	Percent
Acceptable	44	22.0
Questionable	57	28.5
Clearly unethical	93	46.5
Don't know/refused	6	3.0

QUESTION 29

In your opinion, is "going negative" an unethical campaign practice?

	N	Percent
Yes	4	2.0
No	194	97.0
Depends [volunteered]	2	1.0

QUESTION 30[3]

In your own words, what does "going negative" mean?

QUESTION 31

Are campaigns today more likely to "go negative" than they were 10 years ago, less likely, or about as likely?

	N	Percent
More likely	100	50.0
Less likely	4	2.0
About as likely	93	46.5
Don't know/refused	3	1.5

QUESTION 32

Who is responsible for this change? The candidate, their campaign consultants, the media, or the public?

	N	Percent
Candidates	3	1.5
Campaign consultants	37	18.5
The media	16	8.0
The public	26	13.0
All of the above	15	7.5
Other	4	2.0
Don't know/refused	99	49.5

QUESTION 33A

Some consultants say that voters respond more to negatives than to positives. Do you completely agree, mostly agree, mostly disagree, or completely disagree?

	N	Percent
Completely agree	63	31.5
Mostly agree	104	52.0
Mostly disagree	27	13.5
Completely disagree	4	2.0
Don't know/refused	2	1.0

QUESTION 33B

Some consultants say that the news media pay more attention to negatives than to positives. Do you completely agree, mostly agree, mostly disagree, or completely disagree?

	N	Percent
Completely agree	128	64.0
Mostly agree	69	34.5
Mostly disagree	3	1.5
Completely disagree	0	0.0

QUESTION 34

In the typical campaign that goes negative, is it more likely that the candidate or his or her staff will tell the consultants to "go negative" OR that the consultants will make the recommendation to the candidate?

	N	Percent
Candidate or his or her staff will tell consultants	5	2.5
Consultants will recommend to candidate	162	81.0
Neither is more likely	31	15.5
Don't know/refused	2	1.0

QUESTION 35

On another subject, are you a member of the American Association of Political Consultants?

	N	Percent
Yes	102	51.0
No	96	48.0
Don't know/refused	2	1.0

QUESTION 36

Do you think there should or should not be a code of ethics for professionals who work on campaigns?

	N	Percent
Should	149	74.5
There already is one [volunteered]	15	7.5
Should not	23	11.5
Don't know/refused	13	6.5

QUESTION 36A

Do you think there should or should not be a code of ethics for professionals who work on campaigns? [Only asked of those who volunteered in question 36 that a code already exists, N = 15.]

	N	Percent
Should	14	93.3
Don't know/refused	1	6.7

QUESTION 37

As you may know, the American Association of Political Consultants, or AAPC, does have a code of ethics. Do you happen to be familiar with this code? [Only asked of those who did not volunteer in question 36 that a code already exists, N = 185.]

	N	Percent
Yes	113	61.1
No	72	38.9

QUESTION 38

How much of an effect to you think this code has on the behavior of your peers? A great deal, a fair amount, not very much, or none at all? [Only asked of those who in question 37 were familiar with the AAPC code, N = 128.]

	N	Percent
A great deal	0	0.0
A fair amount	15	11.7
Not very much	58	45.3
None at all	46	35.9
Don't know/refused	9	7.0

QUESTION 39

And how much of an effect to you think this code has on your own behavior? A great deal, a fair amount, not very much, or none at all? [Only asked of those who in question 37 were familiar with the AAPC code, N = 128.]

	N	Percent
A great deal	25	19.5
A fair amount	32	11.7
Not very much	28	21.9
None at all	41	32.0
Don't know/refused	2	1.6

QUESTION 40

Should a professional organization be able to censure those who violate a code of ethics for campaign professionals or not? [Not asked of those who in question 36 said there should not be a code of ethics, N = 177.]

	N	Percent
Yes	113	63.8
No	43	24.3
Don't know/refused	21	11.5

DEMOGRAPHIC QUESTION 1

Respondent's sex

	N	Percent
Male	164	82.0
Female	36	18.0

DEMOGRAPHIC QUESTION 2A

Finally, I'd like to ask you a few background questions. Have you ever worked in the office of a federal, state, or local elected official?

	N	Percent
Yes	107	53.5
No	93	46.5

DEMOGRAPHIC QUESTION 2B

Have you ever worked for a national, state, or local political party or party committee?

	N	Percent
Yes	124	62.0
No	76	38.0

DEMOGRAPHIC QUESTION 2C

Have you ever worked in government?

	N	Percent
Yes	108	54.0
No	92	46.0

DEMOGRAPHIC QUESTION 2D

Have you ever worked for a news media organization?

	N	Percent
Yes	60	30.0
No	140	70.0

DEMOGRAPHIC QUESTION 3

Over the past two-year period, that is since 1996, about what percentage of your professional income has come from candidate or political-issue consulting, as opposed to corporate work?

	N	Percent
5% to 25%	18	9.0
26% to 50%	45	22.5
51% to 75%	53	26.5
75% to 100%	83	41.5
Don't know/refused	1	0.5

DEMOGRAPHIC QUESTION 4

What is your age?

	N	Percent
18 to 39	76	38.0
40 to 49	80	40.0
Over 50	43	21.5
Don't know/refused	1	0.5

DEMOGRAPHIC QUESTION 5

What is the last grade or class that you completed in school?

	N	Percent
High school graduate, equivalent, or less	0	0.0
Technical, trade, or business school		
after high school	0	0.0
Some college	13	6.5
Four year college (B.A. or B.S.)	83	41.5
Some graduate school	23	11.5
Master's degree (M.A. or M.S.)	53	26.5
Law degree (J.D.)	13	6.5
Doctorate	15	7.5

DEMOGRAPHIC QUESTION 6

Are you of Hispanic or Latino descent, such as Mexican, Puerto Rican, Cuban, or some other Spanish background?

	N	Percent
Yes	5	2.5
No	194	97.0
Don't know/refused	1	0.5

DEMOGRAPHIC QUESTION 7

What is your race? Are you white, black, Asian, or some other race?

	N	Percent
White	195	97.5
Asian	1	0.5
Other	3	1.5
Don't know/refused	1	0.5

DEMOGRAPHIC QUESTION 8

What is your religious preference? Protestant, Roman Catholic, Jewish, Mormon, or an orthodox church such as the Greek or Russian Orthodox Church?

	N	Percent
Protestant	74	37.0
Roman Catholic	46	23.0
Jewish	23	11.5
Mormon	2	1.0
Orthodox Church	3	1.5
No religion/atheist	44	22.0
Other	3	1.5
Don't know/refused	5	2.5

DEMOGRAPHIC QUESTION 9

Would you describe yourself as a "born-again" or evangelical Christian or not?

	N	Percent
Yes	19	9.5
No	112	56.0
Don't know/refused	69	34.5

DEMOGRAPHIC QUESTION 10

In politics today, do you consider yourself a Republican, Democrat, or Independent?

	N	Percent
Republican	79	39.5
Democrat	115	57.5
Independent	4	2.0
No preference	1	0.5
Other	1	0.5

DEMOGRAPHIC QUESTION 11

In general, would you describe your political views as very conservative, conservative, moderate, liberal, or very liberal?

	N	Percent
Very conservative	14	7.0
Conservative	51	25.5
Moderate	55	27.5
Liberal	52	26.0
Very liberal	25	12.5
Other	2	1.0
Don't know/refused	1	0.5

DEMOGRAPHIC QUESTION 12

Thinking about your total family income in both 1996 and 1997, if you were to AVERAGE the total across these two years, what was your annual family income from all sources before taxes? Just stop me when I get to the right category. [Read]

	N	Percent
Less than $30,000	0	0.0
$30,000 to $49,999	12	6.0
$50,000 to $99,999	33	16.5
$100,000 to $149,999	40	20.0
$150,000 to $199,999	41	20.5
$200,000 to $299,999	34	17.0
$300,000 to $499,999	17	8.5
Over $500,000	12	6.0
Don't know/refused	11	5.5

Notes

1. Note that while this appendix reports all 200 responses to the consultants survey described in chapter 2, the total percentages reported in the tables in that chapter may not match those reported here, for the following reasons: some questions had several "don't know/refused" responses; and the analyses in chapter 2 excluded those who described themselves as "independent" or "direct mail" consultants, because neither group was large enough to perform meaningful statistical tests.

2. In the interest of space, we do not report responses to this open-ended question. Responses can be obtained upon request from the Center for Congressional and Presidential Studies.

3. See note to question 27.

The State Party Survey

This survey should take only a few minutes of your time. Your cooperation is essential to this research. We are interested in your party's past and future relationships with political consultants in very general terms. The code number on this form indicates your party.

1. Does your political party currently have a contract with, or plan to negotiate a contract with, one or more political consultants for the 1998 election cycle?

Yes ——— No ———

2. If the answer to the above question is yes, what sort of political consultants do you have such contracts with? Please check ALL that apply.

☐ Polling
☐ Media production
☐ Media buying
☐ Direct mail
☐ Fundraising
☐ Referenda/Initiatives
☐ Research
☐ General
☐ Other (specify) ————————————————————

3. Which one or two consultant types listed above is the most critical to your party's needs?

_____

4. Approximately how much money will your party spend on consultant services and fees in the entire 1998 cycle? [Note: text was revised to make categories mutually exclusive.]

☐ nothing
☐ $1–$10,000
☐ $10,000–$25,000
☐ $25,000–$50,000
☐ $50,000–$75,000
☐ $75,000–$100,000
☐ greater than $100,000

5. About what percentage of your total expected expenditures for the 1998 election cycle would you say the answer to number four represents?
_____ percent

6. Do you advise your candidates to seek the services of political consultants?

Yes _____   No _____

7. If the answer to number six is yes, how is this done? Please check ALL that apply.

☐ We have a list of preferred consultants/vendors that we give to candidates who pay for the services themselves.
☐ For certain candidates, we pay for the services of our preferred consultants/vendors.
☐ We recommend consultants informally, on a case-by-case basis.

8. What type of consultant do you find your party recommends to candidates most often? Please rank these in from most frequent to least frequent.

☐ Polling
☐ Media production
☐ Media buying
☐ Direct mail
☐ Fundraising
☐ Research
☐ General
☐ Other (specify) _____

9. What functions do political parties perform better than political consultants for candidates?

10. What functions do consultants perform better for their clients than political parties can?

11. How do consultants help fulfill your party's overall goals?

12. Please state any additional comments about the relationship between political parties and political consultants that we may not have asked. (Please use space on back if needed).

Thank you for your time and effort. They make our research possible.

Initiative and Referendum Interviews

Direct Legislation Consultants Interviewed

Mike Arno (July 9, 1997)
  Arno Professional Consulting (signatures)
Brad Bannon (July 9, 1997)
  Bannon Research (polling)
Michael Berman (June 17, 1997)
  Joe Slade White and Company (media)
Max Besler (July 9, 1997)
  Townsend, Raimundo, Besler, and Usher (general)
Wally Clinton (May 1, 1997)
  Clinton Group (telephone)
Barry Fadem (August 11, 1997)
  Bagatelos and Fadem
Peter Fenn (May 1, 1997)
  Fenn, King, Murphy, and Putnam (media)
Les Francis (May 2, 1997)
  Winner/Wagner & Mandabach Campaigns (general)
Ben Goddard (July 8, 1997)
  Goddard/Clausen/First Tuesday (media)
William Hamilton (May 2,1997)
  Hamilton & Staff (polling)
Mac Hansbrough (July 10, 1997)
  National Telecommunications Services (NTS) (telephones)

David Hill (July 11, 1997)
  Hill Research Consultants (polling)
Kelly Kimball (June 26, 1997)
  Kimball Petition Management (signatures)
Dawn Leguens (June 17, 1997)
  Seder-Leguens, Inc. (media)
Paul Mandabach, (July 14, 1997)
  Winner/Wagner & Mandabach Campaigns (general)
Leo McElroy, (July 9, 1997)
  McElroy Communications (media)
Jim McLaughlin (July 16, 1997)
  Fabrizio-McLaughlin and Associates (media)
Bob Meadow (May 2, 1997)
  Decision Research (polling)
Mark Mellman (June 17, 1997)
  The Mellman Group (polling)
Stu Mollrich, (June 26, 1997)
  Stu Mollrich Communications (signatures, media)
Neil Newhouse (May 1, 1997)
  Public Opinion Strategies (polling)
Virgo Chip Nielsen (San Francisco) (August 10, 1997)
  Nielsen and Merksamer
Will Robinson (May 1, 1997)
  MacWilliams, Cosgrove, Snider, Smith Robinson (media)
Larry Sheingold (July 14, 1997)
  Sheingold and Associates (general/media)
Thomas C. Shephard (June 2, 1997)
  Campaign Strategies, Inc. (general)
Jim Weber (June 17, 1997)
  (general)
Marice White (June 26, 1997)
  Nelson Communications Group (media)
Dick Woodward (August 20, 1997)
  Woodward and McDowell

Initiative and Referendum Consultants Survey

1. How many years have you worked in the consulting industry?

   _____

2. Do you have an office located in Washington, D.C.? ☐ Yes ☐ No

3. In what state do you do the most business? *(Please list the state)*

   _____

4. What percentage of your time do you spend working on initiative campaigns? _____%

5. What political parties employ your services?

   ☐ Democrat   ☐ Republican   ☐ Both   ☐ Neither

6. What proportion of your business comes from the following types of groups? *(Please estimate a percentage for each category)*
   ☐ Candidates
   ☐ Special Interest Groups
   ☐ Wealthy Individuals
   ☐ Political Parties
   ☐ Grassroots Campaigns
   ☐ Other (specify) _____

7. Are the groups that employ your services mainly liberal, moderate, or conservative?

   ☐ Liberal   ☐ Moderate   ☐ Conservative

8. Do you work on both candidate and initiative campaigns?

   ☐ Yes   ☐ No

8a. If you answered "yes" to question #8, do you prefer working on candidate or initiative campaigns?

   ☐ Candidate Campaigns   ☐ Initiative Campaigns

   ☐ Prefer both equally

9. What overall effect does the initiative process have on American democracy? *(Circle the answer that best applies)*

   Very Negative   Somewhat Negative   No Effect

   Somewhat Positive   Very Positive

10. What effect does the initiative process have on voter interest in politics? *(Circle the answer that best applies)*

Very Negative   Somewhat Negative   No Effect

Somewhat Positive   Very Positive

11. What effect does the initiative process have on voter participation? *(Circle the answer that best applies)*

Very Negative   Somewhat Negative   No Effect

Somewhat Positive   Very Positive

12. Do you believe that the initiative process checks special interests or expands their power?

☐ Checks Special Interests   ☐ Expands the power of Special Interests

13. What service(s) do you or your firm provide? *(Check all that apply)*

☐ Legal advice
☐ Polling
☐ Media production
☐ Media buying
☐ Direct mail
☐ Fund-raising
☐ Research
☐ Signature-gathering
☐ General campaign management
☐ Other (Please specify) _____

14. Do you believe that virtually any issue could qualify for the ballot if its backers have sufficient funds?

☐ Yes   ☐ No

15. In an initiative campaign, do you receive support or assistance from political parties?

☐ Yes   ☐ No   ☐ Sometimes

15a. If you answered yes or sometimes to question 15, what kinds of support and assistance do you receive from political parties? *(Check all that apply)*

☐ Financial
☐ Organizational
☐ Help with strategy and message
☐ Other (Please specify) _____

16. Do you believe that in the future there will be an increase or a decrease in the number of initiative campaigns?

☐ Increase   ☐ Decrease   ☐ No Change

17. How important to the success of an initiative is the wording of the initiative on the ballot?
(Circle the answer that best applies)

Very Important   Important

Somewhat important   Irrelevant

18. Do you prefer working on the "Yes" side or the "No" side of an initiative campaign?

☐ "Yes" side   ☐ "No" side   ☐ Prefer both equally

19. What effect does a longer ballot have on the success of an initiative? *(Circle the answer that best applies)*

Negative   Somewhat Negative   No Effect

Somewhat Positive   Positive

20. The following list contains reasons why consultants may prefer initiative contests to candidate contests. Please mark whether you strongly agree, agree, disagree, or strongly disagree with each statement.

	Strongly Agree	Agree	Disagree	Strongly Disagree
Initiative campaigns pay better than candidate campaigns	☐	☐	☐	☐
Initiative campaigns are easier to manage	☐	☐	☐	☐
Initiative campaigns are more likely to pay their fees	☐	☐	☐	☐
Initiative campaigns give you more freedom and control	☐	☐	☐	☐

21. When working on initiative campaigns, what two firms for each of the following specializations do you most often work with.

General Management: _____

_____

Polling: _____

_____

Media: _____

_____

Direct Voter Contact
(Mail/Phone): _____

_____

Signature Solicitation: _____

_____

Legal: _____

Thank you very much for your assistance.
Please return in the envelope provided.

Contributors

:

Shaun Bowler is an associate professor in the Department of Political Science at the University of California, Riverside.

David A. Dulio is a doctoral candidate in the Department of Government at American University and is a senior research assistant with the Center for Congressional and Presidential Studies.

David M. Farrell is a senior Jean Monnet lecturer in the Department of Government, University of Manchester, England.

Martin Hamburger is a partner in the consulting firm Laguens, Hamburger, and Stone. He is also program coordinator of American University's Campaign Management Institute.

Paul S. Herrnson is professor of government and politics at the University of Maryland, College Park.

Dennis W. Johnson is associate dean of the Graduate School of Political Management and director of the master of arts in legislative affairs program at George Washington University.

Robin Kolodny is associate professor of political science at Temple University.

David B. Magleby is professor of political science at Brigham Young University.

Stephen K. Medvic is assistant professor of political science at Old Dominion University in Norfolk, Virginia.

Candice J. Nelson is an associate professor of government and academic director of the Campaign Management Institute at American University.

Kelly D. Patterson is an associate professor in the Department of Political Science at Brigham Young University.

James A. Thurber is professor of government at American University and director of the Center for Congressional and Presidential Studies and the center's two institutes.

Index